A CHRISTIAN THEOLOC

The place in which we stand is often taken for granted and ignored
mobile society. Differentiating between place and space, this book argues that place
has very much more influence upon human experience than is generally recognized
and that this lack of recognition, and all that results from it, are dehumanizing.

John Inge presents a rediscovery of the importance of place, drawing on the resources
of the Bible and the Christian tradition to demonstrate how Christian theology should
take place seriously. A renewed understanding of the importance of place from a
theological perspective, has much to offer in working against the dehumanizing
effects of the loss of place. Community and places each build the identity of the other;
this book offers important insights in a world in which the effects of globalization
continue to erode people's rootedness and experience of place.

Explorations in Practical, Pastoral and Empirical Theology

Series Editors: Leslie J. Francis, University of Wales, Bangor, UK
and Jeff Astley, University of Durham and Director of the North of England Institute
for Christian Education, UK

Theological reflection on the church's practice is now recognized as a significant element in theological studies in the academy and seminary. Ashgate's new series in practical, pastoral and empirical theology seeks to foster this resurgence of interest and encourage new developments in practical and applied aspects of theology worldwide. This timely series draws together a wide range of disciplinary approaches and empirical studies to embrace contemporary developments including: the expansion of research in empirical theology, psychological theology, ministry studies, public theology, Christian education and faith development; key issues of contemporary society such as health, ethics and the environment; and more traditional areas of concern such as pastoral care and counselling.

Other titles published in this series:

Ordinary Theology
Looking, Listening and Learning in Theology
Jeff Astley

The 'Empty' Church Revisited
Robin Gill

Sin and Forgiveness
New Responses in a Changing World
Kay Carmichael

God, Human Nature and Education for Peace
New Approaches to Moral and Religious Maturity
Karl Ernst Nipkow

A Christian Theology of Place

JOHN INGE

ASHGATE

Published by
Ashgate Publishing Limited
Gower House
Croft Road
Aldershot
Hampshire GU11 3HR

Ashgate Publishing Company
Suite 420
101 Cherry Street
Burlington, VT 05401-4405
USA

Ashgate website: http//www.ashgate.com

British Library Cataloguing in Publication Data
Inge, John
   A Christian theology of place. – (Explorations in
   practical, pastoral and empirical theology)
   1. Place (Philosophy) 2. Philosophical theology. 3. Sacred
   space
   I. Title
   263'.042'01

Library of Congress Cataloging-in-Publication Data
Inge, John, 1955–
   A Christian theology of place / John Inge.
      p. cm. -- (explorations in practical, pastoral, and empirical theology)
   Includes bibliographical references.
   ISBN 978-0-7546-3498-0 (alk. paper) -- ISBN 978-0-7546-3499-7 (pbk : alk. paper)
      1. Sacred space. I. Title. II. Series.

 BV895.I54 2003
 231.7--dc21

2002043964

ISBN 978-0 7546 3498 0 (Hardback)
ISBN 978-0 9546 3499 7 (Paperback)

Reprinted 2007

Typeset by IML Typographers, Birkenhead, Merseyside and printed in
Great Britain by MPG Books Ltd, Bodmin, Cornwall

To Denise without whom, for me, any place would be impoverished

Contents

Introduction

This book argues that place is very much more significant than is generally recognized. That we all need 'a place to stand' goes without saying, but most people do not perhaps stop to reflect very deeply on what effect such places have upon them and why. It has been my good fortune to live in some remarkable places and, probably as a result of this, I have long been interested in place. I spent my teenage years in Canterbury before living within a stone's throw of Durham Cathedral. From there I moved to Oxford before beginning work within the shadow of Lancing College Chapel, the largest private chapel in the world. I subsequently spent time in Harrow-on-the-Hill before moving to Wallsend, a place with a history to conjure with. Not only was it the place where Hadrian's Wall came to its eastern end, it later developed fame as the place where the *Mauritania* and the *Ark Royal* had been built. In the latter half of the twentieth century, while it was still, in my experience, a wonderful place to be, it had fallen upon hard times and showed many signs of inner-city deprivation.

What made me reflect more systematically about the importance of place was moving from there to minister at Ely Cathedral. It was an interesting transition, and not just because they are very different places indeed. What really set me thinking was the casual manner in which people referred to Ely as a 'holy place'. I began to wonder whether this implied that God approves of some places more than others – a proposition I found rather offensive. However, if it was not the case, I had to work out what possible grounds there could be for calling any place holy. For it seemed to me that Ely Cathedral was indeed a holy place. I began to research what had been written on place in theology, and found it to be very little. My disappointment impelled me towards other disciplines where I encountered the same paucity of material. This struck me as surprising. One could be forgiven for thinking that there would be a great deal of theological writing on place, since its importance in the Bible should be apparent even to the casual reader. But absence of consideration of it in other disciplines puzzled me, too, though. Our existence as embodied beings means that place is as necessary to us as the air we breathe but, more than that, it seems to me that our human experience is shaped by place. Why was place not deemed worthy of consideration?

Meditating on this question I began to realize that place had been eliminated from discourse in Western society by a long and complicated process that I attempt to trace in the first chapter of this book. Not only has there not been much discussion of place in the intellectual arena, but there has been what might be termed a 'loss of place' in human experience for very many people in the recent past. My research – and my experience – led me to believe that this loss is dehumanizing. Moreover, I was convinced that the Bible and the Christian tradition held within them the resources for a rediscovery of the importance of place.

In order to substantiate this claim and to demonstrate that Christian theology should take tyhe concept of place seriously, I turn in Chapter 2 to a detailed examination of the attitude of the scriptures to place. This study confirms that place is a very important category in the Old Testament and that the narrative supports a three-way relationship between God, people and place in which all three are essential. Turning to the New Testament I suggest that, although there is no longer a concentration upon the Holy Land and Jerusalem, the incarnation affirms the importance of the particular, and therefore of place, in God's dealings with humanity. Seen in an incarnational perspective, places are the seat of relations or the place of meeting between God and the world.

In the light of this, Chapter 3 proposes that the most constructive manner in which to view place from a Christian perspective is sacramentally. I examine the concept of sacrament and trace its extension from the Church's sacraments to a wider application in the material world. Agreeing with those who emphasize that the notion of sacrament must be grounded in event, I point to the importance of place in human encounter with the Divine, beginning with Jacob's encounter at Bethel and continuing through the scriptures and tradition. I term such encounters 'sacramental events' and go on to argue that, far from being isolated incidents given only to a few, such 'sacramental events' are a very common part of Christian experience, and that the place in which such events occur is not merely a backdrop to the experience, but an integral part of it. I propose that the relational view of place, people and God, which emerges in Chapter 2 as the biblical paradigm, is retained in such encounters. 'Sacramental encounters' then become built into the story of such places, and I enlist the support of scholars of other disciplines to elucidate how this can happen in a manner which allows for the development of holiness across time and the resulting emergence of 'holy places'.

Chapter 4 looks at the way in which holy places so understood have been an integral part of the Christian tradition from the earliest times, particularly as seen in the phenomenon of pilgrimage. Pilgrimage is a dynamic model which links people, place and God in a manner which is consonant with the biblical paradigm to which I have referred above. Examining its history, I show how pilgrimage to the Holy Land and Jerusalem grew in popularity and was accompanied by the emergence of a sacred geography of holy places across Christendom. Pilgrimage to such holy places, where God's love had been made manifest in 'sacramental encounter' and the resulting witness of holy men and women, was a vital ingredient of Christian life in medieval times, and has remained so for many since the Reformation. Having characterized pilgrimage as an authentic Christian phenomenon, I examine the theology of shrines to which such pilgrimage is made, and look at the manner in which the shrine can act as a memorial to the saving events of Christian history, a prophetic presence in the midst of secular society, and an eschatological sign of God's future. I then go on to suggest that there is a good case for treating all churches as shrines, for if holy places are those in which 'sacramental encounter' takes place, then churches are certainly holy places as a result of regular Eucharistic celebration and the development of a Christian community associated with the place. Churches so regarded can help to root the worshipping community in its faith, nurture its prophetic witness, and speak eschatologically of its destination in a manner which maintains a proper biblical relationship between people, place and God. This means that holy places, as well as the Christian communities associated with them, can then act as a witness to the world.

Finally, in Chapter 5, I look at the manner in which a renewed understanding of the importance of place from a theological perspective has much to offer to attempts by scholars of other disciplines to work against the dehumanizing effects of the loss of place. Churches viewed sacramentally can demonstrate the importance of place in human experience. Further, the relational view of place which emerges as the proper Christian attitude in this study sheds light upon the complex interaction which characterizes the manner in which people interact with the places they inhabit. Community and places each build up the identity of the other. This is an important insight in a world in which the effects of globalization continue to erode people's rootedness and experience of place. Attention given by the Christian community to place in general, and not just to holy places, will not only therefore afford nourishment to the community itself, but will be a powerful prophetic action. However, at the same time, the Church must witness to the fact that all places in this world are penultimate. I conclude, therefore, with an examination of what it might mean to speak of 'ultimate place', and suggest that belief in the resurrection of the body might imply implacement of that body in the hereafter.

This work began, as I intimated above, as an attempt to address the question of what it might mean to call a place 'holy', but that attempt has led me to ask many other questions. I hope that this book will make some small contribution to a recovery of a sense of place in Western society, particularly for those who feel dislocated and displaced. I believe that if we were all able to rediscover the significance of place, vital aspects of our humanity would be renewed. For place is crucial both in the here and now and in eternity: Jesus implies as much when he tells his disciples that he is going to prepare a place for them.

September 2002   John Inge

Acknowledgements

This book grew out of a doctoral thesis, and I am grateful to Ann Loades for all her encouragement in that work. It would not have been completed without a sabbatical, and thanks are due to the Dean and Chapter of Ely for granting me one during the autumn of 2000. During it I was fortunate to have a Visiting Scholarship at Duke University, and I owe a debt of gratitude to Duke, and especially to Geoffrey Wainwright for his assistance in arranging it. Others who have offered help in various ways during the writing of this book include Jeff Astley, Walter Brueggemann, Marianne Felter, David Ford, Daniel Hardy, Stanley Hauerwas, Al McFadyen, Bridget Nichols, Philip Sheldrake and Sam Wells. I offer my thanks to them, and most of all to my wife Denise, whose quiet and unwavering support was more crucial than she knows.

Chapter 1

Place in Western Thought and Practice

The Demise of Place

Place and Space

In order to be clear about the use of terms we need to begin by teasing out the difference between the two terms 'space' and 'place' as I shall use them in what follows. Many people, including theologians, use the terms interchangeably, but this leads to the concept being rather unclarified. Einstein pointed out the difficulty when he wrote that when different authors use words like 'red,' hard' or 'disappointed', no one doubts that they mean more or less the same thing, because 'these words are connected with elementary experiences in a manner which is difficult to misinterpret. But in the case of words such as "place" or "space", whose relation with psychological experience is less direct, there exists a far reaching uncertainty of interpretation'.[1] The situation is complicated by the fact that, as the geographer David Harvey reminds us, the term 'place' has an extraordinary range of metaphorical meanings: 'We talk about the place of art in social life, the place of women in society, our place in the cosmos, and we internalise such notions psychologically in terms of knowing our place, or feeling that we have a place in the affections or esteem of others.'[2] He goes on to remind us that by putting people, events and things in their proper place we express norms, and concludes that 'place' is one of the most multi-purpose words in the English language.

Even when we restrict our attention to *physical* place, we have to contend with the fact that, as another geographer, Yi-Fu Tuan, observes 'space and place are basic components of the lived world; we take them for granted which means that "in experience, the meaning of space often merges with that of place".'[3] However, despite all these difficulties, it is possible to see broad differences between the way in which the words are used, since 'space' is more abstract than 'place'. What begins as undifferentiated space becomes place as we get to know it better and endow it with value. It is from there, from the security and stability of place, we are aware of the openness, freedom and threat of space, and vice versa. These observations elucidate some basic points about the way in which the two words are in general use. When we think of space, most of us will tend to think of 'outer space' and 'infinity', but when we think of place, on the other hand, we will tend to think of locality, a particular spot. What is undifferentiated space becomes for us significant place by virtue of our

---

[1] Albert Einstein in his foreword to Jammer, M. (1969), xii.

[2] Harvey, D. (1993), 3.

[3] Tuan, Y.-F. (1977), 3.

1

familiarity with it. The two terms might be thought of as tending towards opposite ends of a spectrum which has the local at one end and the infinite at the other. Spaces are what are filled with places.

Though some thinkers take a different line,[4] this distinction between the terms 'place' and 'space' is in common usage and has honourable precedent. It is the one which I shall follow as we go on to look at the history of 'place' and 'space' so defined in Western thought.

The Greek Inheritance

In what follows I shall argue that there are two ways in which our approach to place is construed. The first, as intimated above, builds upon our experience. Such experience begins very early. As Tuan expresses it:

> The infant acquires a sense of distance by attending to the sound of a human voice that signals the approach of his mother. A child is walked to school a few times and thereafter he can make the journey on his own, without the help of a map; indeed, he is able to envisage the route. We are in a strange part of town: unknown space stretches ahead of us. In time we know a few landmarks and the routes connecting them. Eventually what was strange town and unknown space becomes familiar place. Abstract space, lacking significance other than strangeness, becomes concrete place, filled with meaning. Much is learned but not through formal instruction.[5]

This is the manner in which we begin to be able to organize our experience and differentiate between what I have described as 'space' and 'place'. However, as our consciousness develops, what we learn from our everyday experience is affected by the manner in which the society in which we live conceives these notions, and such conceptions will be affected by a long history of thought and practice. The philosopher Michel Foucault observed that 'a whole history remains to be written of spaces – which would at the same time be a history of powers – from the great strategies of geopolitics to the little tactics of the habitat'.[6] This equivalence of a history of powers with a history of spaces is obvious in the case of geopolitics. Power has, for example, been concentrated in particular places during colonial eras, and how we conceive of such places is still affected by a colonial perspective. But what Foucault is suggesting here is that this power and space are connected right across the spectrum from such a macro scale to the 'little tactics of the habitat'. We can see at the outset that it will be necessary to allow some flexibility with our definitions, since

---

[4] For example, Michel de Certeau defines the two terms in pretty much exactly the reverse sense to speak of the manner in which places (*lieux*) are practised by their inhabitants so as to have overlaid upon them a multitude of spaces (*espaces*). De Certeau, M. (1984), 117. More recently, however, the French theologian Jean-Yves Lacoste uses the terms as I am suggesting here. He states that 'place (*lieu*) is not another name of space (*espace*). The concept of space is geometric ... place is other than space for it gives us the coordinates of life, or of existence.' Lacoste, J.-Y. (1994), 8. My translation. Some writers seek to avoid the difficulties by using different terms: Anthony Giddens, for example, uses the term 'locale' to mean pretty much what we have defined 'place' to mean. See Cassell, P. (1993), 181.

[5] Tuan, Y.-F. (1977), 199.

[6] Foucault, M. (1980), 149. See also Said, E. (1993).

Foucault's use of the terms 'spaces' and 'habitat' in translation are more or less equivalent to what I have designated a 'place'. In the realm of geopolitics we could say that a nation is better referred to as a place than as a space: none of us would think of the country in which we live primarily as a 'space' because, as we have noted, the word 'space' carries with it connotations of infinity and emptiness, it is something to be filled. These connotations derive both from our own experience, as accrued in the manner Tuan has suggested, and from implicit modes of thinking inherent in our society. Foucault's words, then, imply that we should not be surprised if investigation of the history of the consideration of place reveals hitherto hidden powers at work in contemporary understanding.

Since 'place' and 'space' are an essential part of our experience we would expect them to have been the subject of much contemplation from the earliest times, and this is indeed the case. The manner in which they are conceived in our Western society owes a great deal to the influence of Greek thinking and what developed from it, since until the fourteenth century all theories of space were developments of Aristotle's and Plato's conceptions. It is therefore to these conceptions that we shall now turn our attention.

In Plato's account of creation by the Demiurge in his epic *Timaeus*, space is pre-existent and the task of the Demiurge is to convert this pre-existent 'space' into defined 'places', though Plato does not use these terms in exactly the manner I have been using them above. He talks of creation as occurring in and with a pre-existent body, which he names necessity (*ananke*) and space (*chora*). Space, then, is there in the beginning, and since space *precedes* creation, the Demiurge is far from omnipotent. Plato also uses the term 'receptacle' to describe this space in which creation takes place. This receptacle is a complex thing since it 'appears to possess different qualities at different times', so that it is not a void but a passive medium in which the action of the Demiurge takes place. Although Plato does not always distinguish between *chora* (space) and *topos* (place), he needs to state the difference when he comes to discuss the 'primary bodies' created by the Demiurge. Creation by the Demiurge consists of the configuration of these 'primary bodies' within a previously existing space, which is there as 'a matrix for everything',[7] and the *Timaeus* is thus a story of implacement. This placement is, as Plato himself says, 'ever-lasting'. Hence place is of great importance in Plato's cosmology – and it is possible to see how it can be differentiated from space as I have defined in the latter. Plato's account remained very influential as a standard text in the West for Plato's *Timaeus*, and was succeeded by Aristotle's *Physics* only in the middle of the twelfth century.

In Aristotle's writing we find ourselves moving to a world where Plato's interest in cosmology disappears to give way to the much more down-to-earth approach of the *Physics*, where place is conceived of as a container. Aristotle adopts a characteristically practical as much as a scientific approach to place: he looks at our *experience* of place as a starting point. In book four of the *Physics*, he writes that there are regions or kinds of place – up and down and the others of the six directions. He suggests that such distinctions (up and down, right and left, and so on) do not hold only in relation to us: 'To us they are not always the same but change with the direction in which we are turned: that is why the same thing may be both right and

---

[7] *Timaeus*, 50c.

left, up and down, before and behind ... but in nature each is distinct, taken apart by itself.'[8] His empirical approach led him to construe where something is as a basic metaphysical category but, as Thomas Torrance notes, his analysis was affected by the way in which he misunderstood Plato at two important points:

> He misconstrued the Platonic separation (*chorismos*) as a local or spatial separation, and mistook the Platonic 'receptacle' or 'matrix' for the original stuff or substrate from which bodies are derived. This was due to his very different approach, from the empirical situations where one body is in fact contained by another and is thus 'in place'. He listed 'space' among the categories and so thought out his conception of it within a substance-accidents scheme of things. As a category, then, space was regarded not only as a fundamental way in which we conceive of things but an actual way in which things exist, and so Aristotle associated space with, and sometimes included it in, the category of quantity. This led him to develop a predominantly volumetric conception of space, which was reinforced through the attention he devoted to place, or the specific aspect of space that concerned him in natural science.[9]

Torrance's observations are interesting not only because of his comments on the manner in which the thinking of Plato and Aristotle on place are related, but also because of his revealing description of place as a 'specific aspect of space'. We have already noted a tendency among many thinkers to confuse the two terms. It should be said, however, that Aristotle's doctrine of place in the *Physics* is not a doctrine of space. Since neither here nor elsewhere does Aristotle say much about space – *chora* – he cannot be said to have a theory about it.

In devoting attention to place, Aristotle argues that place must be the boundary of the containing body at the points at which it is in immediate contact with the contained body. He uses the analogy of the vessel to pursue this line of thinking: in the same way as a vessel, say a jug or a cup, holds its contents by surrounding them, so place surrounds the body or group of bodies located within it. Aristotle recognizes, however, that a vessel can be transported whereas a place cannot, and in the light of this he refines his definition to make clear that place is a vessel that cannot be moved around. Place is thus defined as 'the innermost motionless boundary of what contains', in other words the innermost unmoved limit of the container which immediately encompasses each body. Place so defined is determined to be a unique and irreducible part of the material universe. Place, as bounded container, has a dynamic role in enabling a thing to be somewhere, for according to this manner of thinking, without place things would not only fail to be located, they would not even be things. Thus place has for Aristotle a uniquely important role within the material world so that, in his own words, 'the potency of place must be a marvellous thing, and takes precedence of all other things'.[10] However, Torrance reminds us that the most influential part of Aristotle's thinking about place is the idea of the container.

The container was the most prevalent notion of space found in Greek thought and this notion was very powerful in fostering the conviction that place is simply an inert environment in which things happen. A consequence of this view is that if an

---

[8] Aristotle, *Physics*, 208b12–18.

[9] Torrance, T. F. (1969), 7.

[10] Aristotle, *Physics*, see 209b26, 212a20, 208b35.

environment is just an inert container, things might just as well happen in one as in another. So it does not really matter whether I live in Glasgow or Beijing, and what kind of buildings surround me will have no significant effect on me. Other effects served to compound this persistence, as we shall see.

The Eclipse of Place

One such effect was the emergence of the notion of space. In the fifth century BC, about two generations before Plato, Democritus was arguing, in contrast to Aristotle's notion of place as something confining and confined, that there is in fact nothing but atoms and the void. Atoms were conceived as incredibly dense and literally indivisible bits of matter, and the void as a vast open space. In the Hellenistic period of Greek philosophy there emerged neoplatonic thought in which Atomist and Aristotelian notions of place and space jostled with one another for attention. At the same time, there developed in neoplatonic thought a philosophical conception of 'spaceless spirit' which was to be determinative for the West's understanding of the soul. This has bred the conviction that our local embodied relations are to be transcended and left behind – that place is ultimately of no import. In the centuries that followed, concentration on the primacy of space gathered momentum. This complex transition is charted by the philosopher David Casey in *The Fate of Place: A Philosophical History*. He shows that if the Atomists were the first to isolate space in the broadest sense as something which is unlimited and open-ended, an interest in space gradually gained a hold over place which 'solicits questions of limit and boundary, and of location and surrounding'. Space, Casey notes, sets these latter questions aside in favour of a concern with 'the absolute and the infinite, the immense and the indefinitely extended. If place bears on what lies in – in a container, dwelling or vessel – space characteristically moves out, so far as to explode the closely confining perimeters in which Aristotle attempted to ensconce material things. In this unequal battle, spacing out triumphs over placing-in.'[11] Thought about place may have come first, Einstein observed, because place is a psychologically simpler concept than space.[12] However, space won the day, as Casey observes:

> The change took place in an ever-lengthening shadow of preoccupation with space, regarded as absolute and more particularly as infinite (and frequently both together). ... Thus talk of 'space' began in the wake of Aristotle: at first hesitatingly and with a backward glance at Plato (in his employment of *chora* to designate a roominess that *topos* could not sustain); later, and more tellingly, in the invention of *spatium* (and its medieval variant *spacium*) as a way of distinguishing the properly spatial from the merely local (locus taking over the delimited and delimiting role formerly assigned to *topos*). It was in exploring the extensiveness of space, its seemingly undelimitable outspread, its unendingness, that the co-ordinate but distinguishable notions of spatial absoluteness and infinity began to seem irresistible.[13]

---

[11] Casey, E. (1997), 77.

[12] Albert Einstein in his foreword to Jammer, M. (1969), xiii.

[13] Casey (1997), 134. Jammer refers to the work of the Christian neo-Platonist Philoponus (born *c.* 490 AD) and Damascius (born *c.* 480 AD) as being very influential in this process. See Jammer, M. (1969), Chapter 3.

If we ask what effect this development in thought had upon the everyday lives of ordinary people at the time, the answer must be very little. Most people remained bound to one place for the entirety of their lives until the nineteenth and twentieth centuries. In those primitive societies which survive in today's world, place remains very important,[14] and in some working-class societies in the Western world where mobility has not yet caught on, attachment to place is still very strong. When I was Vicar of a church on Tyneside in the early 1990s, remaining in that place was the zenith of the ambition of some young people. Place continued to be of primary human importance for centuries to come, and still does in some instances. However, the importance of the developments in thought charted above is that they set the scene for the development of modernism which, in its later phases, has downgraded the importance of place in people's *experience* as well as in patterns of thought. It is during this period, in other words, that these philosophical developments began to bite.

Place retained its religious significance right through the medieval period, as we shall see when we come to look at the phenomenon of pilgrimage in Chapter 4. However, theological thought about God's omnipotence in medieval times set the scene for a further eclipse of a recognition of the importance of place, and Aristotle reappears at this point in the story. In 1277 – three years after the death of Thomas Aquinas, who had done much to integrate Aristotelian thought into Western theology – the Bishop of Paris issued a series of condemnations which sought to suppress doctrines which limit the power of God, especially the Aristotelian notion of there only being a finite amount of matter in the universe. The problem was that since motion presupposes an infinite immovable body, there must by implication be a point of absolute rest, and God's power is thus limited. The condemnations therefore asserted, against Aristotle, that God is able to move the whole universe through space. In so doing, the possibility of infinite space was opened up: a development which was not seen to compromise God's omnipotence, since God was conceived as being outside time and space and to be Lord of it in terms of his power. This was a very important point for the relationship between space and place for it allowed the emergence of the concepts which underlie Newtonian physics, most notably its commitment to the infinity of the physical universe. Thus place becomes subordinate to space. Casey tells us: 'There can be little doubt that one of the most fateful things condemned by the condemnation was the primacy of place, thereby making room for the apotheosis of space that occurred in the seventeenth century.'[15]

Ironically, although this hugely important occurrence was intended to suppress Aristotelian philosophy, before very long Aristotelian thought gained ground again, so that, as Thomas Torrance puts it, 'the receptacle notion of space was consolidated into the whole structure of medieval theology.'[16] The interplay of theology and philosophy at this juncture was crucial for setting the seal upon the relegation of place to the boundaries of thought, because theology was a hugely important influence in the formulation of physical theories of space from the time of Philo to the Newtonian era and even later. As Casey puts it: 'If God is limitless in power, then his presence in

---

[14] See, for example, Weiner, J. (1991) and Lane, B. L. (1988).

[15] Casey, E. (1997), 107.

[16] Torrance, T. (1969), 25.

the universe at large must also be unlimited. Divine ubiquity thus entails spatial infinity. It further follows that the physical universe itself must be unlimited if it is to be the setting for God's ubiquity as well as the result of his creation.'[17] So it was that the idea of space was victorious over place, and Newton's concept of absolute space became a fundamental prerequisite of every physical investigation.

In an age of enormous change and development in thought the discoveries of Galileo, alongside those of Newton, had a very strong impact in conspiring to make place of no importance. In the words of Michel Foucault:

> The real scandal of Galileo's work lay not so much in his discovery, or rediscovery, that the earth revolved around the sun, but in his constitution of an infinite and infinitely open space. In such a space the place of the Middle Ages turned out to be dissolved, as it were; a thing's place was no longer anything but a point in its movement, just as the stability of a thing was only its movement infinitely slowed down. In other words, starting with Galileo and the seventeenth century, extension was substituted for localisation.[18]

For Galileo as for Newton, then, places were just portions of absolute space and have no interest or significance in their own right. One can see an important effect of these developments on place in the emergence of maps. In the medieval world view a whole sacred geography held sway: people were not only attached to the places in which they lived, but were conditioned to view the world as criss-crossed with holy places to which they made journey, pilgrimage. This disappeared when what Michel de Certeau terms 'itineraries' were replaced by 'maps' in the new configuration of modernity. He writes: 'If one takes the "map" in its current form, we can see that in the course of the period marked by the birth of modern scientific discourse (i.e. the fifteenth to the seventeenth century) the map has slowly disengaged itself from the itineraries that were the condition of its possibility.'[19] William Cavanaugh summarizes de Certeau's insights on the transformation thus:

> Pre-modern representations of space marked out itineraries which told 'spatial stories', for example, the illustration of the route of a pilgrimage which gave instructions on where to pray, where to spend the night , and so on. Rather than surveying them as a whole, the pilgrim moves through particular spaces, tracing a narrative through space and time by his or her movements and practices. … By contrast, modernity gave rise to the mapping of space on a grid, a "formal ensemble of abstract places" from which the itinerant was erased. A map is defined as a 'totalizing stage on which elements of diverse origin are brought together to form a tableau of a "state" of geographical knowledge'. Space itself is rationalised as homogeneous and divided into identical units. Each item on the map occupies its proper place, such that things are set beside one another, and no two things can occupy the same space. The point of view of the map user is detached and universal, allowing the entire space to be seen simultaneously.[20]

A geographer named Brian Jarvis has noted that: 'some critics in the burgeoning field of feminist geography have argued that cartography is inherently authoritarian,

---

[17] Casey, E. (1997), 77.

[18] Foucault, M. (1986), 23.

[19] de Certeau, M. (1984), 120.

[20] Cavanaugh, W. (1999), 183.

tainted by its association with a prohibitive Enlightenment metaphysic that ensures this abolition of difference, automatic complicity with authority and the imposition of standardised patterns of order'. He tells us that he finds this 'an entirely appropriate criticism of the dominant cartographic order'.[21] Within this criticism we can see another indication of the way in which this particular homogenization of space is associated with power.

Throughout the period we have been considering, most people, as we have observed, remained attached to place. However, one might conjecture that it was the very fact that people were bound to particular places which fuelled the very preoccupation with space which I have been cataloguing. Casey suggests that Western thinkers were drawn to meditate upon the vastness of space because, in invidious contrast, place presents itself in what he refers to as stubborn and rebarbative particularity: 'Regarding the particular place that one is in one cannot speculate, much less levitate or miraculate, freely; one has to cope with the exacting demands of being just there, with all its finite historicity and special qualities.'[22] Place can be frustrating and 'rebarbative', and when this frustration strikes it is likely that the 'freedom' represented by a consideration of space will hold a particular attraction. In an age of enforced commitment it is not difficult to see why such restrictions led to a desire to escape in the mind, if not the body. It was a complex mixture of all these factors that led to a burgeoning interest in space and an eclipsing of concern for place.

Yet another factor emerged to consolidate this demise of place, though: time. This again, was a gradual process. Max Jammer asserts that it was only in the late Middle Ages that the role of time as the fundamental viable parameter in physical processes was clearly understood, and points out that by the twentieth century a profound change had taken place, as is evidenced by Carnap's assertion in 1925 that the properties of space are dependent on those of time.[23] What caused this shift? According to Jammer, it was Leibnitz's profound analysis of the concepts of space and time which led to the conviction that the notion of time must precede that of space in the construction of a philosophical system. However it happened, Casey points out how Kant argued in his *Critique of Pure Reason* that objective succession of time is the schematic expression of causality in the physical world order, and suggests that 'by the moment when Kant could assert this, time had won primacy over space. We have been living off this legacy ever since, not only in philosophy and physics but in our daily lives as well.'[24] Practical as well as philosophical considerations also played their part, however: the sociologist Anthony Giddens argues that history and time began to be asserted over geography and space when the mechanical clock began to become widely available at the end of the eighteenth century, since it led to the specific ordering of time as a universal phenomenon.[25] Making a similar point, Casey recounts the fascinating story of the invention of the marine chronometer,[26]

---

[21] Jarvis, B. (1998), 194.

[22] Casey, E. (1997), 338.

[23] Carnap R., referred to in Jammer, M. (1969), 4.

[24] Casey, E. (1993), 7.

[25] See Giddens, A. (1990).

[26] This story has since been popularized by a television production and book. See Sobel, D. (1999).

which solved the problem of the determination of longitude but meant that the 'where' became determined by the 'when'.

The invention solved a pressing problem. In 1707 a fleet of British ships became lost in heavy fog for eleven days on their return to England from Gibraltar. On the twelfth day they ran into the Scilly Isles with the loss of four ships and two thousand men, the navigators having thought that they were safely to the west of Brittany. As a response to this disaster the Government of the day passed a bill offering a reward of £20 000 – a very considerable sum – to 'such person or persons as shall discover the Longitude'. The reward was offered in 1714, but it was not until 1761 that John Harrison was given the coveted prize by the Board of Longitude for his 'No 5 Chronometer'. Casey asserts that concealed within Harrison's triumph was 'a form of domination such as the Western world had never known: the subordination of space to time, or "temprocentrism" as we may call it'.[27]

The gist of the development that I am suggesting occurred is that the subordination of place to space culminated in the seventeenth century, and that the overcoming of space by time continued during the next two-and-a-half centuries. The result is that time came to be conceived in such a way that everything else is made subservient to it, beginning with place and ending with space. At the end of this process, Hans Reichenbach was able to claim in 1958 that 'time is ... logically prior to space'.[28] The situation has been complicated by the dual paradigms of modern physics, Quantum Theory and relativity, which have yet to be reconciled.[29] The former reasserts the importance of the particular, but the implications of it have, to date, barely entered the discourse of non-physicists. Thus we remain in a period where time receives much attention. This is not a happy situation since, 'when events are ordered on a time line – just as Descartes, Leibnitz and Kant all proposed (and as Galilean and Newtonian physics seemed to affirm) we should not expect anything other than the running down or out of these events, their literal ex-haustion. Our lives also run out and down if we conceive them on this kenotic model of self-emptying time.'[30] This observation correlates with my own experience of primitive societies in Africa and traditional working-class communities in England, which leads me to believe that their attitudes to time are much more relaxed than those parts of the world where everyone is rushing 'against' it.

Is the above analysis correct? It is certainly true to say that in the period of modernism 'place' has not been singled out for scrutiny in academic discourse, but Clifford Geertz, acknowledging this fact in his own discipline, anthropology, offers more straightforward reasons for the omission:

> One is surely the simple ubiquity of place and the sense of place in human life. It is difficult to see what is always there. Whoever discovered water, it was not a fish. Also, the diffuseness of the term in ordinary language makes it hard to fix in the mind. The six three-column pages its definition takes up in the Oxford English Dictionary ... is evidence

---

[27] Casey, E. (1993), 7.

[28] Reichenbach, H., quoted in Jammer, M. (1969), 5.

[29] The search for what are termed by physicists 'theories of everything' is something which is greatly occupying many at present. See Barrow, J. (1990).

[30] Casey, E. (1993), 7.

enough that it is not a clear and distinct idea. But the invisibility of place has mainly to do with the fact that it is so difficult to free from subjectiveness and occasions, immediate perceptions and instant cases. Like love or imagination, Place makes a poor abstraction. Separated from it materialisations, it has little meaning.[31]

Against Geertz, we have asserted that place receives so little attention because Western academia has become obsessed with space and then time. It was certainly considered worthy of consideration in pre-modern society, as we have noted, and contemporary studies from primitive societies in Geertz's own discipline have indicated that place does not necessarily have to be such an elusive quality even now, as we shall see. Geertz's comment that place, like love or imagination, makes a poor abstraction is telling, since the development of science is one which is primarily interested in phenomena which can be abstracted. Things which cannot be abstracted lost their appeal during the period of modernity and its search for 'universals'.

Geertz goes on to observe that: 'No one lines up people and asks them to define "place" and list three examples of it. No one really has a theory of it. No one imagines that it is some sort of data set to be sampled, ordered, tabulated, and manipulated.'[32] I would suggest that it is the tyranny of the scientific method, so conspicuously successful in many areas, that it has led modern thinkers to believe that the only academically respectable manner of proceeding with data is to 'sample, order, tabulate and manipulate'. But should we approach all phenomena in the same way? Should we not, too, attend to the insights of those who believe scientific 'objectivity' to be a chimera? One such is the philosopher of science Michael Polanyi who developed an interpretation of what is involved in knowing and understanding that questions all attempts to make the scientific method a privileged way of knowing, utterly different from and more reliable than other human ways of understanding.[33] I would suggest that Geertz's analysis is naive, and that the one which I have summarized is more convincing.

Further support for our alternative account can be found in David Harvey, for example, who speaks of the privileging of time over space in late modernism as 'one of the more startling schisms in our intellectual heritage'. Social theories, he tells us, typically privilege time over space in their formulations: 'They broadly assume either the existence of some pre-existing spatial order within which temporal processes operate, or that spatial barriers have been so reduced as to render space a contingent rather than fundamental aspect of human action.'[34] Harvey points out that though space and time are basic categories of human existence, we rarely debate their meanings: we tend to take them for granted and give them 'common-sense or self-evident attributions'. Harvey observes that it is a tribute to the compartmentalizations in Western thought that this disjunction has for so long passed largely unremarked. He feels that, on the surface, the difference is not too hard to understand since social theory has always focused on processes of social change, modernization and

---

[31] Geertz, C. in Feld, S. and Basso, K. H. (1996), 259.

[32] Geertz, C. in Feld, S. and Basso, K. H. (1996), 260.

[33] Polanyi suggested that scientists are, in fact, very much part of a 'tradition' which conditions their response to data. See Polanyi, M. (1967). See also Kuhn, T. (1962) and Steiner, G. (1989).

[34] Harvey, D. (1990), 205.

revolution (technical, social and political). Pointing out that writings on modernization emphasize temporality rather than spatiality, he suggests that, from the perspective of modernism, 'progress entails the conquest of space, the tearing down of all spatial barriers, and the ultimate annihilation of space through time. The reduction of space to a contingent category is implied in the notion of progress itself.'[35] Harvey's words suggest how the eclipsing of place first by space and then by time in Western thought has been translated into actual experience. In the past it would have taken months to move around the globe: it now takes seconds, and in the process space and time increasingly are compressed. This annihilation of space through time fuelled a preoccupation with time in which place is forced out of the picture. Michel Foucault, a seasoned investigator of hidden tyrannies of thought, writes that a critique could be carried out of 'this devaluation of space that has prevailed for generations. Space was treated as the dead, the fixed, the undialectical, the immobile. Time, on the other hand, was richness, fecundity, life, dialectic.'[36] It is ironic that it was Foucault, who is well known for his insightful historical analyses and thus associated primarily with time, who should note the importance of space and place. The irony melts, however, when one realizes that, like any other phenomenon, one can only really understand the contemporary approach to place by tracking its history. That we have done, and our conclusions correlate with those of Casey, who summarizes what has happened as follows:

> In the past three centuries in the West – the period of 'modernity' – place has come to be not only neglected but actively suppressed. Owing to the triumph of the natural and social sciences in this same period, any serious talk of place has been regarded as regressive or trivial. A discourse has emerged whose exclusive cosmological foci are Time and Space. When the two were combined by twentieth century physicists into the amalgam 'space-time' the overlooking of place was only continued by another means. For an entire epoch, place has been regarded as an impoverished second cousin of Time and Space, those two colossal cosmic partners towering over modernity.[37]

Foucault associates the prevailing view with the discourses of power. Relationships of power are complicated, but it is certainly those with control of wealth and power in the last generation, more than any other, who have seen the annihilation of space through time. This development is, of course, one of the great achievements of modernity. In the last fifty years the possibility of travel has been greater than ever before, both in terms of the ease of travel in a 'global village' and in terms of the number of people who are able to indulge in such travel, for pleasure as well as business. But it is a mixed blessing. I know from my own experience how comforting it can be to travel, how tempting it is to believe that by travelling one will actually be achieving something – if only by 'widening one's horizons' – whereas in fact travel can simply be an escape, literally an escape, from facing the sorts of irritations which Casey refers to as the 'rebarbative particularity' of remaining in one place. I shall later argue that the avoidance of such 'rebarbative particularity' is necessarily dehumanizing.

---

[35] Ibid.

[36] Foucault, M. (1980), 70.

[37] Casey, E. (1993), xiv.

Twenty years ago the annihilation of space through time was being experienced as discussed above, but more spectacularly, in what has been described as 'the conquest of space'. A glance at the entry for 'space' in recent editions of *Encyclopedia Britannica* shows this: the 'space race' is catalogued in great detail – presumably in the belief that this is all people will want to know about – and nothing else is mentioned. Time was, of course, all-important in this latter venture, since if space is to be 'conquered' then the speed at which travel occurs has to be ever faster. However, things have taken an unexpected and dramatic turn in the advent of electronic media. Space and time can now be annihilated *without even moving*. Anthony Giddens argues that localized activities dominated the shaping of space into place by pre-modern societies, but that the situation has changed dramatically since, as Anthony Giddens observes, the advent of modernity 'increasingly tears space away from place by fostering relations between "absent" others, locationally distant from any given situation of face-to-face interaction. In conditions of modernity, place becomes increasingly *phantasmagoric*: that is to say, locales are thoroughly penetrated by and shaped in terms of social influence quite distant to them.'[38]

Those of us with sufficient wealth and power are now able to be in contact with others anywhere on the globe instantaneously. There are new and potent forces at work here, and the consequences, as Giddens indicates, are profound. In a good account of the effects of electronic communications up until 1985, Joshua Meyrowitz points out the enormous effect of electronic media, especially television, on Americans' sense of place: 'Electronic media have combined previously distinct social settings, moving the dividing line between private and public behaviour towards the private, and weakened the relationship between social situations and physical places.'[39] This is not only true of Americans, of course, and the effects Meyrowitz is describing have been multiplied severalfold since 1985. Electronic media have, in the recent past, resulted in coinage of the phrase 'virtual space'. The development of highly sophisticated games in which people can take on imaginary identities and engage in interactive encounters and contests on line mean that the notion of 'placement' has become all the more precarious. Questions of 'where' something is on the Internet, and to whom it belongs, are beginning to engage lawyers at an increasing pace, and these, together with moral questions surrounding the advance of cloning and other genetic techniques, are likely to become a great preoccupation. Cloning represents yet another move away from the *particular*. There is opening up the possibility of moving from a world in which the particularity of places has been eroded by the invasion of Macdonald's and other familiar icons of the homogenization of places to an even more disturbing one in which one might find identical cloned human beings anywhere in the world.

The above influences mean that each geographical 'place' in the world is being realigned in relation to the new global realities, their roles within the wider whole are being reassigned, their boundaries dissolved as they are increasingly crossed by everything from investment flows, to cultural influences, to satellite TV networks. This dramatic change is one to which attention was drawn by Martin Heidegger long before the situation became as acute as it is today:

---

[38] Giddens, A. (1990), 18.

[39] Meyrowitz, J. (1985), 308.

All distances in time and space are shrinking. Man now reaches overnight, by plane, places which formerly took weeks and months of travel. He now receives instant information, by radio, of events which he formerly learned about only years later, if at all.... Man puts the longest distances behind him in the shortest time. He puts the greatest distances behind himself and this puts everything before him in the shortest range. Yet the frantic abolition of all distances brings no nearness; for nearness does not consist in shortness of distance. What is least remote from us in point of distance, by virtue of its picture on film or its sound on radio, can remain far from us. What is incalculably far from us in point of distance can be near to us.... What is happening here when, as a result of the abolition of great distances, everything is equally far and equally near? What is this uniformity in which everything is neither far nor near – is, as it were, without distance? Everything gets lumped together into uniform distancelessness. How? Is not this merging of everything into the distanceless more unearthly than everything bursting apart? ... What is it that unsettles and thus terrifies? It shows itself and hides itself in the way in which everything presences, namely, in the fact that despite all conquest of distances the nearness of things remains absent.[40]

Heidegger summarizes the effects of the demise of place which I have been tracing upon humanity, and corroborates the proposition that the prevailing intellectual discourse at which we have been looking has worked itself out with immense and 'terrifying' effect upon human experience in the twentieth century.

Protests at This Prevailing Discourse

A Phenomenological Approach to Place in Philosophy, Geography and Psychology

Heidegger declares that the manner in which time and distance are shrinking 'unsettles and terrifies'. It is, no doubt, such dis-ease that has brought place back onto the agenda in some circles. There has, in fact, been a rising tide of protest against the hegemony of time and space which so suits the Western world view and its drive towards globalization in the name of greater prosperity for all. This is because such protesters feel the negative as well as the positive effects of this state of affairs on themselves and others.[41] Whilst the wealthy experience the practical if mixed blessings of the annihilation of space through time, the poor in our world experience a loss of place in more malign forms, through the experience of being a refugee or a migrant worker.

Such protests almost invariably begin, like Heidegger's, with phenomenology. Phenomenology is the study of the forms in which something appears or manifests itself, in contrast to studies that seek to explain things, say, from their causal relations, evolutionary processes, theological dogma or some other first principle. I indicated at the beginning of this chapter that our conception of place will be affected both by our own experience and by traditions of thought and practice in our society. Phenomenologists concentrate upon the latter and question the assumptions of

---

[40] Heidegger, M. (1975), 165–6.

[41] For a good analysis of globalization see Waters, M. (1995). Waters characterizes globalization as: 'a social process in which the constraints of geography on social and cultural arrangements recede and in which people become increasingly aware that they are receding' (p.3).

prevailing norms which seem not to correlate with their experience or make sense in the light of it. Casey, to whose analysis of the demise of place I have made reference above, begins from a phenomenological standpoint. He opens his book *The Fate of Place* as follows:

> Whatever is true for space and time, this much is true for place. We are immersed in it and could not do without it. To be at all – to exist in any way – is to be somewhere, and to be somewhere is to be in some kind of place. Place is as requisite as the air we breathe, the ground on which we stand, the bodies we have. We are surrounded by places. We walk over them and through them. We live in places, relate to others in them, die in them. Nothing we do is unplaced. How could it be otherwise? How could we fail to recognise this primal fact?[42]

The answer he gives, as we have seen, is that we do not realize this primal fact because of the predominant discourse in which we are immersed. One of the many things that philosophy has taught us, thanks to the important work of people like Foucault, is that there are certain narratives – discourses – which shape our perceptions. One of these, I have been suggesting, is a forceful one in Western culture that devalues place. I have proposed that just how embedded this is in our thinking is shown by the way in which place has not been considered a topic worthy of consideration in philosophy. People like Casey are enabling us to see that modernism has had inherent in it from the beginning a universalism which, in his words, is 'most starkly evident in the search for ideas, usually labelled "essences", that obtain everywhere and for which a particular *somewhere*, a given place, is presumably irrelevant'.[43] This approach translates into a globalization which, like the modernity from which it springs, brings benefits, but huge concomitant costs. One of them is the disappearance of a recognition of the importance of place not just from the world of ideas, but from the world which people inhabit.

Casey himself acknowledges that it is not only the Western philosophical tradition that has had an effect upon people's experience of place, or lack or it. He suggests that during the last century, at the same time as the West has experienced the 'displacement' of electronic technology which seems to render one's locality irrelevant, there have been other momentous happenings making themselves felt on other sections of the human population, each of which could be argued to encourage a devaluation of place. These include:

> the cataclysmic effects of two world wars, which have acted to undermine any secure sense of place (in fact, to destroy it altogether in the case of a radical anti-place like Auchwitz); the forced migrations of entire peoples, along with the continual drifting on the part of many individuals, suggesting that the world is nothing but a scene of endless displacement. … Each of these phenomena is truly 'cosmic', that is, literally worldwide, and each exhibits a *dromocentrism* that amounts to temporocentrism writ large: not just time but speeded up

---

[42] Casey, E. (1997), ix. Edward Hall has argued that human beings are spatially predisposed, citing as evidence that 20 per cent of the words found in the *Pocket Oxford Dictionary* refer to space. See Hall, E. (1969), 93.

[43] Ibid., xii. For a good account of modernism and its relation to theology and science, see Funkenstein, A. (1986).

time (*dromos* connotes 'running', 'race', 'racecourse') is of the essence of the era. It is as if the acceleration discovered by Galileo to be inherent in falling bodies has come to pervade the earth (conceived as a single scene of communication), rendering the planet a global village not in a positive sense but as a placeless place indeed.[44]

It is, then, not just those in the prosperous West who feel dislocation. Others do, too, but more painfully. Elie Wiesel characterized the twentieth century as the 'age of the expatriate, the refugee, the stateless – and the wanderer'.[45] It is, however, those in the prosperous West who have the time and opportunity to articulate such problems.

It was a phenomenological approach that enabled cultural geographers to look again at the importance of place. This is clear from their own analysis of what drives them. Take Yi-Fu Tuan, for instance: 'Most of us must have first felt the romance of our subject through some real encounter with the colour, odour – the mood – of a place.'[46] He suggests that to deny this would not only be to deny experience, but also to hide our shortcomings under a treacherous figure of speech – 'in the mind' – and imply without justification the achievement of objectivity. Tuan is here appealing to experience and asking his fellow geographers not to overlook the importance of place by discounting personal biography in their academic work, the tendency to do so being a feature of the Western intellectual tradition. It is no accident that it is women, generally much less reluctant to engage with the interface between their own experience and their academic studies than men, who have forced the issue. So, Ann Buttimer acknowledges the influence that early experience of place has had on her:

I'm sure that many of the attitudes I bring to my geography ... derive from my childhood experiences of life in Ireland. It is difficult for me to find words to describe what the experience of living in Ireland still means for me. It is a total experience of milieu which is evoked: I recall the feel of the grass on bare feet, the smells and sounds of various seasons, the places and times I meet friends on walks, the daily ebb and flow of milking time, meals, reading and thinking, sleeping and waking. Most of this experience is not consciously processed through my head – which is why words are so hard to find – for this place allows head and heart, body and spirit, imagination and will to become harmonious and creative.[47]

It is important for us to realize that these views were extremely counter-cultural in the world of geography at the time they were articulated. A small band of cultural geographers fought for an acceptance of the overwhelming importance of place in human experience, and so in geography. In 1976 Edward Relph wrote of the almost total failure of geographers to explore the concept of place and, in going on to do so, employed a phenomenological approach which presupposes that the foundations of geographical knowledge lie in the direct experiences and consciousness of the world we live in.[48] Much later, R. J. Johnston still felt it necessary to declare to his fellow geographers that 'place is central to geography'. He accuses geographers of having

---

[44] Ibid., xiii.

[45] Wiesel, E. (1996), 19.

[46] Tuan, Y.-F. (1972), 535.

[47] Buttimer, A. and Seamon, D. (1980), 172. She quotes similar experiences of other geographers in Buttimer, A. (1993), 29.

[48] Relph, E. (1976), 4.

undertaken no profound analysis of two of their central concepts, region and place, and argues for putting 'place' at the centre of human geography which, he tells us, 'lacks a core'. Johnston moves on to attempt an analysis of place from a geographer's perspective. He believes that place is important since, 'places differ not simply because their physical environments differ but also because, for a variety of reasons, people have responded differently to the opportunities and restraints that those environments offer.' It is not only the physical environment that matters, nor only the people who inhabit that environment – the true picture needs to take account of the complex interplay that takes place between the two. He goes on: 'The nature of their responses is important, because they provide the cultural resources within which societies "develop".... In appreciating the contemporary cultural mosaic, therefore, we must appreciate its foundations in the accommodations between communities and their environments in the creation of social structures as "machines for living".'[49] The fact is that there is no such thing as a physical geography of anywhere divorced from its human geography, and even more so the other way round. Relph suggests that places are thus basic elements in the ordering of our experiences of the world. Tuan uses the word *topophilia* as the title for one of his books, a word which means, literally, 'place-love'. He attempts a study of environmental perception, attitudes, experience and values which, he tells us, are enormously complex. Later he bemoans the fact that 'a large body of experiential data is consigned to oblivion because we cannot fit the data to concepts that are taken over uncritically from the physical sciences. Our understanding of human reality suffers as a result.'[50] He insists that appreciation of place develops very early, and that this means that feelings and ideas concerning place are extremely complex in adult human beings growing, as they do, out of life's unique and shared experiences. Every person starts, however, as an infant, and it is out of the infant's tiny world that there appears in time the adult's world view. The philosopher Susan Langer reinforces this point:

> One of my earliest recollections is that chairs and tables always kept the same look, in a way that people did not and that I was awed by the sameness of that appearance. They symbolised such and such a mood ... to project feelings into outer objects is the first way of symbolising and thus of conceiving those feelings. This activity belongs to about the earliest period of childhood that memory can recover. The concept of 'self', which is usually thought to mark the beginning of actual memory, may possibly depend on this process of symbolically epitomising our feelings.[51]

Sadly, although there has been much work in developmental psychology in relation to objects by Piaget and others on what they call the *object concept*, little mention is made of the physical environment as an important factor in a child's developing concept of self by orthodox psychoanalytic theorists. Interestingly, there is even less discussion of adult conceptions of self and environment in the literature. This is in spite of the fact that it is impossible to talk about the self except in relational terms such as 'here' and 'there', or 'inside' and 'beside'.

---

[49] Johnstone, R. J. (1991), 69, 75, 253.

[50] Tuan, Y.-F. (1974), 92. The later work is Tuan, Y.-F. (1977), 25.

[51] Langer, S. (1953), 100.

The huge but little investigated importance of place in our early years results in it being *internalized*. Such internalization was studied by the French thinker Gaston Bachelard, who proposes what he calls *topoanalysis* to study the psychological importance of place. Bachelard argues that the significance of locality is as important in the mind as it is in the outside world, so that place can be non-physical and yet fully count as place. He insists that the psyche or the soul is the spatial receptacle for images, above all poetic images. Poetic images must exist somewhere, and Bachelard tells us that the place in which they exist is psychical in nature. He works out his theme using the image of the house. Our childhood home, he suggests, is our 'first universe', and therefore becomes 'the topography of our intimate being'. In psychic spatiality, place is everything 'for a knowledge of intimacy, localisation in the spaces of our intimacy is more important than dates'. In other words, as we think of all the images contained within our mind, the date or time at which we came into contact with them is only one way of organizing them, and not one which we would normally use, for the chronology of things gives only 'a sort of external history, for external use, to be communicated to others'.[52] Bachelard is suggesting that in order to understand oneself, what he calls 'topoanalysis', the exploration of self-identity through place, might be more useful than psychoanalysis – though on this account the two are virtually identical.

Such insights represent a rising protest against the dehumanizing effects of the ignoring of place in Western society. The complaint is encapsulated in the analysis of Buttimer that since the Second World War the importance of place has been ignored in practice as much as in theory for the sake of economic values such as mobility, centralization or rationalization. She writes: 'The skyscrapers, airports, freeways and other stereotypical components of modern landscapes – are they not the sacred symbols of a civilisation that has deified reach and derided home?'[53] Relph sees this development as derived from 'an inauthentic attitude to places' which is transmitted through a number of processes or media which directly or indirectly encourage 'placelessness', that is, a weakening of the identity of places to the point where they not only look alike but feel alike and offer the same bland possibilities for experience. These media include 'mass communications, mass culture, big business, powerful central authority, and the economic system which embraces all of these'.[54]

It would not be true to say that protests against the predominant view of space and place have never been seen before. In the same piece by Buttimer from which the above quotation is taken, she contends that the record of interest in place

---

[52] Bachelard, G. (1964), xii, 8, 9. Michel Foucault applauds the work of Bachelard as monumental, and writes that it and the descriptions of other phenomenologists 'have taught us that we do not live in a homogeneous and empty space, but on the contrary in a space thoroughly imbued with quantities and perhaps thoroughly fantasmic as well' (Foucault, M., 1986, 23). Similarly, Paul Tournier emphasizes the importance of the child's surroundings in its first home in the development of human identity. He suggests that psychological dysfunction cannot be considered apart from the physical context in which it is experienced, and that deprivation of love and deprivation of place overlap (Tournier, P., 1968, 27).

[53] Buttimer. A. (1980), 174. Similarly, Benko refers to the fact that many locations have become 'non-places', spaces 'devoid of the symbolic expressions of identity, relations and history: examples include airports, motorways, anonymous hotel rooms, public transport' (see Benko, G., 1997, 23 and Augé, M., 1997).

[54] Relph, E. (1976), 90.

synchronizes fairly well with periods of relatively abrupt change either within the social or physical environment or in the world of ideas. Late eighteenth-century and early nineteenth-century Romantic literature on place, for instance, corresponds roughly with a reaction against a Newtonian world view by those who thought it 'scandalous to impose a "scientific" grid on Nature – to reduce beauty, melody, and fragrance to the sterile metric of mathematics or physics'. Buttimer records that when industrialism and transport systems began to rupture the old harmonies of peasant landscapes 'protest was voiced in the language of place. Urbanisation brought its own wave of rebellion against abrupt change: the old mosaic of artisan districts, open markets, and bourgeois villas became distorted and dismantled as within the city itself former cultural and economic equilibria gave way to the new.'[55] I would suggest that the protests are more common now both because the situation is more acute and because the assumptions of modernism are now being discerned and questioned more thoroughly than before.

Most of the geographers to whom I have made reference above are dependent, to greater or lesser extent, upon the work of Heidegger in helping them to make sense of their observations. For example, David Harvey observes the way in which what he refers to as Heidegger's 'ontological excavations' have inspired a particular approach to social processes. Edward Relph owes much to Heidegger, and David Seamon applauds the latter.[56] For Heidegger, the human person is a *dasein*, literally a 'being there' – so that placedness is of the essence. It 'places' human beings in such a way that it reveals the external bonds of their existence and at the same time the depths of their freedom and reality. Heidegger's thought reacts against what he sees as the sadness that 'science's knowledge, which is compelling within its own sphere, the sphere of objects, already had annihilated things as things long before the atom bomb exploded'.[57] This is because 'the modern attitude toward things has the character of seizing. Things are comprehended by attacking them and capturing them in concepts which express them as objects faced by a subject. Thing or being is no longer a sojourning being, but a representative being i.e. a being as set forward in front of a subject and fitted to his sight.'[58] Thus Seamon is attracted to the integration which Heidegger seems to offer, since 'throughout Heidegger's characterisation of person-in-world is a sense of immersion and inextricable togetherness rooted in time and space. Man is not a subject apart from the world as he is in most traditional philosophies, but an integral, immersed member.'[59] Heidegger believed that the true

---

[55] Buttimer, (1980), 170.

[56] See Relph, E. (1989), 26, and numerous references to Heidegger in Relph, E. (1976). Seamon writes: 'Whereas many approaches to human problems advocated by social and behavioural scientists assume that people can actively forge a better world through material, socioeconomic change, Heidegger, recognising humankind's fragility and participation in a universe of meaning, which he calls Being, seeks to reduce people's sense of anthropomorphism and to usher in a new world view founded on care and openness. The aim is a reintegration of earth, people, and an invigorated spirituality arising from the individual's reflexive awareness of his or her life and mortality. The crux of such a possibility is what Heidegger calls in his later work, *dwelling* – the process through which people make their place of existence a home' (Seamon D., 1984, 45).

[57] Heidegger, M. (1971), 170.

[58] Vycinas, V. (1969), 96.

[59] Seamon, M. in Richardson (1984), 45

understanding of 'things' arises when we let things be and allow them to speak through us. This will lead to what Heidegger called 'disclosure', which is the revelation of a thing as it is in itself. His later work concentrates upon the implications of this for 'dwelling':

> A style of disclosure practised in daily life leads to the Heideggerian notion that perhaps has the most direct practical value for students of environment and place, namely, dwelling. Dwelling is the final conceptualisation of the key aim of Heidegger's work: to resurrect an ontological scheme that relocates person-in-world. Over his life, Heidegger phrases this task differently, and these differences can be spoken of as 'stages', though each stage is not chronologically exclusive but interpenetrates others ... The third stage explores person-in-world more in terms of daily living, and its key is dwelling.[60]

In his essay *Building, Dwelling, Thinking*, Heidegger asks: 'What, then, does *bauen*, "building" *mean*? The Old English and High German word for building, *bauen*, means to dwell. This signifies: to remain, to stay in place. The real meaning of the word *bauen*, namely, to dwell, has been lost to us.'[61] He goes on to point out that a covert trace of it has been retained in the word 'neighbour' which implies to cherish, and protect, to preserve and care for, and suggests that a proper understanding of building would relate to its etymological roots, to dwelling, and that this dwelling would involve a sense of continuity, community and of being 'at home'. Seamon tells us that Heidegger believed that it is 'this basic lack of "dwelling" ... that is another reason for much of the trouble and anxiety of modern times – and also explains the sorry state of some modern architecture.'[62]

With this in mind, we can go on to observe that some work stemming from protests against the loss of place, including that of Seamon whom I quoted above, has been directed towards critical analyses for application in urban planning, environmental design and architecture. The importance of buildings to transform undifferentiated *space* into marked and delimited *place* and the power of architecture are being increasingly recognized. Some architects have joined the fray. Richard Rogers points out that although the cities of Europe have traditionally, by their design, shown the importance of place to the functioning of such cities, nowadays most people associate cities with congestion, crime, pollution and fear. The BBC reported in November 2000 that well over 1000 people a week are leaving English towns and cities to escape from urban life. In all probability, a negative connection will be made in most people's minds between city and quality of living. Rogers' diagnosis of the demise of cities is expressed as follows:

> The essential problem is that cities have been viewed in instrumental or consumerist terms. Those responsible for them have tended to see it as their role to design cities to meet private material needs, rather than foster public life. The result is that cities have been polarised into communities of rich and poor and segregated into ghettos of single minded activity – the business park, the Housing Estate, the residential suburb – or worse still, into giant

---

[60] Ibid.

[61] Heidegger, M. (1971), 146

[62] Seamon, M. in Richardson, M. (1984), 45.

single function buildings like Shopping Centres with their own private streets (which lead nowhere) built in. ... We are witnessing the destruction of the very idea of the city.[63]

The British Government recognized the problem by setting up of an Urban Task Force chaired by Lord Rogers in 1999, which resulted in the publication of a White Paper in 2000. The latter proposed a number of measures designed to promote urban living, including an English Cities Fund, which in partnership with private enterprise will tackle the impact of cars, grime and graffiti. The problem is that places are turning from 'places' into dehumanizing 'spaces'. This is more than anywhere else true in North America, where the 'downtown' areas of most cities have become no-go areas of deprivation, squalor and crime, whilst in the suburbs 'gated housing' estates abound. One of the seldom articulated effects of the tyranny of the market model is the consumerization of space to which Rogers refers, and the proliferation of what Rogers calls 'single minded space' as opposed to 'open minded space'. The market model has been a key player in the demise of place in the recent past, as we shall see. 'Open minded spaces' are places which can foster the shared, public life, and thereby the community. One should add that the socialist model has not done any better than the market model: travelling around Eastern Europe and seeing the devastation of once beautiful cities is a salutary experience.

It has been observed that environments are thought before they are built. This insight may give weight to the proposition that, encouraged and enabled by a long philosophical tradition, the political orthodoxies of our recent past have contributed to the downgrading of 'human' place and this has had severe ramifications in architecture. Once built, the buildings reinforce the prevailing norms. As Winston Churchill put it: 'first we shape our buildings and then our buildings shape us'. We 'breathe in' our surroundings as much as we observe them, and there is no doubt that the modern city is full of barriers, both material and intangible, which conceal or deny that segregated people with different social identities, defined by class or by ethnic characteristics, dwell in the same town. The sociologist E. V. Walker suggests that what has been happening is a 'topomorphic revolution', which he describes as radical shift of topistic structure, a fundamental change in the form of dwelling together. Such revolutions conceal, interrupt, or break the old forms, causing new structures by patterns of exclusion, enclosure, and dissociation.[64] In other words, 'places' are turned into 'spaces' since the manner in which they enrich people's humanity is lost.

A phenomenological approach among scholars in the disciplines at which we have been looking has thus served to raise serious questions about how dehumanizing the loss of place has been in Western society.

Place in Political and Social Theory

Rogers' contention that cities have been viewed in instrumental or consumerist terms moves us to the political dimensions of the protest I have been describing. Criticisms

---

[63] Rogers, R. (1997). The publication by English Heritage in 2000 of a report entitled *The Power of Place. The Future of the Historic Environment* also shows a renewed concern about place.

[64] Walker, E. V. (1988), 23.

of the political dimensions of the downgrading of place are seen most clearly in the works of neo-Marxists like David Harvey, Edward Soja and Peter Jackson. Brian Jarvis tells us that it is gradually being recognized in postmodern times that:

Space/place/landscape is always represented in relation to codes that are embedded in social power structures. The three most significant power structures in contemporary American society are capitalism, patriarchy and white racial hegemony. Accordingly, the subjects of class and capital, gender and sexuality, race and ethnicity, whilst by no means exclusive of other interests, are of critical significance to any study of the workings of the geographical imagination in modern culture.[65]

Even these make use of Heidegger. It might be thought that someone of the latter's political sympathy would be a strange bedfellow for neo-Marxists, but David Harvey quotes a passage from *Poetry, Language, Thought* which, he observes, shows that Heidegger attributes the achieved shift in space relations to commodification and market exchange, and that in so doing invokes an argument remarkably similar to Marx:

The object-character of technological dominion spreads itself over the earth ever more quickly, ruthlessly and completely. Not only does it establish all things as producible in the process of production; it also delivers the products of production by means of the market. In self-assertive production, the humanness of man and the thingness of things dissolve into the calculated market value of a market which not only spans the whole earth as a world market but also, as the will to will, trades in the nature of Being and thus subjects all beings to the trade of a calculation that dominates most tenaciously those areas where there is no need of numbers.[66]

This homogenization of space which dumbs our sense of place and stifles our humanity is seen by Harvey as a crisis:

The tension between fixity and mobility erupts into generalised crises ... when the landscape shaped in relation to a certain phase of development (capitalist or pre-capitalist) becomes a barrier to further accumulation. The landscape must then be reshaped around new transport and communications systems and physical infrastructures, new centres and styles of production and consumption, new agglomerations of labour power and modified social infrastructures (including, for example, systems of governance and regulation of places). Old places have to be devalued, destroyed or redeveloped while new places are created. The cathedral city becomes a heritage centre; the mining community becomes a ghost town; the old industrial centre is deindustrialised; speculative boom towns or gentrified neighbourhoods arise on the frontiers of capitalist development or out of the ashes of deindustrialised communities. The history of capitalism is punctuated by intense phases of spatial reorganisation.[67]

The market model fits well with the modernist notion of development conceived in

---

[65] Jackson, P. (1989), *Maps of Meaning*, London: Routledge, 7. Of Harvey's many works the best known is Harvey, M. (1990). Soja's approach is made clear in Soja, E. W. (1989).

[66] Heidegger, M. (1971), 114–15, quoted in Harvey, M. (1993), 10.

[67] Harvey, M. (1993), 7.

terms of the conquest of space and time, but some of its notable successes have forced huge change – and there has been a considerable cost. This has been seen, as much as anywhere else, in its effect on places. Harvey concurs with what I proposed above, that we have been experiencing, since 1970, an intense phase of time-space compression – compression that has had a disorientating effect upon political-economic practices, the balance of class power, as well as upon cultural and social life. He feels that we have witnessed 'another fierce round in that process of annihilation of space through time that has always lain at the heart of capitalism's dynamic', and points out that one of the results of this is that urban places that once had a secure status find themselves vulnerable and 'residents find themselves forced to ask what kind of place can be remade that will survive within the new matrix of space relations. We worry about the meaning of place when the security of actual places becomes threatened.'[68]

The threat to the security and identity of a particular place because of the forces of which Harvey is speaking is something of which I have firsthand experience. In the early 1990s I was Vicar of the parish in which the Swan Hunter Shipyard at Wallsend on Tyneside was situated. This most prestigious of yards, at which many famous ships had been built, had been in decline for many years but had at the same time increased symbolically in importance as the last remaining shipyard in an area that had once boasted many and, at the beginning of the twentieth century, had built something like one-fifth of the world's ships. The whole identity of the place was determined by shipbuilding. This was threatened when decline turned into crisis and the management was forced to call in the Receivers in 1993. All the workforce was made redundant as a desperate search for a buyer was mounted. The search lasted a full year, during which it was not just economic hardship which characterized the mourning apparent in the local community: there was much soul-searching as to what a town which had identified itself almost exclusively with the building of ships could mean in the face of the demise of that industry. A buyer was eventually found, but not for the building of ships.

Harvey's point is again confirmed by another happening in Wallsend at the same time. After the shipyard crisis there was much rejoicing in the face of a decision by the German company, Siemens, to build a huge semi-conductor factory in the town. The factory, costing many millions of pounds, was open for only eighteen months before the bottom dropped out of the semi-conductor market and Siemens announced that it would close.

Harvey cites other reasons why place has been downgraded in the recent past, including diminishing transport costs, highly mobile capital and the resulting competition between places in order to sell themselves to prospective investors. What is significant is the role that money plays. It is the capitalist system which has precipitated all this, in Harvey's view: 'Place is becoming important to the degree that the authenticity of dwelling is being undermined by political-economic processes of spatial transformation and place construction.'[69]

Keith and Pile argue that the reassertion of place in protest against this is politically vital to the picture because it is 'mobilizing a territorialized sense of place and

---

[68] Ibid.
[69] Ibid.

community identity' that can enable local people to force themselves onto the political agenda. They use such examples as the Docklands dispute in 1992 to affirm the importance of place seen as a potent force for resistance to powerful economic forces. This consideration leads them into an attempt to understand the manner in which conceptions of space and place can have enormous political and economic consequences. The conclusion of their project is that 'space is constitutive of the social; spatiality is constitutive of the person and the political; new radical geographies must demystify the manner in which oppressions are naturalised through concepts of spaces and spatialities and recover progressive articulations of place and the politics of identity.'[70]

Edward Soja, whose thinking is not dissimilar to the above, states the objective of his recent publication, *Thirdspace*, directly to the reader at the outset: 'It is to encourage you to think differently about the meanings and significance of space and those related concepts that compose and comprise the inherent spatiality of human life: place, location, locality, landscape, environment, home, city, region, territory, and geography.' He goes on to assert his belief that the spatial dimension of our lives has never been of greater practical and political relevance than it is now:

> Whether we are attempting to deal with the increasing intervention of electronic media in our daily routines; seeking ways to act politically to deal with growing problems of poverty, racism, sexual discrimination, and environmental degradation; or trying to understand the multiplying geopolitical conflicts around the globe, we are becoming increasingly aware that we are, and always have been, intrinsically spatial beings, active participants in the social construction of our embracing spatialities. Perhaps more than ever before, a strategic awareness of this collectively created spatiality and its social consequences has become a vital part of making both theoretical and practical sense of our contemporary life-worlds at all scales, from the most intimate to the most global.[71]

Soja draws heavily on the work of Henri LeFebvre, as does David Harvey. LeFebvre is important to their Marxist critique because, though he rarely uses the term 'place' in his writings, he means much the same thing in his understanding of 'everyday life'. He presents this latter, rather than Marx's workplace, as the locus where alienation and mystification are to be found and struggled against. LeFebvre's *The Production of Space* argues that space cannot be represented by a neutral and passive geometry, but is *produced* and represents the site and the outcome of social, political and economic struggle. He distinguishes between different types of space – physical, mental and social – but it is the economic and political upon which Harvey and others have concentrated. LeFebvre's conceptions of *space* make their effects felt in *places*. LeFebvre asks: 'Is space a medium? A milieu? An intermediary? It is doubtless all of these, but its role is less and less neutral, more and more active, both as instrument and as goal, as means and as end. Confining it in so narrow a category as that of 'medium' is thus woefully inadequate.'[72] This is a direct assault on the notion of place as receptacle. Soja refers us to LeFebvre's starting point which was, once again, phenomenological. The latter states that his research on place started in childhood

---

[70] Keith, M. and Pile, S. (1993), 225.
[71] Soja, E. W. (1996), 1.
[72] LeFebvre, H. (1991), 410.

because he could not understand the philosophical separation of subject and object, the body and the world, for the boundary between them did not appear to him so clear and clean.

It should be said that although the writings of neo-Marxists like Soja and Harvey have been applauded by critics on the left, they can be read very differently. Brian Jarvis, for example, writes that they could be seen as 'symptomatic of a crisis of faith in the grand narratives of classical Marxist prophecy. It may be far from coincidental that the upsurge in spatial politics flows rapidly on the heels of a series of devastating disappointments for the left on the historical stage.'[73] We might respond that even if the motivation of the neo-Marxist critique is suspect, this does not necessarily negate all its insights, any more than a recognition of the validity of those insights requires the wholehearted embracing of a neo-Marxist position. Jarvis also reminds us that Soja has been attacked by Gillian Rose for failing to recognize that spatiality has not been universally disregarded in favour of historicity. She writes: 'Geography was central to anti-colonial movements from the eighteenth century onwards and, as countless feminist historians argue, feminist projects too have been organised over geographical networks, have used institutional spaces in which to try and create women's culture, and have struggled against the patriarchal spatial imagery of the public/private division.'[74] What Jarvis does not acknowledge is that, far from repudiating the assertion that place is of huge importance, Rose is simply clear that feminists got there first: she writes elsewhere that feminism, through its awareness of the politics of the everyday, 'has always had a very keen awareness of the intersection of space and power – and knowledge. As de Lauretis says, there is "the epistemological priority which feminism has located in the personal, the subjective, the body, the symptomatic, the quotidian, as the very site of material inscription of the ideological".'[75]

Much of the thinking to which I have referred above among these 'protests' about the devaluing of place fits loosely into what might be termed 'postmodern'. A consequence of postmodern suspicion of grand narratives is an attempt to recover a sense of the importance of the *particular*. One aspect of the particular is place, and much postmodern writing recognizes the significance of spatial factors in human experience which was lost in modernity. Keith and Pile criticize rather sloppy use of spatial metaphors like 'position, location, situation, mapping, geometries of domination, centre–margin, open–closed, inside–outside, global–local; liminal space, third space, not-space, impossible space; the city' in postmodern writing,[76] but despite such criticisms they, too, are clear that place is of huge importance. Lurking in the background of much of such postmodern thinking is Michel Foucault, to whom I have already made reference on more than one occasion. He was one of the first to recognize the huge importance of spatial questions to the condition of late twentieth-century society. Foucault was clear that: 'we do not live in a kind of void inside of

---

[73] Jarvis, B. (1998), 45.

[74] Rose, G. (1998), *Review of Postmodern Geographies* and *The Condition of Postmodernity* in *Journal of Historical Geography*, quoted in Jarvis, B. (1998), 47.

[75] Rose, G. (1993), *Feminism and Geography*, Cambridge: Polity Press, 142. See also Duncan, J. and Ley, D. (1993), and Massey, D. (1994).

[76] Keith, M. and Pile, S. (1993), 2.

which we could place individuals and things. We do not live inside a void that could be coloured with various shades of light, we live inside a set of relations that delineates sites which are irreducible to one another and absolutely not superimposable one on another.' He even went so far as to suggest that whereas in the nineteenth century the great obsession was history, 'the anxiety of our era has to do fundamentally with space, no doubt a great deal more than with time. Time probably appears to us only as one of the various distributive operations that are possible for the elements that are spread out in space.'[77] So, for Soja, for example, Foucault uncovers:

> the persistent overprivileging of the powers of the historical imagination and the traditions of critical historiography, and the degree to which this privileging of historicality has silenced or subsumed potentially equivalent powers of critical spatial thought. Breaking down the controlling effects of this particular form of historicism becomes a key step in radically opening up the spatial imagination and in rebalancing the trialectics of historicality-sociality-spatiality.[78]

The anxiety to which Foucault refers was recorded by the psychologist Paul Tournier when he found that a recurring theme in the dreams of modern men and women is that of the seat that cannot be found. The consequences of the 'loss of a sense of place' run deep into the psyche.

The importance of place in social theory is gradually being recognized. In his *Central Problems in Social Theory*, Anthony Giddens, whom I have already cited, wrote that the importance of place has been ignored in social theory: 'Most forms of social theory have failed to take seriously enough not only the temporality of social conduct but also its spatial attributes ... neither time nor space have been incorporated into the centre of social theory; rather, they are ordinarily treated more as "environments" in which social theory is enacted.'[79] By 'space' in this context he means the place where things happen. He not only pointed out the marginalization of time and place from social theory, but announced his intention to put them at the very core of his own social theory, and in works published since then he has attempted to realize this theoretical aim. Giddens' insight is not just that time and place are topics worthy of consideration by those interested in the social sciences. What he argues is much more radical: that excluding them from social analysis, or privileging one above the other a priori, distorts our understanding of the way in which social reality is constituted. He uses the term 'locale' rather than that of that of 'place', for he sees it carrying 'something of the connotation of space used as a setting for interaction'. Philip Cassell explains how Giddens' work makes clear that:

> the setting of interaction is not some neutral backdrop to events that are unfolding independently in the foreground. 'Locales' enter into the very fabric of interaction in a multiplicity of ways. They figure in the normative basis of action – implicit rules cover what one might and might not do in a given place; and they serve as sources of meaning – aspects of the setting are routinely incorporated, usually implicitly, in conversation.[80]

[77] Foucault, M. (1986), 23.

[78] Soja, E. (1996), 49.

[79] Giddens, A. (1979), 201.

[80] Cassell, P. (1993), 19.

Giddens' contention is that travelling through time and place is inseparable from the very being of individual agents, institutions, organizations and indeed nations. This is very much the same sort of conclusion as that proposed by LeFebvre, which we considered above. Similarly, Michel de Certeau talks in terms of narratives, telling us that 'narrative structures have the status of spatial syntaxes. By means of a whole panoply of codes, ordered ways of proceeding and constraints, they regulate changes in space (or moves from one place to another) made by stories in the form of places put in linear or interlaced series.' He goes on to propose that 'every story is a travel story – a spatial practice'.[81]

E. V. Walker confirms our contention about the 'loss of place'. He suggests that in everyday life people are very conscious of places. They talk about how a neighbourhood has changed, when a particular building went up, what it was like in the old days, how it feels to live in a certain place now. However, he feels that 'today, the experience of place is often out of balance. Preoccupations with the logic of space tend to suppress the feeling of place. There is a tendency in modern Western thinking to separate the feelings, symbolic meanings, moral sentiments, and intuitions of a place from the intellectual rational features. The expressive dimension gets lost in systems design and management.'[82] These words are consonant with what I have been arguing: that our intellectual traditions and the effects of them have flown in the face of what our experience tells us – that place is of primary importance to our humanity. Walker develops a theory of 'placeways' which seeks to reintegrate rational understandings of place with the manner in which people experience it. The significance of places, he tells us, is profound:

> The totality of what people do, think, and feel in a specific location gives identity to a place, and through its physique and morale it shapes a reality which is unique to places – different from the reality of an object or a person. Human experience makes a place, but a place lives in its own way. If form of experience occupies persons – the place locates experience in people. A place is a matrix of energies, generating representations and causing changes in awareness.[83]

This, together with much of the above, draws us to a *relational* view of place and to say that any conception of place is inseparable from the relationships that are associated with it.

I have proposed that place was lost during modernity, and among the social sciences anthropology can be of great assistance to us in reinforcing our understanding of the fact that our own culture has lost a sense of place. There remain societies in the world which have not been so affected, and observation of these can sharpen our own critical analysis. So, for example, James Weiner's study of the Foi of Papua New Guinea leads him to suggest that 'a society's place names schematically image a people's intentional transformation of their habitat from a sheer physical terrain into a pattern of historically experienced and constituted space and time'. He suggests that: 'language and place are a unity. The manner in which human action and

---

[81] de Certeau , M. (1984), 115.

[82] Walker, E. (1988), 2.

[83] Ibid., 131.

purposive appropriation inscribes itself upon the earth is an iconography of human intentions. Its mirror image is speech itself, which in the act of naming, memorialises these intentions, makes of them a history-in-dialogue.'[84] However, anthropologists, like most other scholars, have come late to an appreciation of place. Clifford Geertz points out that: 'if you should look into the table of contents or, for that matter, into the index of a standard textbook or monograph in anthropology, you would not find there a category called place.'[85] A collection of essays entitled *Place: Experience and Symbol* by ethnographers and human geographers (including Tuan, Buttimer and Seamon, whom I cited above) began a series of endeavours to understand social identities in terms of place. Subsequent work has begun to understand place in similar terms to some of the geographers above from the standpoint of its contestation and its linkage to local and global power relations. In a recent collection of essays, Steven Feld and Keith Basso suggest:

> Whatever else this may involve, this development surely reflects the now acute world conditions of exile, displacement, diasporas, and inflamed borders – to say nothing of the increasingly tumultuous struggles by indigenous peoples and cultural minorities for ancestral homelands, land rights, and retention of sacred places. These days, narrative of place once presented under such gentle rubrics as 'national integration' and 'political evolution' are being framed in decidedly harsher terms: as economic development by state invasion and occupation, or as the extraction of transnational wealth at escalating costs in human suffering, cultural destruction and environmental degradation.[86]

Like some of the geographers cited above, anthropologists have thus come to worry less about place in broad philosophical terms than about places as sites of power struggles or about displacement as history of annexation, absorption and resistance. Thus, ethnography's stories of place are increasingly about contestation, and this makes them consistent with a larger narrative in which previously absent 'others' are now portrayed as with us, no longer a presumed and distant 'them' removed from a vague and tacit 'us'. Margaret Rodman recognizes that 'places are not inert containers. They are politicized, culturally relative, historically specific, local and multiple constructions.'[87]

Recognizing this, Gupta and Ferguson identify problems which have resulted from the assumed isomorphism of space, place and culture. For example, they characterize 'multiculturalism' as 'a feeble acknowledgement of the fact that cultures have lost their moorings in definite places' and hold that conventional accounts of ethnicity rely upon an unproblematic link between identity and place. They engage with post colonialism and ask: 'to which places do the hybrid cultures of post-coloniality belong?' They go on to point out that: 'The rapidly expanding and quickening mobility of people combines with a profound sense of loss of territorial roots, of an erosion of the cultural distinctiveness of places, and of ferment in anthropological theory.'[88] More recently, the essays in Feld and Basso's *Senses of Place* have the

---

[84] Weiner, J. (1991), 32, 50.

[85] Geertz, C. in Feld, S. and Basso, K. (1996), 259.

[86] Feld, S. and Basso, K. (1996), 4.

[87] Rodman, M. C. (1994), 641.

[88] Gupta, A. and Ferguson, J. (1992), 7.

declared aim of aim describing and interpreting some ways in which people encounter places, perceive them and invest them with significance. They conclude: 'As people fashion places, so, too, do they fashion themselves. People don't just dwell in comfort or in misery, in centres or in margins, in place or out of place, empowered or disempowered. People everywhere act on the integrity of their dwelling.'[89] Similarly, a recent fascinating study by anthropologist and theologian Timothy Jenkins allows 'the importance of the cosmological and religious to be recast as the values that arise among people when they marry, have children, live near each other, identify themselves with places and use their understanding of local history to inform and justify their self-regard and respect, or withholding of respect, for others'.[90]

Having surveyed the scene as far as attitudes to place in political and social theory is concerned, the above comment might lead us to ask what is the position of contemporary theology on place.

The Position of Contemporary Theology on Place

I have charted an emerging protest from scholars in a variety of disciplines who are beginning to see that what I have termed 'the loss of place' is a feature of modernism which has had, and is having, painful consequences for vast numbers of people. We might now ask: 'Where have theologians been in all this?' The answer, I fear, is more or less entirely immersed in the norms of modernity, at least as far as the lack of recognition of the importance of place is concerned. A notable exception is Oliver O'Donovan, to whom I have already made reference, who concurs with my proposition that 'contemporary Western society is marked by a loss of the sense of place, and its intellectual traditions, far from controlling the loss, have encouraged it'. He suggests that 'local roots and rootlessness should be, one would think, a major topic of conversation among theologians who habitually read the Bible',[91] but that it is not. Why is this? It may be partly to do with the fact that it was from theology that modernity emerged. It is no accident that the discoveries of Newton and Galileo arose, as we saw, from a theology which was interested in the infinite and the all-powerful rather than the particular. It is no coincidence either that in the same epoch as these scientists were working, the Reformation was separating theology from the material and the particular. In medieval times locality had been a vital ingredient of a world view which, as I have already intimated, enabled the sustenance of a 'spiritual geography', but Reformed thought would have no truck with what came to be

---

[89] Feld, S. and Basso, K. (1996), 11.

[90] Foreword by Parkin, D. to Jenkins, T. (1999), xiv.

[91] O'Donovan, O. (1989), 48, 44. His article is an excellent one, but he has not, to my knowledge, returned to the theme. Philip Sheldrake is another lonely voice in this field. His insightful 2000 Hulsean lectures on the theme of place have been published as Sheldrake, P. (2001), *Spaces for the Sacred: Place, Memory and Identity*, London: S.C.M. Press. He notes that 'in current debates about the future of place, the Christian theological voice contributes very little apart from occasional reference to specifically environmental issues' (p.2). Similarly, a recent article by Andrew Rumsey makes the point that 'there have been few studies which address the impact of place on contemporary western religious experience' (Rumsey, A., 2001, 102).

regarded as superstition. As O'Donovan reminds us, it became an axiom of Protestant theology that God's revelation in Christ broke down elective particularity, not only of race, but of place.

This inheritance is most clearly illustrated in terms of thinking about 'holy places', the study of which will be a central concern of what follows. In a rare foray into this area, Susan White points out in a piece entitled *The Theology of Sacred Space* that one would be hard pressed to find consideration of the question of place in the writings of any systematic theologians in the recent past. She should be given credit for raising the question of what a theology of sacred space might look like. Many other theologians would seem to be so inculturated that the question of place is a long way from their thoughts and writings. White observes that the only ones who have been interested in 'sacred space' have tended to be liturgists and historians of religion, whose approach:

> is taken over almost wholesale from studies of how sacred places function in tribal religions, sometimes (but not always) with Christian terms interpolated here and there. Eliade is a good example. In general, there has been a lot of talk about ley-lines and mandalas, and poles of the universe and aboriginal dreaming-places and such. Some of this is intertwined with depth-psychology and semiotics, which no doubt is interesting to be sure, but it should not be mistaken for Christian theology. So the problem is that up to now Christian theology of sacred space has not been very theological; and the second problem is that the Christian theology of sacred space has not been very Christian.[92]

Whatever the rights and wrongs of her evident prejudice against any interdisciplinary study, it is undoubtedly true that those who have written about place have been motivated by a phenomenological starting point. Eliade is exclusively phenomenological. Others attempt to mix phenomenological insights with those derived from the Christian tradition. Geoffrey Lilburne, for example, in a book entitled *A Sense of Place: A Christian Theology of the Land*, freely mixes biblical insights with those of the Aboriginal people without making clear at any stage what authority he suggests should be given to each and for what reason. Interestingly, Susan White quotes from Lilburne's book one of the few passages which suit the direction of her writing. Similarly, Belden Lane's beautiful *Landscapes of the Sacred: Geography and Narrative in American Spirituality*[93] contains many good things, but his recounting of the experiences of native North Americans and that of various Christian settlers is analysed using 'axioms for the study of sacred place' which he draws from his own experience. He does not attempt to find support for these axioms from the Christian tradition or to relate them to it. A recent piece by Ron Di Santo looks at the threat of commodity consciousness to human dignity, and outlines the problem well. In order to address the threat, however, he suggests adopting the 'noble eightfold path' from the Buddhist tradition.[94] In a book which has as the subtitle 'The Catholic Vision of Human Destiny' this seems strange, to say the least. The approach of all these writers is phenomenological, and while this may be a

---

[92] White, S. (1995), 36.

[93] Lilburne, G. R. (1989).

[94] Di Santo, R. (1999), 79.

reasonable starting point which may alert them to the problem, Susan White is surely right in suggesting that theology demands an approach which begins not *just* with experience, but also with the scriptures and tradition.

However, whilst agreeing with Susan White's prognosis of the problem, we might question her solution. In the face of the evident lacuna which she identifies, she goes on to attempt to begin to construct such a theology and offers what she refers to as a 'biblical' approach which, she tells us 'after Barth, is suspicious of allowing the natural world to speak for itself'. The conclusion of her project can be summarized in her closing sentences, which read as follows:

> I can say that the ugly concrete block worship-space in Telford can be a holy place, because it is occupied by and associated with a community of Christian people who are known, publicly known, for their acts of charity and peacemaking and who have drawn their building into the struggle for a radical openness to the will of God. And I would argue that to root the holiness of Christian sacred space in anything else is to be involved either in idolatry or in magic.[95]

Susan White suggests, in other words, that place is of negligible importance in theology, even though an 'ugly block worship space' is hardly 'the natural world' and implicit in White's assessment is the fact that a humanly constructed environment can have an effect on people, though this is something of which White is unaware or chooses to ignore. As far as she is concerned, whether a place can be deemed sacred is entirely a function of the virtues of the particular people associated with it at any particular time. A church is thus a 'space' and not a 'place', it is a receptacle, it is a commodity to be used. Nor can it be said that this is a view peculiar to her or to the Reformed tradition. The effect of Vatican II and associated liturgical reform has been to emphasize the 'community' aspects of liturgy to the exclusion or downplaying of the 'formal' and, it could be argued, 'transcendent'. The documents make reference to the fact that the Council 'established principles for the reform of the rites of the sacrifice of the Mass so as to encourage the full and active participation of the faithful in the celebration of this mystery.'[96] The ecclesiastical and liturgical consequences of Vatican II have served to concentrate attention upon people and community, and although this has resulted in many good things, there has been an accompanying shift away from the appreciation of the significance of place. Certain places are very important in Catholic piety, of course, but are not a major consideration in Roman Catholic theology. I shall return to this point in Chapter 4.

The approach to sacred space which Susan White proclaims strongly is very fashionable nowadays and represents the only basis upon which many people would be prepared to designate a place 'holy': place is totally subordinate to ethics, and a place cannot be deemed holy unless it be frequented by radically holy people in the here and now.[97] There are exceptions, as we shall see, just as there are in other

---

[95] White, S. in Brown, D. and Loades, A. (1995), 42.

[96] Flannery, A. (1975), 100.

[97] The theologian Christopher Rowland, for example, tells us that buildings are of little theological significance, and quotes Susan White's words about the 'ugly, concrete block worship-space' approvingly. He feels that British cathedrals are dangerous 'friends of Albion'. See Rowland, C., 'Friends of Albion?', in Platten, S. and Lewis, C. (1998), 33.

disciplines, but the majority view is clear: in effect, it is only people who can be holy, and not places. Less systematic and informed theologians and churchpeople than Susan White would want to insist upon the oft-stated maxim that 'the Church is people and not buildings', and would concur with her view that it is on people that any respectable theology must concentrate. Place as a category has thus more or less disappeared from sight – something which might be thought strange in view of the important role it plays in both the scriptures and tradition – but wholly understandable in the light of the effects of the influences I have been discussing above. I would suggest that, in the wake of the disappearance of place from Western thought and the 'commodification' of place, Susan White and others have taken on the assumptions of the prevailing discourse which I have described and baptized them – a process which, from her Barthian stance, she condemns in others.

It was H. Richard Niebuhr who suggested in *Christ and Culture* that in our understanding of the faith we are more likely to be affected by our culture than we would sometimes like to allow.[98] The downgrading of the importance of place in theology, I would argue, owes less to a diligent engagement with the Christian scriptures and tradition than it does to the influences I have outlined above. Ironically, Reinhold and H. Richard Niebuhr have themselves been under fire for being in thrall to prevailing culture in recent years. At any rate, Susan White, who from her professed Barthian perspective would probably applaud such a critique, has proclaimed the necessity of producing a Christian theology of sacred space which is both theological and Christian. Strange, however, that she has not used either scripture or the tradition in order to formulate such a theology but could, rather, be accused of being in thrall to a 'market' culture. It takes someone from a discipline other than theology, like E. V. Walker, a social theorist, to suggest that:

> we take for granted ritual and doctrine as theological subjects, but we tend to overlook the theology of building, settling, and dwelling. As expressions of religious experience, sacred places are as important as doctrine and ritual. They energise and shape religious meaning. They help to make religious experience intelligible. A sacred place is not only an environment of sensory phenomena, but a moral environment as well.[99]

There has been some small interest in space from a theological perspective in, for example, Iain Mackenzie's book the *Dynamism of Space*. But the picture on the front cover – an impressive collection of stars, planets and other features of outer space – betrays what sort of space the book will be about. I would not want to suggest that such a topic – the relationship between the God revealed in Christ and the complex immensity of the universe – is not worthy of investigation. But I am interested that Mackenzie takes the trouble to distinguish between place and space in his prologue and in so doing tells us that *'place is significant space'* (his italics). However, having

---

[98] His argument is summarized in the following passage: 'Christ claims no man purely as a natural being, but always as one who has become a human in culture; who is not only in culture, but into whom culture has penetrated. Man not only speaks but thinks with the aid of the language of culture. Not only has the natural world about him been modified by human achievement; but the forms and attitudes of his mind which allow him to make sense of the natural world have been given him by culture.' Niebuhr, H. R. (1951), 27.

[99] Walker, E. (1988), 77

made important (and very sensible, in my view) observations about the nature of 'place',[100] Mackenzie himself offers barely any further thought on the subject. Mackenzie is nothing if not a diligent student of the scriptures. If he had continued with this line of thought on place as significant space he would have found much to commend it in the biblical narrative, but he does not. By concentrating upon 'space' he merely continues the collusion of contemporary theology with what I have characterized to be the predominant discourse of modernity.

Conclusion

In this chapter I have attempted to show that, although place was of importance in Greek thought, the Western intellectual tradition has tended to downgrade it, place being eclipsed by an emphasis first upon space, and second upon time. This prevailing discourse has worked itself out in the development of Western society, the process reaching a dehumanizing culmination in the twentieth century.

I have looked at a rising tide of protest from scholars in a variety of disciplines who have uncovered the demise of place and pointed to its negative effects upon human experience. I have argued that theologians, in the main, have not given much attention to place, and have, in this respect, remained wedded to the norms of modernity which are being questioned in other disciplines. I have suggested that their attitude owes more to secular assumptions than to Christian insights. In order to substantiate this latter claim, what is needed is a reassessment of the Christian approach to place in scripture and tradition, and it is that to which I now turn.

---

[100] He writes: 'First, that it is identifiable space. Second, that the identity does not depend on measurement. Third, that the identity does depend upon events. Fourth that these events are the expression of existence or existences. Fifth, place is the space or room which these existences make for themselves and determine by their presence and activity. Sixth, place is therefore that which is qualified by the nature of the existences and their activities. Seventh, that place is quantified is only secondary and tenuous on that quality if it is possible at all. Eighth, if it is quantifiable, it is only in terms of where the activities and existences peculiar to one thing or sets of things either cease or give way to other existences of things in their particular and differing activities. Ninth, place is to be described dynamically, therefore. Tenth, measurement is static if treated as the primary way to define place and leads to a false appreciation of what place is' (Mackenzie, I., 1995, 5).

Chapter 2

Place and the Scriptures

The Old Testament

Place as a Primary Category of Biblical Faith

One only needs to open the Bible at the beginning of Genesis and read a few pages to be left with the impression that place is important to the writer. The second creation account (Genesis 2) revolves around *place*: the Garden of Eden is not just the location where the drama happens to unfold, it is central to the narrative. This is not surprising in view of some of the insights at which we looked in the last chapter and summarized by Giddens' insight that 'the setting of interaction is not some neutral backdrop to events that are unfolding independently in the foreground. "Locales" enter into the very fabric of interaction in a multiplicity of ways.'[1] It has been said that gardens mirror certain cosmic values and I would suggest that this image resonates with our deepest dis-placed selves within the human consciousness – 'the laughter in the garden, echoed ecstasy', as T. S. Eliot would have it.[2] This beginning sets the tone for what I shall argue is the importance of place throughout the scriptures, concluding with the descent of the heavenly Jerusalem at the consummation of all things at the end of time in the penultimate chapter of the Book of Revelation.

In the first part of this chapter I shall attempt to investigate how place relates to a reading of the Old Testament. In doing so I shall draw on the work of Walter Brueggemann who, at the beginning of his book *The Land: Place as Gift, Promise and Challenge in Biblical Faith*, criticizes what he refers to as the dominant categories of Biblical theology, the existentialist and 'mighty deeds of God in history' formulations. The former, he tells us, has been exclusively concerned with 'the urgent possibility of personal decision-making in which one chooses a faith context' and the latter on 'normative events around which Israel's faith has clustered'. Concerns about existentialist decisions and transforming events have, he feels, made interpreters insensitive to 'the preoccupation of the Bible for placement'. This exclusive concern is entirely in accord with what I have characterized as the domination of theology and other disciplines by the predominant mores of our culture. Existentialism was, of course, one of the absorptions of mid-twentieth-century philosophy and theology, and preoccupation with events is a result of understanding the Christian faith in terms of what has been termed 'Salvation History'. This latter approach has, in my view, much to commend it if it takes account of place as well as time in the drama of salvation. However, it generally does not, and this is not surprising in an epoch in

---

[1] Cassell, P. (1993), 19.
[2] Eliot, T. S. (1969), 180.

which time has had hegemony over both space and place. This makes the publication of Brueggemann's book in 1977 all the more remarkable, and it is a tribute to him that he was able to speak so prophetically and insightfully to outline an alternative hermeneutic.

Brueggemann's book is well known but, though respected as innovative, has been regarded as rather idiosyncratic by mainstream Biblical scholarship and therefore not engaged with except by those very few theologians who have an interest in place. However, several more recent works have taken up the theme. There is some reference to the Old Testament material in Geoffrey Lilburne's *A Sense of Place: A Christian Theology of the Land* which seeks biblical insight which will be of help in a situation of rural crisis, land degradation, and conflict over land rights. Jamie Scott and Paul Simpson-Housley published a collection of essays which looks at the 'geographics of religion' and seeks to build bridges with other disciplines.[3] A more recent publication by Norman Habel breaks new ground in looking at the land issue in recognizing the importance of ideology as compared with theology in the text. As Habel writes:

> A distinction, subtle though it may be, can be made between theology and ideology as schemas of thought in the Bible. By a biblical theology I mean the doctrine and discourse about God expressed within a biblical literary unit that reflects the living faith of a given community. Biblical ideology refers to a wider complex of images and ideas that may employ theological doctrines, traditions or symbols to justify and promote the social, economic and political interests of a group within society.[4]

In an Editor's Foreword to Habel's work, Brueggemann himself recognizes that Habel's use of the governing term ideology reflects an important turn in scholarship in the last two decades. Habel identifies six different ideologies woven into the biblical texts, and in so doing makes the important point that most biblical texts push a point. They seek to convince the implied audience and persuade those who hear the message that the beliefs proclaimed in the texts are authoritative and true. This applies to interpretation of texts as much as it does to the texts themselves, of course: Habel acknowledges that his interest in social justice issues may have influenced his interpretation, since recent studies have, he reminds us, made us 'acutely aware of ourselves as readers who construct meaning with the stuff of the text'.[5] The background to his writing is what he refers to as the social, political and religious context of the current land rights debate, his hope being that his volume would illuminate texts often used as 'significant sources for developing land theologies or position statements on the land rights of indigenous peoples'.[6] The starting point of each of the writers mentioned is phenomenological, but they then go on to attempt a thorough engagement with the texts. Although our approach here will, after Brueggemann, be largely chronological, it is important to acknowledge Habel's insight that different pressures are brought to bear upon the text by its writers in terms

---

[3] Scott, J. and Simpson-Housley, P. (eds) (1991), *Sacred Places and Profane Spaces: Essays in the Geographies of Judaism, Christianity and Islam*, New York: Greenwood Press.

[4] Habel, N. (1995), 10.

[5] Ibid., 6. He directs us particularly to McKnight, E. V. (1988).

[6] Ibid., 7.

of understanding the relationship Israel is to have to the land. However, although attitudes to land vary according to the perspective of the writers, there is one central ideology which is common to each approach: that of the vitality of place in the life of Israel.

As Habel begins with issues surrounding land rights, Brueggemann's phenomonological starting point that alerted him to new interpretative possibilities was the failure of an 'urban promise'. The 'urban promise' of which he speaks concerned 'human persons who could lead detached, unrooted lives of endless choice and no commitment. It was glamorised around the virtues of mobility and anonymity which seem so full of freedom and self-actualisation.'[7] In speaking of the failure of such a promise Brueggemann refers to Harvey Cox's 1965 publication *The Secular City*, in which the latter extols the virtues of the city by citing two of its major gifts as anonymity and mobility. Against Cox, Brueggemann concurs with some of the secular insights we have looked at above in concluding that: 'more sober reflection indicates that they are sources of anomie and the undoing of our common humanness.' The existentialist quest for meaning, he tells us, fails to recognize that: 'it is rootlessness and not meaninglessness that characterises the current crisis. There are no meanings apart from roots.'[8] Thus, the failure of this promise is that it does not recognize that there is a human hunger for *a sense of place* which it cannot meet. Brueggemann's creative work was thus born out of an impatience with predominant culture and a feeling that theology was in thrall to it, just as the work of the scholars whose witness I enlisted in the last chapter felt that their disciplines had been consumed by the predominant discourse which denigrates place. For Brueggemann, the central problem in our age is 'not emancipation but rootage, not meaning but belonging, not separation from community but location within it, not isolation from others but placement deliberately between the generation of promise and fulfilment.'[9] This sentiment has much in common with all that we have studied, the conclusion of which could be summed up in Foucault's observation that 'the anxiety of our era has to do fundamentally with space'. This anxiety, I have proposed, is a result of the dehumanizing effects of loss of a sense of place.

Brueggemann encourages us to take a fresh look at the Bible to see that place is a 'primary category of faith' and that 'land is a central, if not *the central theme* of biblical faith'. He proposes that the narrative of the Old Testament centres around land, and that the importance of this land is that it is a particular *place* which has been promised. Though this is an approach which finds support in passing references by other scholars, Brueggemann goes on to examine the whole narrative through the prism of land and his engagement with the text suggests to him that the Bible is addressed to the central human problem of homelessness (anomie) and seeks to respond to that agenda in terms of grasp and gift.[10] Brueggemann does not confuse space and place but, following Dillistone, clearly articulates what he understands to be the difference between the two as follows:

---

[7] Brueggemann, W. (1977), 10.

[8] Ibid., 4.

[9] Ibid., 4.

[10] Ibid., 187.

'Space' means an area of freedom, without coercion or accountability, free of pressures and void of authority. Space may be imagined as week-end, holiday, a vacation, and is characterised by a kind of neutrality or emptiness waiting to be filled by our choosing. Such a concern appeals to a desire to get out from under meaningless routine and subjection. But 'place' is a very different matter. Place is space which has historical meanings, where some things have happened which are now remembered and which provide continuity and identity across generations. Place is space in which important words have been spoken which have established identity, defined vocation and envisioned destiny. Place is space in which vows have been exchanged, promises have been made, and demands have been issued. Place is indeed a protest against the unpromising pursuit of space. It is a declaration that our humanness cannot be found in escape, detachment, absence of commitment, and undefined freedom.[11]

This approach coincides with our own definition as I outlined it at the beginning of Chapter 1. As far as the Old Testament is concerned, Brueggemann is clear that being human, as biblical faith promises it, will be found in belonging to and referring to that particular place in which the historicity of a community has been experienced and to which recourse is made for purposes of orientation, assurance and empowerment. The Promised Land is always a place with Yahweh, a place filled with memories of life with him, with his promises and vows made to him. Possession of the land was of overriding importance to the people of Israel, but this land is not just a piece of 'real estate': it was a place with memories as well as hopes, with a past as well as a future; it was, in other words, a *place* and not a space, and as such it was a *storied* place. The fact is that if God has to do with Israel in a special way, then he has also to do with this historical place in a special way. This insight might be expressed by positing a three-way relationship between God, his people, and place: biblical faith as it is presented in the Old Testament suggests that it will not do to leave any one of these out of the equation, for the narrative would suggest that the consequences of so doing are disastrous for the wellbeing of God's people. I shall return to this proposal a little later in this chapter. First, though, having established the importance of place to Old Testament faith in general terms, I shall look at the Old Testament narrative in more detail.

Genesis and Wilderness

If place is central right at the beginning of the Bible, its importance, as I have already suggested, does not diminish. Brueggemann directs our attention to the fact that as the narrative of the Book of Genesis unfolds there are expressed two paradigms of relationship to place as it divides into two histories. The first, in Genesis 1:11, is one which describes how people living securely in a paradisal place face expulsion from it. The second, in Genesis 12:50, concerns Abraham and his family moving towards possession of a place which has been promised. In the beginning, when 'everything was very good', that goodness had to do with God's people being in a particular place, the Garden of Eden, with their creator. Their lack of obedience, which resulted in expulsion from the garden (and the unfaithfulness of Cain and Abel, the generation of Noah and the people of Sodom), can be contrasted with the faithfulness of Abraham

---

[11] Ibid., 5.

which enabled his journey towards the land of promise. Brueggemann goes on to suggest that this sets the parameters for the theology of the Old Testament as seen through the prism of the land and that these parameters are not remote from contemporary experience of Western culture: 'The two histories are never far from each other, either in the Bible or in modern experience ... The history of anticipation, as soon as it is satisfied, lives at the brink of the history of expulsion.'[12]

'Abd Al Tafahum has noted that the centrality of the land in the Old Testament has implications for other peoples, for we do not rightly understand the Old Testament's sense of place and people 'unless we know that it mirrors and educates the self awareness of all lands and dwellers. The nationhood of Israel, the love of Zion, has its counterparts in every continent. Its uniqueness lies, not in the emotional experience, but the theological intensity.'[13] Thus our own lives, in this perspective, are lived between the experience of estrangement and anticipation. But the biblical narrative suggests that hope is appropriate in this situation since if our experience now is predominantly that of loss and estrangement, that is not the way that things will finally be. The will of God for his people to dwell secure overcomes the power of expulsion. The anticipation, the promise, is of landedness, a *place* which is rooted in the word of God. God speaks a new word which calls his people to a new consciousness:

> Such a word spoken gives identity and personhood, and we could not have invented it. It is the voice of the prophet – or the poet if you wish – who calls a name, bestows a vision, summons a pilgrimage. This is not the detached prattle of a computer; not the empty language of a quota or a formula or a rule; but it is a word spoken which lets no one be the same again. Land-expelling history could live by coercive language but land-anticipating history can only begin with One who in his speaking makes all things new. That is what Gen 12.1 does in the Bible. It makes all things new when all things had become old and weary and hopeless. Creation begins anew, as a history of anticipation of the land.[14]

From then on Israel is a people on a journey because of a promise, and the kernel of all its promises from Yahweh is to be given the land, to be *placed*. In Brueggemann's view, the whole history of Israel is best understood in terms of hope in and response to that promise. Faith is presented in this second part of the Genesis narrative in terms of being willing to accept the radical demand of God to become a sojourner on the way to a new place of promise. As the author of the Epistle to the Hebrews puts it: 'By faith Abraham obeyed when he was called to go out to a place which he was to receive as an inheritance; and he went out, not knowing where he was to go' (Hebrews 3:8).

The journey was long. In a brief intervening period of settlement in Egypt, a foreign land, under Joseph, Israel was given the best of the land (Genesis 47:6) and prospered and multiplied (Genesis 47:27), but this experience soon gave way to slavery. Sojourn was followed by wandering in the wilderness for forty years during which the promise of land seemed a distant one in the struggle for survival. Wilderness is presented as a place where desolation is as much psychological as

---

[12] Ibid., 16.

[13] 'Abd Al-Tafahum, (1966), quoted in Davies, W. D. (1974), 15.

[14] Brueggemann, W. (1977), 17.

physical. Both have resonances with our own time, where displacement is experienced as rootless anxiety. Brueggemann describes the wilderness as a place of complete desolation, which is the opposite of a storied place – it is a place without memory or meaning. But there is a paradox here, as Belden Lane points out: 'There is an unaccountable solace that fierce landscapes offer to the soul. They heal, as well as mirror, the brokenness we find within. Moving apprehensively into the desert's emptiness, up the mountain's height, you discover in wild terrain a metaphor of your deepest fears.'[15]

Lane is here describing the apophatic tradition, or 'negative way', which eschews attachment to place and which 'naturally returns again and again to the suggestive image of Sinai. There, in flashes of lightning on red granite, Moses watches for God in the cleft of the rock, his mind stripped of images and his tongue rendered mute.'[16] However, the very language Lane uses exemplifies the curious irony that although emphasizing the 'placelessness' of God, this tradition has made frequent use of particular sorts of places – most notably mountain and desert landscapes – in its concern to teach the relinquishment of control that is necessary for approaching God. Brueggemann asks the crucial question: 'Is this what God finally wills for his people? Is wilderness an in-between moment without him? Or is wilderness a place which he prefers for his peculiar presence because of his peculiar character? Could it be that he is a god who most desires the interactions of the wilderness?'[17] The final answer to that question in the biblical narrative is quite definitely the promise of a place. In the intervening period in the wilderness, as in the apophatic tradition of desert spirituality that flows from it, Yahweh answers the people of Israel by assuring them of his presence and giving them sustenance: 'And as Aaron spoke to the whole congregation of the people of Israel, they looked in the wilderness, and behold, the glory of the Lord appeared in a cloud' (Exodus 16:10). Although seen in a cloud and not fully, his appearance in the wilderness is a certain sign that he is with his people in their sense of abandonment, transforming the situation by that presence. Thus, there was comfort in the midst of chaos and the hope that faithfulness would allow deliverance: 'What we are confronted with, then, is a foreign land, a passage through a desert; testing and discernment. But in this same land, from which God is not absent, the seed of a new spirituality can germinate.'[18] These words of Gustavo Gutierrez refer to the spirituality associated with Liberation Theology, the inspiration for which, like apophatic spirituality, derives very much from the experience of Israel as it is recorded in the Old Testament:

> The breakthrough of the poor into Latin American history and the Latin American church is based on a new and profound grasp of the experience of estrangement. The exploited and marginalised are today becoming increasingly conscious of living in a foreign land that is hostile to them, a land of death, a land that has no concern for their most legitimate interests and serves only as a tool for their oppressors, a land that is alien to their hopes and is owned by those who seek to terrorize them. ... Exiled, therefore, by unjust social structures from a land that in the final analysis belongs to God alone – 'all the earth is mine' (Exod 19.5, cf.

---

[15] Lane, B. (1998), 216.

[16] Ibid., 216.

[17] Brueggemann, W. (1977), 40.

[18] Gutierrez, G. (1983), 19.

Deut 10.14) – but aware now that they have been despoiled of it, the poor are actively entering into Latin American history and are taking part in an exodus that will restore to them what is rightfully their own.[19]

Using biblical images of slavery, exodus, wilderness and exile, Gutierrez here confirms that just as Israel's history can be seen to be about land as much as about anything else, so too redemption, seen in this light, has fundamentally to do with relationship to God *and with place*. The insights of Liberation Theology show us that emphasis on the locatory aspects of the scriptures is far from the reactionary stance it is sometimes characterized to be. It can be deeply prophetic. As such, this biblical narrative has given inspiration and hope not just to Liberation Theologians, but to many peoples exiled and oppressed in a foreign land. This great epic of deliverance has been celebrated in many generations as a sign of hope. As Robert Wilken puts it: 'Whether that redemption be from the occupation of Eretz Israel by the Romans or from cruel and arbitrary mistreatment at the hands of Soviet apparatchiks. Christians, too, from Oliver Cromwell in seventeenth-century England to Martin Luther King in the twentieth century have evoked the Exodus as the paradigmatic story of redemption.'[20] But if place is integral to the Exodus narrative and all that surrounds it, it is at least equally so to what follows as the people of Israel arrive in the Promised Land.

The Promised Land: Arrival, Exile and Restoration

At the conclusion of the wilderness experience deliverance reached its fulfilment when the people of Israel arrived in the land which they had been promised, and this land, which had been idealized as 'flowing with milk and honey' (Exodus 3:8) turned out to be as good as the word of the Lord had predicted: 'A land of brooks and water, of fountains and springs, flowing forth from valleys and hills, a land of wheat and barley, of vine and fig trees and pomegranates, a land of olive trees and honey, a land in which you will eat bread without scarcity, in which you will lack nothing' (Deuteronomy 8:7–10). Habel, among the various ideologies he identifies, characterizes Deuteronomic history as representative of a 'conditional ideology'. In this account Yahweh has conquered the land for Israel's occupation, and in so doing has inaugurated a theocracy which requires the indebtedness of Israel and justifies the dispossession of its original inhabitants. Survival in the land requires faithfulness to Yahweh, as interpreted by the Levites. This, Habel suggests, is in marked contrast to the Abraham 'charter narratives', which represent what he terms an 'immigrant ideology' in which the Promised Land is presented as a host country inhabited by a range of peoples whose rights and cultures Abraham is expected to respect.[21] Oliver O'Donovan gives us a different perspective on the Deuteronomic history:

> The relationship between Yahweh and the land is depicted with the greatest care, in order to avoid any possible confusion between Yahweh and the Baalim of the settled Canaanite

---

[19] Ibid., 19.

[20] Wilken, R. L. (1992), 3.

[21] Habel, N. (1995), 115ff.

communities. The possession of the land was the climax of a sequence of mighty acts performed by Yahweh, who had ever been a *melek*, leader of his wandering followers, not a *baal*, localised and limited. This is one of the lesson taught by the battle stories, which are tales, not of military prowess but of miraculous delivery, always remarkable, sometimes even whimsical. Yahweh is not born in that land, he enters it with his people, and laid hold of it by his strong right arm. Yet there is another aspect to the role of battle in the book. It also represents the act of *consecration*, by which the community gives itself to receive the gift.[22]

This consecration requires deep faithfulness on the part of Israel, and will necessitate a very careful balance in the three-way relationship between people, place, and God. It is a balance that was soon lost. Unfaithfulness to Yahweh while in the land meant that almost as soon as the promise has been fulfilled and Israel has arrived in the Promised Land it is on the way to exile. Indeed, Brueggemann characterizes arrival at the Jordan as the juncture between two histories. The first begins with God's promise to Abraham in Genesis 12, which was fulfilled when 'the Lord gave to Israel all the land which he swore to give to their fathers' (Joshua 21:43–45). It is a narrative of landlessness on the way to land, promise to fulfilment. The second, of landedness leading to exile, begins almost immediately when Joshua dismissed the people and the people of Israel went each to his inheritance to take possession of the land (Judges 2:6). It concludes with the exile which resulted from Israel's unfaithfulness. The problem, Brueggemann explains, was that 'the very land that promised to create space for human joy and freedom became the very source of dehumanizing exploitation and oppression. Land was indeed a problem in Israel. Time after time, Israel saw the land of promise become the land of a problem.'[23]

Though the prophets warned continually that the certain result of idolatry and harlotry would be exile, the kings and their people had begun to manage the land in their own way, to serve their own self-seeking purposes, and the law of the Lord had been forgotten. We have already seen that, though many of the blessings associated with the land are this-worldly, as often as the scriptures speak of 'possessing the land' they speak of 'walking in the ways of the Lord' (Deuteronomy 8:6), of 'harkening to God's voice' and 'keeping all the words of the law' (Deuteronomy 17:1). Place is not inert: it offers opportunity and challenge and it would seem that it is the land which enables the people to be established by God as a 'people holy to himself' (Deuteronomy 28:9). Responsibility to the land as well as to Yahweh is important in this three-way relationship. The Lord, people and place are inextricably woven together in harmony: 'And because you hearken to these ordinances and keep and do them, the Lord God will keep with you the covenant and the steadfast love which he swore to your fathers to keep; he will love you, bless you, and multiply you' (Deuteronomy 7:12–13). It was the failure of the people to hearken to the ordinances of the Lord which, as the prophets warned, led to displacement.

It could be construed that the place of Jerusalem in the scheme of things is not irrelevant to imposition of exile. In the original promise of the land, the city had played no part, and it was only after the city had been captured by David from the Jebusites (2 Samuel 5:6) in the tenth century that this small town of little importance

---

[22] O'Donovan (1989), 51.

[23] Brueggemann, W. (1977), 73.

rose to prominence. One of David's first acts after subjugating Jerusalem was to take the Ark of the Covenant there from Shiloh in the hill country to the north. As the Ark, symbol of God's presence in Israel, arrived in Jerusalem there was much celebration as David 'leaped and danced' before the Lord. David, we are told, was dissuaded from building a permanent house for the Ark (2 Samuel 7), but in the reign of his son, Solomon, a temple was built on a high outcrop of rock above the city, a threshing floor of Araunah, a Jebusite whose quarry had been bought by David. Once the Ark of the Covenant had been placed in the inner sanctuary of the house, God's mysterious and glorious presence would dwell there. As the priests came out of this holy place, 'a cloud filled the house of the Lord, so that the priests could not stand to minister because of the cloud; for the glory of the Lord filled the house of the Lord' (1 Kings 8:10–11).

In his 1977 work, Brueggemann does not have much time for the temple. He tells us that it served to give theological legitimacy and visible religiosity to the entire programme of the regime so that it becomes a cult for a static God, lacking in the power, vigour and freedom of the God of the old traditions. Brueggemann suggests that God who had promised and given the land becomes, in the Solomonic period, patron of the King, and religion becomes a decoration rather than a foundation. This approach is certainly consonant with Habel's less than flattering description of the 'Royal Ideology' reflected in 1 Kings 3–10 and the royal psalms, the promulgation of which, he suggests, supports the vested interests of the monarch and the royal court to the extent that the people as a whole have no rights over the land.[24] Criticism of Jerusalem – and the temple in particular – is not new, as Harold Turner observes: 'All great religious traditions have their internal sources of self-criticism and throw up their own reformers, but there can be no people in history who have examined their temples in the way that Israel and the Jews defended or opposed, reformed or re-interpreted or even discarded the sanctuary that stood at the centre and basis of their existence for more than a millennium.'[25]

Part of what we see here is a continuing tension between place and placelessness evident in the scriptures. Although the people of Israel were rooted to the land, we must not be blind to the fact that it is not just the New Testament that insists upon what Belden Lane characterized as the supra-locative character of the divine–human encounter:

> Yahweh, unlike the mountain and fertility gods of the ancient Canaanites, refuses to be bound by any geographical locale. All of the 'high places' pretending to capture the divine presence must be torn down as idolatrous in the highest degree. The prophet Nathan warns David, as he plans to build the temple, that no-one can presume to build a house for God. Yahweh, the one who dwells in thick darkness, will not remain 'on call' in Jerusalem, at the behest of the king (2 Samuel 7). A theology of transcendence will never be fully comfortable with place. Hence, the tension between place and placelessness remains a fiercely vigorous one, struggling to understand the truth of a great and transcendent God revealed in the particularity of place.[26]

---

[24] Habel, N. (1995), 17–32.

[25] Turner, H. W. (1979), 68.

[26] Lane, B. L. (1992), 5.

Whilst noting this, we should also be aware that there are many texts which speak of Yahweh choosing to make himself known in particular locales which then become holy, for example to Moses at the burning bush (Genesis 28:16–17) and Jacob at Bethel (Exodus 3:1–5). The abhorrence of 'high places' is a result of their dedication to foreign gods, not antipathy to holiness of place. Similarly, against Nathan's warning to David we must set the huge importance that Jerusalem and the temple develop in the biblical narrative from here on. It would be a bold exegesis which would be prepared to write all this off as an aberration. However, Lane is right to draw attention to the tensions, and we must concede that a delicate balance is necessary. In conversations with me, Walter Brueggemann has suggested that he is now more sympathetic to the importance of Jerusalem, particularly in the post-exilic period. Although the place of Jerusalem in the scheme of things is a complex question, it is certainly true that the hopes of the people of Israel became more and more concentrated in Jerusalem, which seemed to become the focus of their sense of place. For better or for worse, Jerusalem looms large in the scriptures, and we must therefore pay attention to it.

Solomon, temple builder, had been told by Yahweh in his youth that if he would: 'walk before me, as David your father walked, with integrity of heart and uprightness, doing according to all that I have commanded you, and keeping my statutes and ordinances, then I will establish your royal throne over Israel for ever' (Psalm 89, Proverbs 8:30, Isaiah 11:4–5). Solomon forgot this, however, as he forgot the conditions for dwelling in the land: and it was left, ironically, to the Queen of Sheba, a foreigner, to articulate them. There were three facets of the covenant, as we saw – Yahweh, the land, and the people – and when Yahweh began to be left out of the equation, whatever the status of Jerusalem, it was inevitable that exile would follow. This necessity is articulated in the prophetic writings, and the importance of the land and attitudes to it is made clearest in the writings of Jeremiah. Jeremiah recites the whole history of Israel as the history of land. He explains that the people of Israel went far from the Lord, and 'went after worthlessness and became worthless' (Jeremiah 2:6–7). Habel characterizes Jeremiah's writings as representing an ideology which might best be described as a symbiotic relationship between Yahweh, the land and the people of Israel in which the land is seen as a personal gift from Yahweh.[27] The land, he suggests, might almost be thought of as a third party in the relationship. In all the ideologies Habel identifies, this is the one in which we see the three-way relationship to which I have referred operating most clearly.

Neglect of the Lord meant that Israel had become foolish and stupid (Jeremiah 4:22) and became so bad that, according to Jeremiah, Yahweh had no alternative but to force the people into exile. Faithfulness in this situation meant submitting to his will: 'Like these good figs, so I will regard as good the exiles from Judah, whom I have sent away from this place to the land of the Chaldeans. I will set my eyes upon them for good, and I will bring them back to this land. I will build them up and not tear them down; I will plant them and not uproot them' (Jeremiah 24:4–6). The prophet Jeremiah was not the last person to meditate upon the experience of exile.

---

[27] Habel, N. (1995), 75.

The words of the *Salve Regina*,[28] which refer to us as poor banished children of Eve, exiled in this vale of tears, have ensured that the notion of exile has become a powerful image for Christians through the centuries. Only the Jews, however, have made exile a central metaphor in their lives. In reminding us of this, Wilken quotes the words of the medieval Jewish poet Judah Halevi, who describes the Jews as being 'captives of desire'. Wilken goes on to say:

> This yearning to return has been nourished over the centuries by men and women who never saw the land or nurtured any realistic hope they would see it in their lifetimes. In poetry and works of devotion, in drawings on marriage contracts, in the bunting to festoon houses and booths during the celebration of Sukkoth, in paintings on the Torah shrine and carvings on copper plates used for Passover, Jews have displayed their longing. A marriage contract from eighteenth-century Italy, for example, used the traditional benediction, 'May the voice of the bridegroom and bride be heard in the cities of Judah and in the streets of Jerusalem' as well as the psalm, 'If I forget you, O Jerusalem, let my right hand wither' (Ps 137). Marriage contracts were illustrated with a picture of the holy city, Jerusalem.[29]

But exile remains a desperate reality for many in today's world. I noted in the last chapter how the demise of place has made itself felt to disastrous consequence in the lives of displaced people in the twentieth century. That century has been described as the century of the refugee: during it many millions suffered the agonies of sojourning in a refugee camp, almost always through no fault of their own. As Mark Raper, who works among refugees, reminds us: 'The number of refugees, that is, those persons forced to leave their countries because of war, famine, persecution and conflict, the traditional wellsprings of refugees, is today at least three times that of the early eighties. Over ninety per cent of the world's refugees come from the world's poorest countries and are hosted by them.'[30] In the biblical narrative, however, God's faithfulness was experienced even in exile: the Lord allowed history to begin anew for the hopeless exiles. There are resonances here with current experience. Mark Raper reminds us that it is important not to romanticize the experience of refugees today, nor to idealize the experience of those who work with them, but points out that, ironically, the most grace-filled encounters for both parties seem to occur at the most inconvenient moments. They are mediated by the most unlikely of messengers. Positive things take place in exile, just as they did for Israel, awful though the experience is.

During the exile, synagogues or 'gathering places' evolved for regular meetings, and these had spread to almost every settlement in the Diaspora by the time of Jesus. In addition, the home, which had from earliest times been a place for blessing and prayer, acquired a new significance as time went on. This development was to prove vital for the survival of Judaism for it meant that the destruction of the temple in 70 AD

---

[28] The words of the *Salve Regina* in English are: 'Hail, holy Queen, mother of mercy. Hail, our life, our sweetness and our hope. To thee do we cry, poor banished children of Eve; to thee do we send up our sighs, mourning and weeping, in this vale of tears. Turn then, most gracious advocate, thine eyes of mercy towards us; and after this our exile, show unto us the blessed fruit of thy womb, Jesus. O clement, O loving, O sweet virgin Mary.'

[29] Wilken, R. (1992), 3.

[30] Raper, M. (1999), 29.

did not mean the end of Judaism. However, biblical faith holds out the promise of restoration and the enjoyment of a sense of place. Seeking after righteousness and justice in a strange land will bring its reward for, as Jeremiah puts it: 'I will be found by you, says the Lord, and I will restore your fortunes and gather you from all the nations and all the places where I have driven you, says the Lord, and I will bring you back to the place from which I sent you into exile'(Jeremiah 29:14). Brueggemann draws our attention to the significance of this promise:

> That is the ultimate word of biblical faith. It is the word spoken to the first fathers in exile (Gen 12:1–3) and the affirmation of the last man at Calvary. It is the surprise of Easter which lies beyond all our landless and landed expectations. Exile ended history because the two are antithetical. But exile did not end Yahweh's will for history, and he will, as he has before, begin anew to make another history. The Bible never denies there is landlessness, but it rejects every suggestion that landlessness is finally the will of Yahweh. Exiles, like the old sojourners, live in this hope and for this plan which outdistances all reasonable hypotheses about history. The exiles know about endings and about waiting. They find it to be a beginning beyond expectation, nearly beyond celebration, but so his plan always is.[31]

Israel did indeed return to the Promised Land and to the holy city, but the ending of the exile was not an occasion for great rejoicing since those who were able to do so returned to a land under the control of new masters, the Persians. It was something less than full freedom in which Israel covenanted again for land (Nehemiah 9:38), since Judea was simply a province of the Persian Empire. In contrast to the period of the monarchy, careful, respectful intention to honour the covenant for being in the land characterized the Ezra community, which believed that the land could be kept by obedience. In the face of a less than satisfactory restoration, one of Israel's responses was apocalyptic, and in this the imagery of the land is central, as it had been throughout Jewish history. Here storied place, the holy land, with which Israel's history is inextricably entwined, remains a central image of salvation:

> On that day the Lord their God will save them
> For they are the flock of his people;
> for like the jewels of a crown
> they shall shine on his land.
> How good and how fair it shall be!
> Grain shall make the young men flourish,
> and new wine the maidens. (Zechariah 9:16–17)

This apocalyptic vision contrasts land in hope with land in possession. Brueggemann concludes his consideration with the following comments:

> This hope for transformed land, renewed land, new land, became a central point for expectant Israel (which is to be sharply contrasted to possessing, possessive Israel). They were indeed 'prisoners of hope' (Zech 9:12). They were enslaved to an expectation that the present arrangement of disinheritance could not endure. And so they waited. They waited with radical confidence because they did not believe that the meek Torah-keepers would finally be denied their land. The Hellenistic world had created a keen sense of alienation.

---

[31] Brueggemann, W. (1977), 126.

The promise was for luxuriant at-homeness. And they waited. They could neither explain nor understand, but they had a rhetoric which both required and bestowed hope upon them. And it was this Promised Land which gave them identity and even sanity in a context where everything was denied. They waited for the new land which seemed unlikely and which required the dismantling of everything now so stable. They waited. Jerusalem for some was a present possession to be jealously guarded. For others it was a passionate hope, urgently awaited and surely promised.[32]

I shall look at the significance and implications of this apocalyptic approach to place when I turn to the New Testament material. Here, however, we can note that it is of great importance in later Old Testament writings, and that placedness is held out as the final promise in these writings as in others. Place remains central.

The notion of 'possessing the land' develops great poignancy when one contemplates the relationship between the Jewish people, newly returned to the Promised Land at the conclusion of the Second World War after centuries in exile, and the Palestinian people. One could be forgiven for thinking that society in Israel today is consumed by a 'frantic effort of the landed to hold onto the turf', to use a phrase of Brueggemann's, and the treatment of Palestinians by the Jewish people as being characterized by dehumanizing exploitation and oppression. This is not new: an analogous situation pertained at the time of the possession of the Promised Land by Joshua, for the land of Canaan had to be 'dispossessed' before it could be 'possessed' (Judges 11:24) and this could only be accomplished by driving out other peoples (Deuteronomy 9:4) and blotting out all signs of their presence (Deuteronomy 25:19). These words have uncomfortable resonances with what is happening in the Middle East in our own day. Twentieth-century Zionism uses the promised return from Exile as a rationale for the sustenance of political and military suppression of the Palestinian people. As Kenneth Cragg observes, Zionism in the twentieth century 'fulfils' biblical promises in that it:

> expresses their age-long sense of inalienable habitat, from which exile is inauthentic and therefore necessarily terminable. Jewishness can never be, as it were, 'departicularised' either ethnically or land-wise. Identity is always *sui generis qua* people and land-tied *qua* geography, however widely dispersion scatters it. Judaism counts divine-people relation without land as a Christian aberration, the church being esteemed overly 'spiritual' in supposing that 'people of God' could have no necessary physical address. For Jews it is as if Yahweh himself has 'an address on earth'.[33]

However, what is new, as Rabbi Dan Cohn-Sherbok points out, is that increasingly, for Jewry, a void exists where once the people experienced God's presence. And the result is that 'the State of Israel has been invested with many of the attributes previously reserved for the Deity. It is the land of Israel that is seen as being ultimately capable of providing a safe haven for those in need. Israel, not the God of history, is seen as protector of the Jewish nation.'[34] This is a radical departure from what the biblical narrative demands of the people of Israel, and its insistence upon a three-way relationship between Yahweh, land, and people.

---

[32] Ibid., 166.

[33] Cragg, K. (1997), 79.

[34] Cohn-Sherbok, D. (1998) in *The Church Times*, 1 May

Even without this latter development, the situation in the Middle East would seem to be intractable if one sees the Old Testament as a document intended to refer for all time to the relationship between God, the chosen people and *this* land, rather than treating the land motif as symbolic of the importance of place in our relations with God and with one another. My analysis in this book looks at the scriptures from a Christian perspective, and it is not appropriate here to comment upon what a way forward in the unhappiness of the Holy Land might be from a Jewish perspective, though we might note that Habel's analysis of Old Testament ideologies is instructive, since not all of the six ideologies identified by him require outright possession and expulsion of other peoples from the Promised Land. This exegesis is by a Christian theologian, however, not a Jew. Whatever the way forward, a Christian would surely wish to agree with Kenneth Cragg that communities must somehow learn to find identities which are participatory as well as distinctive: 'Our particularities of birth and land and story are inescapable. But their sanctions must be within and not against the human whole. This is why the "territorial" must also be the "terrestial". There are few tasks more spiritually strenuous than those which have to do with the Judaic part and the human whole.'[35]

A Relational View of Place

It would be tempting, in view of the intractable problems still being encountered in the Holy Land as a result of a 'high' theology of the land, to jettison the notion that God's way with the world is as located as our examination has suggested. But that would not be true to the text as we have studied it. The basic lesson that we can learn from our analysis of the Old Testament material is that place is a hugely important biblical category – and that it has been greatly underrated. The Old Testament can, as we have seen, be read as the story of God's people with God's land. It would appear from what we have seen of the Old Testament narrative that the latter suggests, first, that place is a fundamental category of human experience, and that, second, there is a threefold relationship between God, his people, and place. This conclusion finds support from W. D. Davies, who tells us that 'the Jewish faith might be defined as "a fortunate blend of a people, a land and their God"', and Habel, who speaks of the land–God–people relationship as characterizing some of the most important strands of the material.[36] In all this we can observe this same threefold relationship between Yahweh, his people, and place which has much potential, I think, for helping us to understand how place should be properly understood from a Christian perspective.

These conclusions would suggest that a proper biblical attitude to place will entail acknowledging that a relational view of it, inextricably bound up with both God and humanity, is essential. Such a view could be expressed diagramatically as follows:

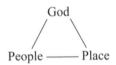

[35] Cragg, K. in Davies, W. D. (1991), 102.

[36] Habel, N. (1995), 75.

The importance of place on this account is relational. It is bound up not just with its relationship to God the creator, but with the creatures to whom that God is bound in covenantal love. Our reading of the Old Testament leads us to believe that the narrative would find foreign any notion that place is not integral to our experience of God or the world but simply exists alongside us as an added extra, so to speak, a view which could be expressed as follows:

This representation is roughly equivalent to that adumbrated by Susan White to which I referred in the last chapter, which suggests that place is entirely subordinate to ethics, that it really does not matter where God relates to us or we to each other. This is also, as we have seen, the predominant view of modernity.

The Old Testament material would not, either, suggest that God's relationship to place is prior to human encounter there and that God privileges some places over and against others. Geoffrey Lilburne, who sees Brueggemann's approach to the Old Testament material as 'overly dependent upon history and human activity as the distinguishing characteristics of place', complains that the latter 'roots the definition of place in the human activity which "hallows" or "qualifies" the otherwise empty space'.[37] Lilburne argues that a sense of place is as much a function of the nature of the places themselves as it is of human activity. This view might be expressed diagrammatically as follows:

I see no evidence for this in the Old Testament narrative, and Lilburne himself does not produce any. The conclusion of our engagement with the Old Testament narrative is thus an understanding of place as relational to both God and his people. We now take this three-way understanding of God, people and place and test it against the New Testament witness.

The New Testament

Place in the Narrative

A remarkable passage in the New Testament comes in the first chapter of St John's Gospel. Philip finds Nathaniel, and says to him: ' "We have found him of whom Moses in the law and also the prophets wrote, Jesus of Nazareth, the son of Joseph." Nathaniel's reply is "Can anything good come out of Nazareth?" ' (John 1:46). This brief exchange centres around the concept of place, and what it can do for a person in a corpus which is sometimes portrayed as having no interest in place.

---

[37] Lilburne, G. (1989), 26.

I shall maintain that the question of the importance of place is one which looms large in the New Testament, particularly with regard to the centrality or otherwise of Jerusalem, which had by New Testament times become central in Judaism's understanding of itself. Any discussion on the significance of place in general and land in particular in the New Testament is bound to make reference to W. D. Davies's study, *The Gospel and the Land*. There is no other work of substance, largely because scholars do not seem to feel that 'place' is a category of sufficient importance in the New Testament to warrant their attention. In his book, Davies surveys the Old Testament background and then looks in detail at the New Testament material. It provides a useful starting point for a discussion flowing from the above chapter, and I shall summarize his findings before analysing them and drawing conclusions.

Davies notes that there is an absence of explicit references to the land in the Pauline epistles. He records that in Paul's own account of the good news in 1 Corinthians 15:3–8 there appears to be no interest in geography. It was apparently of no concern to Paul that his conversion had taken place outside 'the land'. Davies points out that Paul does not include 'the land' in his list of advantages enjoyed by the chosen people in his letter to the Romans (Romans 9:14) and that in his invocation of Abraham in order to claim the extension of God's grace beyond the Jewish people in Christ, Paul did not make much of the promise of the land. God's promise is now for all people in all places. Davies concedes that political considerations may have played their part in this as far as the Epistle to the Romans was concerned, but not that to the Galatians. Paul does not explicitly reject the significance of the Jerusalem Temple but makes it clear on more than one occasion (1 Corinthians 3:16–17 and 2 Corinthians 6:14–18) that the Spirit dwells not there, but in the church. He cites Jerusalem as the centre from which his missionary work expanded (Romans 15:9), and Davies believes that: 'Zion or Jerusalem was for the Jew, Paul, the centre of the world, the symbol of the land itself and the focal point for the Messianic Age. The likelihood is that, at first at least, it occupied the same place in his life as a Christian. 2 Thessalonians 2, and possibly Romans 11.26, and probably Romans 9.26 confirm this.'[38]

Davies goes on to say, however, that Paul is ambivalent in his attitude to the church at Jerusalem. He wishes to assert his independence from the apostles in Jerusalem, and though 'that city remains the city of the End, Paul is no longer governed by concern with it as the centre of his activity. Rather, Jerusalem has become the place where the unity of the "Israel of God", not the end of history, is to be revealed.' As his theology developed, 'Paul apparently felt no incongruity between retaining his apocalyptic geography, centred on Jerusalem, even though, since he was 'in Christ', it had become otiose. Theologically he no longer had any need of it: his geographical identity was subordinated to that of being "in Christ", in whom was neither Jew nor Greek.'[39] Being a new creation 'in Christ', Paul had been set free from the Law, and therefore, from the land. His silence on the matter of the land is in keeping with the place of the Law as he describes it in Galatians and Romans. The role of the Law was purely provisional (Galatians 3:19ff) and in the fulfilment of the promise in Christ was no longer necessary (Galatians 3:10–14, 23–26). Paul's understanding of Christ

---

[38] Davies, W. D. (1974), 196.

[39] Ibid., 200, 208, 220.

and his missionary endeavours made it inescapable that 'the people of Israel living in the land had been replaced as the people of God by a universal community which had no special territorial attachment'.[40] Although I would not want to dissent from the gist of what Davies says about Paul's attitude to the land we should not, perhaps, be too hasty in determining that the place of his conversion was of no significance to him. I shall return to this question in Chapter 4, when we look at the role of place in religious experience.

In examining the land issue in Mark and Matthew, Davies looks in detail at the thesis of some scholars that there is, in the Synoptics: 'a connection between locality and doctrine, an emphasis (in Mark and Matthew) on Galilee as the sphere of revelation and redemption, and in both Gospels (though perhaps to a lesser degree in Matthew) an emphasis on Jerusalem as the place of rejection'. He is not convinced by it, and concludes that the two gospels 'lend little, if any, support to the view that preoccupation with Galilee had led to its elevation to *terra Christiana*'.[41] There is in Mark and Matthew, he believes, an unexpressed assumption that Jerusalem was the 'inevitable' Messianic centre (Mark 10:31ff, Matthew 21:10, Matthew 16:21). Such references as that to the dead raised at the time of the crucifixion going into the holy city and appearing to many (Matthew 27:53) leave Davies in no doubt that Jerusalem was, for Matthew, 'the city of the great king, the setting of the great eschatological drama'.[42] The sin of Jerusalem is very real to Matthew, however: there is no uncritical elevation of it. Davies notes that for Matthew it has become the guilty city, and that some have gone so far as to interpret the *parousia* in Matthew as the divine judgement on Judaism in the fall of Jerusalem.

Davies attacks the land question in Luke–Acts through an investigation of the work of Conzelmann who, in his *The Theology of St Luke*, claimed that: 'to this picture of the scene of Jesus life must be added the "typical" localities, mountain, lake, plain, desert, the Jordan, each especially employed in a way peculiar to Luke. In a word the process by which the scene became stylised into the "Holy Land" has begun.'[43] Davies is suspicious of the schematization that Conzelmann uses to advance his thesis that Luke had a geographical theology. He notes, however, that Jerusalem is of importance to Luke: there are twice as many appearances of the word 'Jerusalem' in Luke as there are in each of the other gospels. It occurs at crucial points – most important, perhaps, as the scene for resurrection appearances. Luke chose to ignore the Galilee appearances. As Davies himself says: 'Luke, a Gentile concerned above all with the Gentile mission, was aware that Christianity arose out of the boiling cauldron of eschatological anticipations of first-century Judaism, and emphasised the significance for its beginning of the city around which those hopes had clustered.' However, as he goes on to observe:

> Though Luke recognises Jerusalem as the geographic centre of Christian beginnings; he also knows its mystique. But he deliberately and clinically transcends this spatial dimension. Christianity is a Way which began at Jerusalem but passes through it. True,

[40] Ibid., 182.
[41] Ibid., 243.
[42] Ibid., 242.
[43] Conzelmann, H., *The Theology of St Luke*, 70.

Luke retains the cry of Jesus over Jerusalem in 19.41–44. But, despite the weeping, it is clear eyed and unsentimental: Luke recognised that Jerusalem had chosen the way of political nationalism which led to war with Rome. In the coming of Jesus, God had decisively visited Jerusalem, but it was in judgement. Despite his awareness of the mystique of Jerusalem, Luke was not as susceptible to it as was Paul. A Gentile, even a Gentile Christian, Luke could be clinical about Jerusalem in a way that Paul never achieved.[44]

Davies believes that in the seventh chapter of The Acts of the Apostles we have Luke's articulation of his belief that Christianity should not be too narrowly and rigidly bound to Judaism, the Temple, and Jerusalem and the land. In this chapter the land does not receive much mention. Why? Because by the time Luke was writing, the number of Gentiles in the Church would have greatly outnumbered the number of Jews, and the former would have had precious little interest in the land. In addition, for Luke to have discussed the separation of the Gospel from the land directly 'would have undermined two of the purposes which he dearly cherished, and which led him to concentrate so much on Jerusalem – first, the recognition of the theological continuity between Gentile Christianity and Judaism, and, second, the political necessity to emphasise this'.[45]

Moving to the fourth gospel, Davies suggests that the author makes it clear that the central place for Jewish worship, the temple, is to be replaced, or rather transcended, by Christ. He goes on to argue that the same applies to other 'holy places' like Bethel, Samaritan Holy Places, Bethzatha and the Pool of Siloam. He concludes his survey of St John's gospel as follows:

> Our discussion of the fourth gospel drives us back to the beginning of the gospel to 1.14 where the flesh of Jesus of Nazareth is said to be the seat of the Logos. That Logos, whether as Wisdom or as Torah, is no longer attached to a land, as was the Torah, but to a person who came to his own land, and was not received. To judge from our examination, the fourth Gospel was not especially concerned with the particular relation of Jesus of Nazareth to his own geographical land.[46]

Davies's examination of much of the New Testament material, then, leads him to find in it, alongside the acknowledgement of the historical role of the land as the scene of the life, death and resurrection of Jesus, a growing recognition that the Gospel demanded a breaking out of its 'territorial chrysalis'. The central thrust of his study is towards a clear conclusion that land is of no importance in the New Testament. There is, as he says above, a 'concern' with the realities of the land, Jerusalem and the temple but these are ultimately transcended in Christ so that: 'in sum, for the holiness of place, Christianity has fundamentally, though not consistently, substituted the holiness of person: it has Christified holy space.' He believes that Christianity has, in the main, only been interested in place to the extent that it has been interested in Jesus:

---

[44] Davies, W. D. (1974), 255, 260.

[45] Ibid., 368.

[46] Ibid., 333.

The witness of the New Testament is, therefore, twofold: it transcends the land, Jerusalem, the Temple. Yes: but its History and Theology demand a concern with these realities also. Is there a reconciling principle in these apparently contradictory attitudes? There is. By implication, it has already been suggested, the New Testament finds holy space wherever Christ is or has been: it personalises 'holy space' in Christ who, as a figure of History, is rooted in the land; he cleansed the Temple and died in Jerusalem, and lends his glory to these and to the places where he was but, as Living Lord, he is also free to move wherever he wills. To do justice to the personalism of the New Testament, that is, to its Christocentricity, is to find a clue to the various strata of tradition that we have traced and to the attitudes they reveal: to their freedom from space and their attachment to spaces.[47]

Thus, as another scholar, Bauerschmidt, puts it: 'The sacred geography of Israel is not simply left behind, but continues to serve Christians both as a source of images and of metaphors which provide the stage upon which the Christian drama is enacted.'[48] I would not want to argue with Davies' conclusions about the land question, and would agree with him about the Christocentricity of the New Testament. However, I believe that there is a way of reconciling this insight with the importance of place as it is recorded in the Old Testament: I do not believe that the two Testaments need to be regarded as being at loggerheads on this question.

The Incarnation

At the end of his discussion of the fourth gospel, Davies himself tells us that 'the Jesus of the fourth gospel is not a disincarnate spirit, but a man of flesh and blood who hungered and thirsted and was weary with his journey. His flesh was real flesh, and he was geographically conditioned as all men. But, although John presents us with itineraries of Jesus to some extent, and although these were real, it was not the horizontal geographical movements that mattered to him. Rather, what was significant to John was the descent of Jesus from above, and his ascent thither. The fundamental spatial symbolism of the fourth gospel was not horizontal, but vertical'.[49]

The vertical dimension is, of course, what Christians refer to as the incarnation, which is central to the New Testament witness and the Christian faith that springs from it, and the fact that Jesus was not a disincarnate spirit has profound implications. 'The Word became flesh,' St John tells us, 'and we have beheld his glory' (John 1:14). Thomas Torrance writes that the 'relation established between God and man in Jesus Christ constitutes Him as the place in all space and time where God meets with man in the actualities of human existence, and man meets with God and knows Him in His own divine Being'. It is in this that our hope is founded for 'unless the eternal breaks into the temporal and the boundless being of God breaks into the *spatial* existence of man and takes up dwelling within it, the vertical dimension vanishes out of a man's life and becomes quite strange to him – and man loses his place under the sun'.[50] In their grappling with the significance of the New Testament material, the Church Fathers understood well that space and time had been 'Christified', to use Davies'

---

[47] Ibid., 367.

[48] Bauerschmidt, F. C. (1996), 507.

[49] Davies, W. D. (1974), 335.

[50] Torrance, T. F. (1969).

term. The Nicene Fathers departed from an Aristotelian 'receptacle' view of place to which I referred in the last chapter, so that the Church Fathers' view of place was one which was at odds with the predominant inheritance of the Western philosophical tradition. Proper attention to the incarnation forced Patristic theology to suggest that place is of great importance in the Christian scheme of things, for in defining places as the seat of relations and of meeting and activity between God and humanity it allowed for the significance of places in human experience to be recognized:

> While the incarnation does not mean that God is limited by space and time, *it asserts the reality of space and time for God in the actuality of His relations with us*, and at the same time binds us to space and time in our relations with Him. We can no more contract out of space and time than we can contract out of the creature–Creator relationship and God 'can' no more contract out of space and time than He 'can' go back on the Incarnation of His Son or retreat from the love in which He made the world, with which he loves it, through which He redeems it, and by which He is pledged to uphold it – pledged, that is, by the very love that God himself is and which He has once for all embodied in our existence in the person and being of Jesus Christ.[51]

I noted in Chapter 1 that Torrance uses the two terms 'space' and 'place' interchangeably and confusingly. There is an equivalence between the sense in which he is using the word 'space' here with what I have defined 'place' to mean. We might say, therefore, that it is clear from the incarnation that *places are the seat of relations or the place of meeting and activity in the interaction between God and the world*, and argue further that place is therefore a fundamental category of human and spiritual experience. In defining the locus of God's relations with humanity to be focused in one particular individual the incarnation asserts the importance of place in a way different from, but not less important than, the Old Testament. It entails a movement away from a concentration upon the Holy Land and Jerusalem but at the same time initiates an unprecedented celebration of materiality and therefore of place in God's relations with humanity. The fact that, as Torrance points out, neither we nor God can contract out of space and time, necessarily implies the importance of place since it affirms the importance of place and time for God in his relations with us. As William Temple says: 'In the great affirmation that "The word became flesh and we beheld his glory" (John 1.14) is implicit a whole theory of the relation between spirit and matter.'[52] There are far-reaching implications here not only for the *material*, but also for the *particular*. On this latter, O'Donovan writes:

> 'The word became flesh …' (John 1.14). Among the ever-unfolding paradoxes of that pregnant saying, there is, perhaps, none more startling than this: that the divine Word, the intelligibility of God, is unlike the intelligibility of the world, in that it communicates itself in the particular, God makes himself known in election, the principle of particularity, and yet without prejudice to his universal processes of love. The phrase 'Universal love' expresses the ultimate paradox of the divine presence for the world; for, in all our experience of it, love is not universal but particular, intimate and selective. The attempt to depict a form of human love which is without particularity, reciprocity or preference has

---

[51] Ibid., 67. My italics.
[52] Temple, W. (1935), xx.

never yielded anything but a cold-blooded monstrosity. The most that we can do with our love is to be open with it, ready to give it to those who come across our paths and show their need of it. But even that is not, in any sense, universality.[53]

The 'Christification' of space and the notion of the Word becoming flesh have importance for considerations of the body. The fact is that, among other factors, the downgrading of the particular in Western thought and practice has meant that the body has been ignored as much as if not more than place. LeFebvre has harsh things to say about the Western philosophical tradition's approach to the body:

> Western philosophy has betrayed the body; it has actively participated in the great process of metaphorization that has abandoned the body; and it has denied the body. The living body, being at once 'subject' and 'object', cannot tolerate such conceptual division, and consequently philosophical concepts fall into the category of the 'signs of non-body'. Under the reign of King Logos, the reign of true space, the mental and the social were sundered, as were the directly lived and the conceived, and the subject and the object. New attempts were forever being made to reduce the external to the internal, or the social to the mental, by means of one ingenious typology or another. Net result? Complete failure! Abstract spatiality and practical spatiality contemplated one another from afar, in thrall to the visual realm.[54]

These words will have disturbing resonance for many of us within the Christian tradition who are aware of theology's collusion in all this. Talk of the importance of the body has revived in academic circles in recent years, and the impetus of the incarnation for a more positive consideration of the body has been on the agenda in theology, too. What is almost always ignored, however, is that if we are to reassert the importance of the body, we must, by implication, reassert the importance of place, and vice versa. The two are inseparable, since place is always there at the first level of human experience: just as there is no experience of place without body, so there is no experience of body without place. It is fascinating that although the importance of the body is increasingly recognized in theology and other disciplines, the obvious interrelationship between place and body, and therefore the importance of place itself in human experience, is scarcely commented on in theology.

Although I shall not be able to consider here all the implications of the incarnation for the body, we should note with Geoffrey Wainwright that the Word of God came to expression in the thick texture of human life: 'His "flesh" is constituted not only by his body, born of Mary, but by an entire range of words and deeds, by his interactions with his historical contemporaries and by the events which surround and mark his career.' Wainright goes on to conclude that, as a result of this utterly corporeal life lived by the Word of God for the redemption of the world, 'it is entirely congruous that he should choose to keep coming to his church by material means for the sake of our salvation.[55] This is why the sacrilizing of storied places is both possible and

---

[53] O'Donovan, O. (1989), 53. Compare the comment of Clifford Geertz quoted on page 10: 'Like love or imagination, Place makes a poor abstraction.' The secular world has never been able to live with the paradox at the heart of the Christian revelation.

[54] LeFebvre, H. (1991), 407.

[55] Wainwright, G. (1997), 10.

important in the Christian scheme of things. It is a process whereby, as we shall see, particular places associated with salvation history can be perceived as potent mediators of divine presence. But, as O'Donovan reminds us, there is a balance to be kept here:

> The 'transitory promises' of particular election, upon which Old Testament faith is based, are not abolished by Christian faith into pure universality, but their exclusivity is taken up; they are, as it were, replicated. They become the matrix for the forms in which God universally meets humankind. It is still the case that human beings meet God within relations of particular belonging; for this reason the church has always to be structured as a local church; yet God is not tied to any one particular other than the name of Jesus Christ, but can make himself known through many and through all; for that reason the church has always to be a universal church. The redeemed universal humanity (to which the universal church bears its imperfect witness) is not intended to abolish the structures of particular familiarity, but to challenge their false claims to autonomy, by 'breaking down the wall of partition', the wall which causes them to express their differences in mutual antagonism rather than in mutual service.[56]

Despite this ongoing tension between place and placelessless (or universality) the incarnation implies that place is of great importance not just in an Old Testament but also in a New Testament perspective, and there is continuity between the two. How this is worked out theologically and practically in the experience of the Church – and what implications it might have for the world – I shall explore in the following chapters, but for the moment we note that 'Christification' is not at odds with Walter Brueggemann's findings:

> In the Old Testament there is no timeless space, but there is also no spaceless time. There is rather *storied place*, that is a place which has meaning because of the history lodged there. There are stories which have authority because they are located in a place. This means that biblical faith cannot be presented simply as an historical movement indifferent to place which could have happened in one setting as well as another, because it is undeniably fixed in this place with this meaning. And for all its apparent 'spiritualising', the New Testament does not escape this rootage.[57]

Before examining how this balance might be kept in the next chapter, I shall consider further the role of Jerusalem in the New Testament writings.

Spiritualization and the Place of Jerusalem: Eschatology

Questions about place when asked by Christians have tended to concentrate upon the

---

[56] O'Donovan, O. (1989), 54.

[57] Brueggemann, W. (1978), 187, So, also, Belden Lane reminds us: 'One necessarily reads the scriptures with map in hand. Yahweh is disclosed, not just anywhere, but on the slopes of Mt Sinai, at Bethel and Shiloh, at the Temple in Jerusalem. The God of Old and New Testaments is one who "tabernacles" with God's people, always made known in particular locales. When Paul celebrates the "scandal of the gospel", this is a reality geographically rooted in Jesus, a crucified Jew from Nazareth, of all places. The offence, the particularity of place, becomes intrinsic to the incarnational character of Christian faith' (Lane, B., 1992, 5).

status of Jerusalem and the Holy Land. Peter Walker is one scholar who has looked at such questions carefully.[58] He does not question the sacredness of Jerusalem in the Old Testament, and speaks of David's choice of Jerusalem and the establishment of Solomon's temple there as the place 'where his name dwelt' (1 Kings 8:29), as having been 'endorsed by God', so that Mount Zion became a symbol of God's dwelling among his people. He points out that this was affirmed by the earthly Jesus when he spoke of Jerusalem being the 'city of the great King' (Matthew 5:35) and of the temple being 'truly God's house' (Mark 11:17; John 2:16). However, he notes that when speaking to the Samaritan woman, Jesus not only confirmed the centrality of Jerusalem (John 4:22), but also told her that 'a time is coming where you will worship the Father neither on this mountain nor in Jerusalem' (John 4:21). Walker goes on to argue that the coming of Jesus significantly changed the status of Jerusalem and that Jesus himself claimed to be 'greater that the temple' (Matthew 12:6).[59]

We know from The Acts of the Apostles that the early Christians continued to worship in the temple, but changing attitudes are made clear as early as Stephen's trial before the Sanhedrin (Acts 7). Among New Testament authors there is a clear consensus that Jesus is the new temple, that the genuine mercy seat, the true place of God's presence, is no longer the Ark of the Covenant, but Christ crucified. God was in Christ reconciling the world to himself (2 Corinthians 5:19), and as such Christ not only brought the temple system to a close, he is himself the spiritual temple, the new dwelling place of God. There is a further development in the first letter of Peter, where Christ remains the central figure but Christians themselves become 'living stones' to be built with Christ (1 Peter 2). Where the temple had offered annual atonement for sins and reconciliation between the human and the divine, Christ's sacrifice did away with the necessity of both the sacrificial system and the mediating role of the temple priesthood. Further, Walker uses the manner in which the temple is seen by the author of the letter to the Hebrews as only a 'copy and shadow' of the reality now found in Christ and the access to God's presence now enabled through his sacrificial death (Hebrews 9:28; 10:10, 19–20) as an example of the way in which the Old Testament material on the theme of Jerusalem can only be rightly understood when read through the lens of the New Testament. The Jerusalem temple, as an integral part of the 'first covenant' (Hebrews 8:7) has lost its previous status (Hebrews 9:8) and will soon disappear (Hebrews 8:13). This is a theme echoed in St John's gospel where we learn that Jesus is the true 'tabernacle' or 'temple' (John 1:14; 2:21) and St Paul identifies Christian believers as God's temple (1 Corinthians 3:17; 6:19). Further, in the Book of Revelation we read that the 'New Jerusalem' has no temple because 'the Lord God Almighty and the Lamb are its temple' (Revelation 21:22).

Walker uses all these references to demonstrate the re-evaluation of the temple by

---

[58] So, for example, Peter Walker asks: 'In what sense, if any, can we talk of Jerusalem having been "special" to God in the Old Testament, or having a distinctive theological status? Or is the city's holiness in any age merely a human construct? However, if it is affirmed that there was indeed a divine involvement with Jerusalem during the Old Testament period what is the relationship between it and the Jerusalem of the New Testament? Should Christians understand the crucifixion and then the fall of Jerusalem to have indicated a divine judgement on the city which is final and irrevocable? Or can they preserve their belief in the city's essential holiness and specialness by emphasising its privileged involvement with the Incarnation and Resurrection' (Walker, P. W. L, 1990, viii).

[59] Walker, P. W. L. (1996), 1.

New Testament writers. He suggests that the reference to the 'river of the water of life' in the Book of Revelation (Revelation 22:1–2) indicates that this prophecy is a re-working of that of Ezekiel which had spoken of a renewed temple (Ezekiel 40ff). Since the author of the Book of Revelation understands this Ezekiel passage to be a reference to the New Jerusalem and the Lamb (who is its temple), Walker argues that the New Testament writers did not subscribe to a 'restorationist' approach to Jerusalem seen in some later Christians who expected the rebuilding of the temple in Jerusalem in the 'end-time', for Jesus was now that temple.[60] There can be little doubt that Walker's assessment is a fair one – it is very difficult to make out that there is a place within the Christian tradition for a 'religion of the temple' understood in biblical terms. As Walker himself puts it: 'Whether the temple is thought of as the place which embodies God's presence on earth or as the place of sacrifice, the New Testament affirms that both aspects have been fulfilled in Jesus: his death is the true sacrifice and his person the true locus of God's dwelling.' He continues: 'By extension Christian believers too may be seen as a temple. A temple in Jerusalem is therefore no longer necessary, for God's eternal purposes have now been revealed in Christ.'[61]

Having disposed of the temple, however, Walker goes on to do the same for the city of Jerusalem and cites the observation of St Paul that 'the present city of Jerusalem ... is in slavery with her children' (Galatians 4:25) as evidence that Paul wanted Jerusalem to be viewed in a new light. However, some of the other material which Walker quotes from the New Testament could be seen as support *both* for his thesis that the status of Jerusalem itself has changed in the New Testament *and* ours that the Christian faith affirms the importance of place. Walker reminds us that St Paul tells us that for Christians the focus is now to be upon 'the Jerusalem that is above ... and *she* is our mother' (Galatians 4:26) and tells us that 'this proves to be an opening salvo of a re-evaluation of Jerusalem which is to be found in all the NT writers'.[62] There can be no doubt that there is a shift away from emphasis upon the earthly Jerusalem but salvation is still represented here in terms of a *place*. The culmination of the heavenly vision is the descent of the New Jerusalem, coming down out of heaven from God (Revelation 21:10), resembling a gigantic hall in the form of a cube with sides measuring about 1500 miles (Revelation 21:15–17), constructed of precious materials (Revelation 21:18–21), and on each side there are three gates (Revelation 21:12–13). The light of this city is the glory of the Lord God and the Lamb (Revelation 21:23) who sit at the centre of the city and from the throne flows the river of the water of life (Revelation 22:1), and at each side of it are the tree of life (Revelation 22:2), and the fruit giving spiritual rather than physical nourishment (Revelation 22:2). The images here are most certainly of a place, and the character of the place is something between a city and a garden. Implicit in the description is that trinity of God, people, and place which I have deemed to be central to the Old Testament narrative.

The city is described in detail and the reader is left in no doubt that it is with *this place* that the consummation of all things is associated. I would want to say that the

---

[60] Ibid., 2.

[61] Ibid., 3.

[62] Ibid., 2.

fact that this heavenly Jerusalem is central to the identity of Christianity is confirmation of the recognition of the New Testament that *it is very difficult for us to imagine salvation in terms of anything other than place.* This realization comes to us most starkly when we read the picture of salvation presented to us in the Book of Revelation, which is quoted by Walker simply as another example of the downgrading of the status of the earthly Jerusalem. But other references support our contention. The author of the Letter to the Hebrews focuses the reader's attention upon the 'heavenly Jerusalem' (Hebrews 12:12). Here we see heaven portrayed as the eschatological goal of the people of God. As Marie Isaacs puts it:

> The author of Hebrews begins and ends with the theme of heaven. What opens with an affirmation of Jesus' session in heaven continues and ends with an exhortation to his audience to make heaven their goal also. The motif of Christ's present exaltation in heaven continues throughout the homily, and is held out as encouragement to a Christian community who are feeling weighed down by the circumstances of their present territorial existence. They are exhorted not to lose confidence in that celestial reality which is the son's present abode, since if they do not waver, it will soon be theirs.[63]

The texts seem to confirm the assertion that the New Testament consistently represents salvation to us in terms of place. The emergence of the literary genre to which Thomas More's *Utopia* gave its name, of which well over a hundred specimens have been published, is evidence of the fact that it is very difficult for us to imagine salvation in terms other than those of place. As Jesus himself puts it: 'There are many rooms in my Father's house; if there were not I would have told you. I am going now to prepare a place for you' (John 4:14). The words focus upon *place* as an eschatological hope. It is, I would suggest, of great significance that the New Testament affirms the importance of place in this manner and the fact that this interest would be characterized by people like Davies as spiritualization does not, in my view diminish that significance.

The conclusion of the above is that a proper Christian attitude to the importance of place derives directly from the New Testament witness to the incarnation as well as from the Old Testament's preoccupation with place, and that the spiritualization of place does not detract from this assessment. In Christ, God has hallowed the material world we inhabit and made it the home of his divinity. It is true to say that, although the happenings described in the New Testament are geographically grounded in particular places, the force of the text suggests that the importance of particular geographical location as it is understood in the Old Testament has been superseded by the person of Jesus Christ: space has been 'Christified' by the incarnation. However, just as our examination of the Old Testament material led us to suggest that there is a three-way relationship between God, people, and place, we see here that if it is true to say, developing Torrance's approach, that the incarnation implies that *places are the seat of relations or the place of meeting and activity in the interaction between God and the world*, then this balance is maintained by an incarnational perspective.

Further, we note that our earlier emphasis on relationality as a result of our engagement with the Old Testament text is confirmed by the contention that places

---

[63] Isaacs, M. (1992), 205.

are the seat of relations between God and the world. God relates *to* people *in* places, and the places are not irrelevant to that relationship but, rather, are integral to divine human encounter. The same holds true, as we might expect, for the relations of people to one another in places. This is a conclusion that follows directly from the incarnation. The significance of Jerusalem as a pivotal image from the conclusion of the scriptures is as a symbol of what is to come. The spiritualization of place in this eschatological strand of the narrative is not equivalent to its being rendered redundant in the divine scheme of things. It is, rather, a very important part of the picture. The New Testament material would suggest, therefore, that a high view of place flows from the incarnation and that place is important psychologically and eschatologically as well as physically. The final promise, in the New Testament as in the Old, is of *placedeness*.

Conclusion

We have looked at the Old Testament material and concluded that 'place' is a primary category of Old Testament faith. I have suggested that the narrative supports a relational view in which God, people, and place are all important. Although emphasis upon the Holy Land and Jerusalem recedes in the New Testament, the incarnation – and the particularity of God's relationship with humanity which flows from it – supports the notion of place retaining vital significance in God's dealings with humanity, since places can be thought of as the seat of relations, or the place of meeting and activity in the interaction between God and the world.

How, though, are we to maintain a balance between a gospel conviction that Christ has redeemed all places, that he is Lord of space and time but, at the same time, hold on to the importance of the incarnation in inviting us to value place? The best way forward, I shall argue in the next chapter, is to make use of a vitally important component of the Christian tradition, and view place *sacramentally*. This will enable us to maintain a proper balance for understanding the importance of place in the Christian scheme of things.

Chapter 3

Place and the Christian Tradition: A Sacramental Approach

The Sacramental World View

The Concept of Sacrament

One might, at first glance, be forgiven for thinking that quite a leap will have to be made from a study of New Testament material to consideration of 'sacramentality'. After all, the word 'sacrament' derives from the Latin *sacramentum*, and is therefore not to be found in the New Testament, it being always a rendering of the Greek *mysterion* (which is sometimes not translated, but transliterated to *mysterium*). C. K. Barrett, referring to the earliest known reference to the word used in this sense by Eusebius in the fourth century, contends that it was quite late that *mysterion* came to be the word in Greek Christian usage to denote what we call sacraments, though two references, one in the *Didache* and one by Ignatius, could be read in this way. However, as Barrett concedes, it would not be sensible to assume that 'just because the New Testament lacked a word for it, it was without the thing that the word signifies'.[1] The obvious references to the Eucharist in the Acts of the Apostles and the letters of St Paul, particularly the first letter to the Corinthians, mean that this cannot be the case. A more subtle reading of the New Testament reveals much more, however. For example, David Brown and Ann Loades contend that, just as the first chapter of John's Gospel can be seen as laying the foundations for all Christian sacramentalism in the idea of the incarnation as sacrament, 'so chapter six may be viewed as legitimating the extension of that principle to what are more conventionally known as sacraments, through that incarnational body now working its effects mysteriously upon our own'.[2] However, to talk of 'biblical sacraments' would be anachronistic, not only because the term is not used in the New Testament itself, but also because even as late as the end of the fourth century in the writings of St Ambrose of Milan, the two words 'sacraments' and 'mysteries' are used interchangeably, and as Elizabeth Rees points out: 'For St Augustine, in the fifth Century, sacraments and symbols were fairly interchangeable concepts. Augustine described sacraments as "visible forms of invisible grace", and included a wide variety of actions and objects in his list: the kiss of peace, the font of baptism, blessed salt, the Our Father, the ashes of penance.' She suggests that he was

---

[1] Barrett, C. K. (1985), 56.
[2] Brown, D. and Loades, A. (1996), 75.

convinced that 'all organic and inorganic things in nature bear spiritual messages through their distinctive forms and characteristics'.[3]

The restricting of the number of sacraments to seven happened as late as the twelfth century, and was accompanied by a narrowing down of the whole notion of sacrament and a concentration upon precise definitions of what was happening in particular sacramental rites. The Council of Trent in the sixteenth century reiterated scholastic teachings about the sacraments: that there are seven of the New Laws instituted and entrusted to the Church by Christ, some directly and some indirectly. Trent also affirmed the thirteenth-century teaching of Thomas Aquinas that sacraments are instrumental causes of grace, a privileged manner of God's interaction with humanity, and that they confer the grace they signify *ex opere operato* – independently of the state of the minister. The Protestant reformers objected to the definition 'sacrament' applied to those rites they were unable to identify in scripture, and therefore restricted the number of sacraments to two. Debates about exactly what was going on in sacramental rite, and the Eucharist in particular, began quite early, as Ann Loades points out:

> The options were already in view as early as the ninth century. One line to take was that characteristic of later reformers – that human beings were united in a saving relationship with Christ by faith. The 'sacrament/sign' (bread and wine for instance) remained what it was. The 'reality' was saving union, evident for instance in reconciliation with the church. 'Sacrament' still meant the rite. For others, however, because what was used in the rite was consecrated by words, including the invocation of the Trinity, the things both remained what they appeared and also became a different reality. In the case of the Eucharist, the bread and wine were now held to 'contain' the 'real presence' of Christ, so 'sacrament' came to be used not only of the rite but of the consecrated things themselves. Associated with the name of Berengar in the eleventh century was the understanding that a sacrament was the visible form of an invisible grace. This covered sacrament as a rite, but not of a thing. In the event, Berengar's understanding of sacrament was transmitted into English-speaking culture via the Book of Common Prayer and the work of Richard Hooker. So in the 1604 catechism, the answer to be given to the question 'What meanest thou by this word Sacrament?' is 'I mean the outward and visible sign of an inward and spiritual grace given unto us, ordained by Christ himself, as a means by which we receive the same, and a pledge to assure us thereof'.[4]

The notion of a sacrament as an 'outward and visible sign' which partakes of the reality to which it points gave rise to some important developments in twentieth-century sacramental theology, which proposed Christ himself in sacramental terms. Edward Schillibeeckx wrote a seminal work, *Christ the Sacrament of the Encounter with God*, in which he asserted that 'the man Jesus, as the personal, visible realisation of the divine grace of redemption, is the sacrament, the primordial sacrament, because this man, the son of God himself, is intended to be in his humanity the only way to the actuality of redemption'.[5] Identification of the Church as sacrament has

---

[3] Rees, E. (1992), 14.

[4] Loades, A. (2000), 635.

[5] Schillebeeckx, E. (1963), 15. Since then there has been much reference to Christ as the 'archetypal sacrament', and in a key passage in *The Church and the Sacraments*, Karl Rahner writes that in Christ: 'there is the spatio-temporal sign that effects what it points to. Christ in his historical existence is both

been very evident in the post-Vatican II Roman Catholic Church: the Encyclical *Gaudium et Spes* states that 'the Church is the "universal sacrament of salvation," simultaneously manifesting and exercising the mystery of God's love for man'. Fr Guilou, member of the International Theological Commission and an expert on Vatican II, was able to write: 'If anyone were to ask me what is the key concept of Vatican II, I would reply without hesitation that it is the concept of the church as sacrament. This idea embraces all the schemata in their very depths. It unites all the conciliar documents, whether constitutions, decrees or declarations.'[6]

The recognition that Christians are called to see Christ in one another has led to the yet further extension of the notion of sacrament to individual human beings, so that, for example, von Balthasar could write of 'the brother as sacrament'.[7] In similar vein, the assertion of catholic theology that the creation is good and that God is to be experienced through it has been emphasized by those expounding Benedictine spirituality: 'Human life is whole, and everything in creation is good. There is no aspect of life in this world that cannot, if rightly understood and used, contribute to leading us to our final end. Temporal reality and human endeavour are reflections of the perfections of God. Material things are *sacramenta*, symbols that reveal the goodness and beauty of the creator.'[8]

This resonates with the ancient Eastern Christian tradition which articulates a difference between the 'energies' of God and his 'essence'. In his essence, God is transcendent and wholly unknowable, but the creation is penetrated by God's energy through his activity and operation. Basil the Great writes that: 'no-one has ever seen the essence of God, but we believe in the essence because we experience the energy.'[9] It is not an approach which is confined to catholic and orthodox spirituality, however, as Belden Lane points out:

It was Martin Luther who explored the other side of that idea of the holy – its *fascinans* as well as its *tremendum*. He insisted that God's naked, awful majesty could never be pursued directly. In order to shield human beings from the unapproachable light of God's glory, God always remains hidden, veiled by a mask (*larva*). Though not seen face to face, this god is yet encountered with a striking immediacy in the *larvae Dei* – the created marvels of God's hand, the bread and wine at Mass, even the twisted mystery of one's own self as created being. They all 'contain Christ', himself the veiled incarnate God. Of course, they form only a 'dark glass' at best. None of them can be read with clarity. They serve to tantalise, to intrigue, to lead always beyond themselves. Yet, because of Christ, all ordinary things assume new importance. They are masks of the holy: not sterile occasions for rationally

---

reality and sign, *sacramentum* and *res sacramenti* of the redemptive grace of God, which through him no longer, as it did before his coming, rules high over the world as yet hidden will of the remote, transcendent God, but in him is given and established in the world and manifested there.' He goes on to say that the Church, as 'the continuance of Christ's presence in the world is the fundamental sacrament of the eschatologically triumphant mercy of God', and emphasizes that he calls the Church the fundamental sacrament, 'not by a vague borrowing of the concept of sacrament known to us already from the current teaching about the sacraments, but by deriving our concept from Christology' (Rahner, K., 1963, 23).

[6] See Beguerie, P. and Decheschau, C. (1991), 16.

[7] Von Balthazar, H. (1958), 142–55.

[8] Fry, T. (1981), 370.

[9] Basil the Great, quoted in Ware, K. (1979), 27.

inferring the existence and attributes of God, but vivid, if broken, means by which God as Mother of creation comes to meet us.[10]

As Lane reminds us, Luther uses the term *larva*, which suggests that the creator is deliberately concealed by his works and yet, at the same time, the *larvae Dei* are media of divine revelation since, as Luther himself puts it: 'All created ordinances are masks or allegories wherewith God depicts his theology; they are meant, as it were, to contain Christ.'[11] Thus, they are more like a dark glass, to use the Pauline analogy as it has come to us in the Authorised Version, than masks. Even Calvin, noted neither for his natural theology nor his sacramental approach, referred to the natural world as *theatrum gloriae dei*,[12] a theatre in which the glory of God is manifested.

The Reformers were, after all, steeped in the scriptures, and were not ignorant of the psalmist's assertion that 'the heavens are telling the glory of God' (Psalm 19:1), or of St Paul's observation in the first chapter of the Letter to the Romans that: 'Ever since the creation of the world his invisible nature, namely, his eternal power and deity, has been clearly perceived in the things that have been made' (Romans 1:20). Although Protestantism came to stress the wickedness of the world in its determination to concentrate upon the salvific work of Christ in the atonement, a much more creative and far-reaching sacramental theology developed in the Anglican Church. This is represented in the following plea by William Temple:

> The real presence in the Eucharist is a fact, but it is not unique. The Word of God is everywhere present and active. … The bread and wine have a symbolic meaning before they are consecrated – they are the gift of God rendered serviceable by the labour of man; and that is what we 'offer' at the 'offertory'. It is this that the Lord takes to make the special vehicle of His universal presence. No words can exaggerate the reverence due to this divinely appointed means of grace; but it is easy to confine our reverence when we ought to extend it.[13]

So Timothy Gorringe refers to the sacraments being 'extroverted', this being: 'the beautiful meaning preserved in the term "mass", from the last words of the Latin rite: *Ita, missa est*, "Go, it is the dismissal." Having gathered for a short while, you are sent out. The sacraments, like the gospel, are not about religious satisfaction but about changing reality.' Having been fed with the sacramental elements of bread and wine, through which Christ nourishes us with his body and blood, we are to go out to find Christ in the people and places of our everyday life. The physicality of the use of bread, wine and oil in the sacraments are 'an affirmation of the material, as the assertion, consonant with the incarnation, that you cannot go round, or beyond, matter, but that you must go through it'.[14] This 'looking outwards' developed very early in the Anglican tradition, as is evidenced in some of the writings of Lancelot

---

[10] Lane (1988), 39.

[11] Luther, M., Werke, *Kritische Gesamtausgabe*, XL.1, 463.9

[12] Calvin, J., *Institutio Christianae Religionis*, I.xiv.20 and II.vi.1.

[13] Temple, W. (1935).

[14] Gorringe, T. (1989), 168.

Andrewes.[15] Brian Horne suggests that the development of such a sacramental theology in Anglicanism has resulted from the fact that Anglicans have paid more attention to the doctrine of creation than any other Church in the West, and that, he believes, is largely because of Richard Hooker. In suggesting that Hooker's theology involved a belief that the whole natural order praised and revealed God, he quotes the following passage:

> All other things that are of God have God in them and he them in himself likewise. ... God hath his influence into the very essence of all things, without which influence of Deity supporting them their utter annihilation could not choose but follow. Of him all things have both received their first being and their continuance to be that which they are. All things therefore are partakers of God, they are his offspring, his influence is in them, and the personal wisdom of God for that very cause is said to excel in nimbleness or agility, to pierce into all intellectual pure, and subtile spirits, to go through all, and to reach unto everything that is. Otherwise, how should the same wisdom be that which supporteth, beareth up, sustaineth all?[16]

Horne points out that this reading of the creation in which the glory of the creator shines through never disappeared from Anglican theology and devotion. He points to its presence in the writings of Hooker's contemporaries, Lancelot Andrewes and George Herbert, and its appearance later in the seventeenth century in John Pearson's *Exposition of the Creed* and Thomas Traherne's *Centuries of Meditation*. In the latter, Traherne even goes so far as to suggest that the world might be thought of as God's body, a theme to which he returns in other writings: 'How do we know, but the World is that Body, which the Deity hath assumed to manifest His beauty, and by which He maketh Himself as visible, as it is possible He should?'[17] Horne records how this strand in the tradition rose strongly to the surface again two centuries later in the theology and devotion of the Oxford Movement, and how when John Keble edited Hooker's works in the 1830s, he believed that he had found the basis of a sacramental theology that was not only the spiritual heritage of the Church of England, but was firmly grounded in the traditions of the early Church. He points out that, in Keble's own poetry, 'the frequency of allusions to nature and the manner in which these are

---

[15] For example, at the conclusion of a sermon preached on Christmas Day, Andrewes writes of the Eucharist in the following terms: 'For, as there is a recapitulation of all in heaven and earth and in Christ, so there is a recapitulation of all in Christ in the Holy Sacrament. You may see it clearly. There is Christ in the Word eternal, for things in heaven; there is also flesh, for things on earth. Semblably, the sacrament consisteth of a heavenly and of a terrene part (it is Irenaeus' own words); the heavenly – there the world too, the abstract of the other; the earthly – the element. And in the elements, you may observe there is a fulness of the seasons of the natural year; of the corn-flour or harvest in the one, bread; of the wine-press or vintage in the other, wine. And in the heavenly, of the wheatcorn whereto he compareth himself – bread, even the Living bread that came down from heaven; the true Manna, whereof we may gather each his gomer. And again, of him, the true Vine, as he calls himself – the blood of the grapes of that vine. And both these issuing out of this day's recapitulation, both in corpus *autem aptasti mihi* of this day' (Andrewes, L., 1841, 281).

[16] Horne, B. (1993), 10.

[17] Traherne, T. (1966), 223. See also Traherne, T., *The Kingdom of God*, Lambeth Palace Library Manuscript 1360 (unpublished), 270v and *Select Meditation*, iv.34 in Traherne, T. (1997), 132.

turned into images of divine revelation demonstrates as powerfully as his theological essays the underlying assumption of the sacramental principle in Keble's thought.'[18]

Contemporary support for this approach among theologians can be found clearly expressed in, for example, the work of Stephen Sykes: 'In becoming man, God becomes matter (Pierre Teilhard de Chardin). In other words the chosen way of divine self-revelation is in the materiality of human fleshliness, God's presence in which he consecrates not merely humankind but the very stuff of created order. Consistent with an incarnational faith is the sacramentality of the universe.'[19] Sykes appeals to William Temple's *Nature, Man and God* as 'a classic of its kind' which presents a sacramental relation of spirit and matter. Brian Horne speaks of this same work by Temple as the most comprehensive exposition of the sacramental principle in Anglican theology. In it Temple asserts:

> It may safely be said that one ground for the hope of Christianity that it may make good its claim to be the true faith lies in the fact that it is the most avowedly materialist of all the great religions. ... Its own most central saying is: 'The Word was made flesh', where the last term was, no doubt, chosen because of its specially materialistic associations. By the very nature of its central doctrine Christianity is committed to a belief in the ultimate significance of the historical process, and in the reality of matter and its place in the divine scheme.[20]

Elsewhere Temple speaks of Christianity being the most materialistic of all great religions. Whereas others hope to achieve spiritual reality by ignoring matter – calling it illusion, or suggesting that it does not exist – Christianity is crucially different since, based as it is on the incarnation, it 'regards matter as destined to be the vehicle and instrument of spirit, and spirit as fully actual as far as it controls and directs matter'.[21] Temple's sacramental approach to reality permeated all of his theology, for he believed that it is in the sacramental view of the universe, both of its material and of its spiritual elements, that there is to be found hope of making human both politics and economics, and of making effectual both faith and love.

John Habgood makes a similar point when he writes: 'Indeed, the world itself only has meaning and value when seen as the sacrament of God's living presence. The secular vision of the world is a lie. It tells of emptiness and meaninglessness.'[22] In seeking support for this same sacramental principle, Habgood goes on to quote Alexander Schmemann, who wrote that Christianity declares the possibility of living in the world and 'seeing everything in it as the revelation of God, as a sign of his presence, the joy of his coming, the call to communion with him'. Schmemann was seeking, as I have been above, to explore how the Church's sacraments relate to the rest of our experience of the world – something which the Church has not always been good at doing. He articulates a view of humanity that both receives the world from God and offers it back to him, and that 'the world was created as the "matter" of

---

[18] Horne , B. (1993), 10.

[19] Address given by S. Sykes at a conference, *The Holy Place: Mission and Conservation*, Keele University, 25–26 June 1996.

[20] Temple, W. (1935), 478.

[21] Ibid., xxi.

[22] Habgood, J. in Brown, D. and Loades, A. (1995), 20.

one all-embracing Eucharist, and man was created as the priest of this cosmic sacrament'.[23]

In developing such an approach, Arthur Peacocke makes use of Oliver Quick's seminal work on the sacraments, *The Christian Sacraments*, written over seventy years ago, which drew attention to the distinction we draw in ordinary life between 'outward' things, which occupy space and time and are, in principle, perceptible by the senses, and 'inward' things or realities, which are not. Quick noted how material objects which constitute part of our 'outward' reality can be thought of either as instruments whose character is defined by what is done with them, or symbols whose character is defined by what is known by them. So, too, Quick argued, the world can be thought of as the instrument with which God is effecting his cosmic purpose and the symbol through which God is expressing his nature for those who will have eyes to see. Arthur Peacocke suggests that, viewed through the eyes of evolution and of faith, the world and its cosmic evolutionary processes can be seen both as *instruments* and *symbols* of God's purposes. The insights of evolution imply that we must see God as continuously creating, and so recover a dynamic view of creation inherent in the scriptures, since: 'God is creating at every moment of the world's existence in and through the perpetually endowed creativity of the very stuff of the world. God indeed "makes things make themselves".' He goes on to conclude that the evolution of matter into humanity demonstrates the ability of matter to display properties for which we have to use such special terms as 'mental', spiritual', 'personal'. He relates this to the Christ event as actualization of the potentiality of humanity already incompletely manifested in evolving humanity. Thus, he argues, there is a: 'real convergence between, on the one hand, the implications of the scientific perspective for the spiritual capabilities of matter and, on the other hand, the sacramental view of matter which Christians have adopted as a natural consequence of the meaning they attach to Jesus' life and the continued existence of the church.' Not only does this give 'a new relevance to Christian sacramental worship, which is now seen not to be representing some magical, cabbalistic and esoteric doctrine but to be expressing, in a communal context, the basic nature of the cosmic process', its convergence also encourages the Christian to see the created world as a symbol because:

> it is a mode of God's revelation, an expression of his truth and beauty, which are 'spiritual' aspects of its reality. It is also valued by them for what God is effecting instrumentally through it, what God does in it and through it. But these two functions of matter, the symbolic and the instrumental, also constitute the special character of the use of matter in particular Christian sacraments. There is, in each sacrament, a universal reference to this double character of created physical reality and, correspondingly, meaning can be attached to speaking of the created world as a sacrament or, at least, as sacramental.[24]

This is very different from the 'Gaia' hypothesis, which sees the world as a living organism and might be described as scientific paganism. It is different, too, from a pantheistic view, which sees God as being exclusively identified with the world and

---

[23] Schmemann, A. (1965), *The World as Sacrament*, London: Darton Longman and Todd, 16, quoted by Habgood in Brown, D. and Loades, A. (1995), 42. This approach is very similar to the one adopted by Pierre Teilhard de Chardin a few years earlier, as Habgood reminds us. See Teilhard de Chardin, P. (1970).

[24] Peacocke, A. (2000), 25.

coterminous with it. A Christian approach to matter is one which neither exalts it to the extent of believing it to be the only true reality, as in Scientific Materialism, nor demotes it to the extent of believing it to be something of no real or lasting significance which must simply be 'overcome', as do some more extreme strands of the reformed tradition. Orthodox Christianity steers a middle course between all these extremes for, as John Polkinghorne (another scientist) points out: 'There are distinctions between God and the world that Christian theology cannot afford to blur. They lie at the root of the religious claim that a meeting with God involves personal encounter, not just communing with the cosmos.'[25] John Habgood summarizes the manner in which he suggests that the sacramental principle can be related to the natural world in a manner consonant with orthodox theology in that natural things 'can be clothed with new meaning by relating them to Christ. The world which would be meaningless by itself, becomes a purposeful place as men make it so; and they are enabled to do this because they find a purpose for their lives in the man whose life was wholly one with God.'[26]

We have established, then, that there is a noble tradition of extending the notion of sacramentality from the Church's sacraments to Christ, the Church and the world. However, we must not ignore that there are severe difficulties with such an approach. Are we simply to assert that the whole world is 'sacramental'? Do all material things, all places, speak equally of God? If so, does that mean that the incarnation simply confirms the creation as it is? If not, according to what criteria do we determine the extent to which they do or do not do so? To set arbitrary limits on what may or may not be sacraments might make us guilty of what has been described as 'ecclesiastical impertinence'. Those who warn us of these dangers include Timothy Gorringe, who tells us to be wary of talk of a 'sacramental principle' which means that 'nature and society' are God's symbols and signs. Gorringe believes that such writing reveals:

> a deep seated confusion which cuts at the root of sacramental thinking. … In this view the created order, the situations of nature and society, constituted extrinsic symbols mediating between God and man, But if everything is a sign, nothing is. It is perhaps true that anything in the created order can become a sign: in particular persons become signs of God's engagement to persons, and invests rings, flowers, and other covenantal symbols with sacramental significance. But in the sacraments as the church has generally understood them we have to do with the freedom of God with signs of a very specific directness in human history.[27]

Similarly, Rowan Williams suggests that to talk of 'some general principle of the world as "naturally" sacramental or epiphanic: a pot-pourri of Jung, Teilhard de Chardin and a certain kind of anthropology, sometimes evoked as a prelude to sacramental theology, will run the risk of obscuring the fact that signs and symbols are made – even in response to some sense that the world is charged with glory'.[28] Temple himself had to counter criticisms from those who accused him of nature-

---

[25] Polkinghorne, J. (1989), 16.

[26] Habgood, J. in Brown, D. and Loades, A. (1995), 21. Habgood wrote these words thirty years previously.

[27] Gorringe, T. (1989), 159.

[28] Williams, R. (2000), 201.

mysticism, which would not only bypass the history of salvation, but also evade the question of sin and the problem of the disorder of the natural world. The question is, how are we to decide which things are behaving sacramentally, and when?

Sacramental Events

In order to extricate ourselves from this impasse, we need to be clear that although God reveals himself in the world, sacramentality does not mean that the world itself is self-revelatory of God in a general and indiscriminate manner. Rather, it means that the world in all its diverse aspects can be the place of God's own self-revelation to us. This is because, as Gorringe puts it, sacraments should be seen as:

> those rents in the opacity of history where God's concrete engagement to change the world becomes visible. It is therefore to speak of the Holy Spirit, which is to say the awareness of events which are wholly worldly, opaque and ordinary on the one hand and wholly divine, radiant and mysterious on the other, for such a duality is the mark of the Spirit. Sacraments are reminders, if we need reminders, that matter and spirit, body and soul are not opposites, not temporarily and unfortunately mismatched, but proper expression of each other.[29]

If we are to heed Williams' warning against beginning with some general principle of the world as naturally sacramental or epiphanic, and Gorringe's assertion that sacraments should be seen as rents in the opacity of history where God's concrete engagement to change the world becomes visible, we must begin with *events* when talking of sacrament. This is true for the Church's sacraments of Baptism and the Eucharist – whatever material sacramentality might derive from those sacramental events – and it must be equally true of any sacramentality we might encounter in the world. I noted in the last chapter how the incarnation has profound implications not only as far as the *material* is concerned, but also as far as the *particular* is concerned. Examination of the scriptures might lead us to expect to experience the numinous not just in a general and undiscerning sense of 'the heavens telling the glory of God', but in a particular sense *and in particular places*, too. For example, Jacob had a dream at 'a certain place between Beersheba and Haran'. Jacob wakes from his sleep and says: 'Surely the Lord is in this place; and I did not know it.' And he was afraid and said, 'How awesome is this place! This is none other than the house of God and this is the gate of heaven' (Genesis 28:16–17). He takes the stone which he had put under his head and sets it up for a pillar and pours oil on top of it. He calls the name of the place Bethel. This place is consecrated for future generations because of the revelation that has happened there, and it becomes a sign to others of the reality of the God who reveals himself, a tradition that has continued in the consecration of many shrines and holy places since.

In the Book of the Exodus we learn of a moment of revelation given to Moses, who was keeping the flock of his father-in-law, Jethro, the priest of Midian, and as he led his flock to the west side of the wilderness, he came to Horeb, the mountain of God: 'And the angel of the Lord appeared to him in a flame of fire out of a bush; and he looked, and lo, the bush was burning, yet not consumed. And Moses said, "I will turn

---

[29] Gorringe, T. (1989), 165.

aside and see this great sight, why the bush is not burnt." When the Lord saw that he turned aside to see, God called to him out of the bush, "Moses, Moses!" and he said, "Do not come near; put off your shoes from your feet for the place on which you are standing is holy ground"' (Exodus 3:2–5). Here we see how crucially biblical stress on the importance of place is interwoven into the experience of revelation, and we can even read back into these Old Testament experiences a sacramental understanding. As John Macquarrie puts it: 'That bush was for him (Moses) a sacrament of God. At the bush God encountered him, manifesting himself in and through the bush. We could say that in and through the particular being of this bush, Moses became aware of Being itself, the mysterious power of ultimate creative Being, the ground of all particular beings.'[30]

In the very early days of the Church, we read in the Acts of the Apostles, Saul, the arch-persecutor of the Church, was on his way to Damascus to search out followers of 'the Way' when, as he approached Damascus: 'a light from heaven flashed about him. And he fell to the ground and heard a voice saying to him, "Saul, Saul, why do you persecute me?" And he said, "Who are you, Lord?" And he said, "I am Jesus, whom you are persecuting; but rise, and enter the city, and you will be told what you are to do"' (Acts 9:3–6). The conversion of St Paul must be one of the best-known in history, and rightly so, since, as has often been observed, it was St Paul who went on to transform the nascent Church from a minor Jewish sect into an unstoppable force within the Gentile world. It is noteworthy that this conversion occurred at a particular *place* just outside Damascus on the road from Jerusalem, and St Luke records this fact in a New Testament whose writers it is often alleged, as we have seen, have no interest in place. St Paul himself, as recorded in Acts, makes very specific reference to the place where his conversion occurred when speaking about it (Acts 22:6–8, Acts 26:12–16). It was a crucial factor in that experience. The fact is, of course, that it was not just the appearance of the risen Lord to this 'one untimely born' that occurred in a particular place: the same was true for all the resurrection appearances for, as we have determined, *places are the seat of relations and of meeting and activity between God and the world.*

Some of the most crucial developments in the Church's history have been initiated by such moments, which I shall term 'sacramental events'. A very influential one took place on 28 October 312 AD in the vicinity of the Milvian Bridge outside Rome, as the Emperor Constantine and his army faced the forces of Maxentius. Eusebius recounts the prelude to his entry into the city:

> Accordingly, he called on him in his prayers, begging and asking that he reveal to him who he was, and that he stretch out his right hand to help him in his current tasks. And while the Emperor was thus praying and supplicating with a fervent heart, a most wonderful sign appeared to him from heaven. … He said that, at about the noon-tide sun, when the day was already on its downward slope, he saw with his own eyes the trophy of the cross, consisting of light, in the heavens and placed above the sun, and that next to it there was a writing which said: 'By this, conquer'; moreover, he said that he was struck with amazement at the sign of the wonder, and so was the whole army, which was following him on the march and witnessed the marvel.[31]

---

[30] Macquarrie, J. (1997), 9.

[31] Eusebius, *Vita Constantini*, I, 26–40.

Shortly afterwards, Constantine entered the Imperial city in triumph. Many have questioned the contemporary accounts of Eusebius and, from Gibbon's *The Decline and Fall of the Roman Empire* onwards, people have doubted the authenticity of the vision. However, no one would dispute that after this supposed vision Constantine behaved as though something extraordinary had happened to him and acted as if he had become a Christian by putting an end to all persecution and giving this newly found faith everything that he had.

Many of these experiences, like Constantine's, have sparked enormous change and renewal, and in each of them the place at which such revelation occurs is far from irrelevant to the person who is undergoing the experience. Another well-known example is the vision of St Francis at the Church of St Damiano in the early thirteenth century.[32] In this instance the place of the revelation remained important to Francis and he returned to it throughout his life. It helped him to be in touch with the reality of the Lord who had revealed himself to him.

Such encounters are not, of course, the exclusive preserve of the pre-Reformation and catholic traditions. What is sometimes referred to as the 'birthday of Methodism', described in the diaries of John Wesley, is another such instance which was to have an enormous effect upon the Church in England. Most days in his journal warrant only a few lines. However, 24 May 1738 is singled out as being of particular importance by him, for six pages are devoted to it and these are introduced with the words: 'What occurred on Wednesday, 24, I think it best to relate at large.' The heart of that entry is numbered fourteen. He writes: 'In the evening I went very unwillingly to a society in Aldersgate Street, where one was reading Luther's preface to the Epistle to the Romans. About a quarter before nine, while he was describing the change which God works in the hearts through faith in Christ, I felt my heart strangely warmed.'[33] It all began in Aldersgate Street. It happened there and nowhere else. Such experiences may not always be of great significance to the life of the Church, as in the above, but they certainly remain of importance to the individual to whom they are given, and examples abound. Thomas Merton describes an experience he had in which he was suddenly overwhelmed with the realization that:

> I loved all these people, that they were mine and I theirs ... it was like waking from a dream of separateness ... to take your place as a member of the human race. I had the immense joy of being man, a member of the race in which God himself had become incarnate. If only everybody could realise this. But it cannot be explained. There is no way of telling people that they are all walking around shining like the sun.[34]

---

[32] The recounting of the story by the 'Three Companions' can be found in many texts. One reads as follows: 'A few days after this, while he was walking near the Church of San Damiano, an inner voice bade him go in and pray. He obeyed, and kneeling before an image of the crucified Saviour, he began to pray most devoutly. A tender, compassionate voice then spoke to him: "Francis, do you not see that my house is falling into ruin? Go and repair it for me." Trembling and amazed Francis replied: "Gladly I will do so, O Lord." He had understood that the Lord was speaking of that very church which on account of its age was indeed falling into ruin. ... On leaving the church he found the priest who had charge of it sitting outside, and taking a handful of money from his purse he said, "I beg you, Father, to buy oil and keep the lamp before this image of Christ constantly alight. When this is spent I will give you as much as you need"' (Mockler, A., 1976, 79).

[33] Wesley, J. (1870), 46, 51.

[34] Merton, T. (1977), 153.

All these experiences could be characterized as 'rents in the opacity of history where God's concrete engagement to change the world becomes visible', to use Gorringe's phrase. They affirm the importance of the particular inherent in the incarnation, the greatest of all gifts and rents in opacity, in that they happen at a particular time and in a particular place. Further, they make clear that *sacramentality is pure gift*. The place where such events occur is always of importance to the person recounting the experience. Merton is quite precise about this: it happened in Louisville, at the corner of Fourth and Walnut. The fact is that invariably those who recount what they believe to have been what we might term a 'sacramental experience' never forget the location of that experience for, as Belden Lane puts it: 'Repeatedly, it is place which lends structure, contextuality, and vividness of memory to the narrative of spiritual experience.'[35] This is not surprising either in view of the incarnation or of place in human experience generally, which is gradually being recognized by social scientists at whose writings we looked in Chapter 1. There we established, with Giddens, that the setting of interaction is not some neutral backdrop to events that are unfolding independently in the foreground. Places enter into the very fabric of interaction in a multiplicity of ways. We can conclude, therefore, that 'sacramental experiences' of the sort that I have been describing are a very important part of the Christian tradition, and that place is an integral part of such experiences.

A Surprisingly Common Phenomenon

But if we are to talk of sacramentality in terms of events, does this not mean that it will have to be a very restricted notion, since events of these kinds are rare? I would suggest not. All of the accounts detailed above might be characterized as containing what might loosely be termed 'religious experience', a phrase reputedly coined by the American philosophe, William James in his Gifford Lectures of 1897 on its varieties and later immortalized in his classic text *The Varieties of Religious Experience*. Much empirical research on such experience has been done over the last few years by such organizations as the Religious Experience Research Unit at Manchester College, Oxford, later renamed after its creator as the Alister Hardy Research Centre. Hardy was convinced that the sort of experiences to which I have been referring above were much more common than is generally supposed. Determined to test this hypothesis, he set up the unit in 1969 at the age of 73, having retired from a lifetime as a scientist, latterly as Professor of Zoology at Oxford University. During his life he had harboured an interest in religious experience, and as far back as 1925 had started to collect press cuttings that referred to them. It is likely that this interest stemmed from sacramental encounters of his own while a boy for he records that: 'there was a little lane leading off the Northampton road to Park Wood as it was called. ... I especially liked walking along the banks of various streams. ... I wandered along all their banks, at times almost with a feeling of ecstasy.' At the age of 88 he noted something concerning these walks that he had never spoken of before:

> Just occasionally when I was sure no-one could see me, I became so overcome with the glory of the natural scene that for a moment or two I fell on my knees in prayer – not

---

[35] Lane, B. (1992), 6.

praying for anything but thanking God, who felt very real to me, for the glories of his kingdom and allowing me to feel them. It was always by the running waterside that I did this, perhaps in front of a great foam of Meadow Sweet or a mass of Purple Loosestrife.[36]

Hardy's unit collected many thousands of responses in answer to the question: 'Have you ever been aware of, or influenced by, a presence or power, whether you call it God or not, which is different from your everyday self?' An analysis of the first 3000 accounts was published by Hardy in 1979 in *The Spiritual Nature of Man*,[37] and the number of people who answered the above question in the affirmative was surprisingly high. David Hay and Ann Morisy, who furthered Hardy's work, found in a national survey that over one-third of all adults in Britain claimed to have had experience of this kind, this proportion later increasing in another survey to over half and, if one includes those claiming some sort of premonition, to an astonishing two-thirds. The character of such experiences is very variable and they can happen in any number of situations. There appears to be no discernible common trigger to them. A few, like the following, derive initially from an aesthetic experience which then transmutes into a religious sense of judgement and contrition:

A friend persuaded me to go to Ely Cathedral to hear a performance of Bach's B Minor Mass. I had heard the work, indeed I knew Bach's choral works pretty well. ... The music thrilled me, until we got to the great Sanctus. I find this experience difficult to define. It was primarily a warning – I was frightened. I was trembling from head to foot and wanted to cry. Actually I think I did. I heard no 'voice' except the music; I saw nothing; but the warning was very definite. I was not able to interpret this experience satisfactorily until I read some months later Rudolf Otto's *Das Heilige*. Here I found it: the 'Numinous'. I was before the judgement Seat. I was being weighed in the balance and found wanting.[38]

Some of them were recorded as happening quite early in childhood:

My father used to take all the family for a walk on Sunday evenings. On one such walk, we wandered across a narrow path through a field of high, ripe corn. I lagged behind, and found myself alone. Suddenly, heaven blazed on me. I was enveloped in golden light, I was conscious of a presence, so kind, so loving, so bright, so consoling, so commanding, existing apart from me but so close. I heard no sound. But words fell into my mind quite clearly – 'Everything is all right. Everybody will be all right.'[39]

John V. Taylor quotes a radio talk broadcast in 1961 by the poet Ruth Pitter in which she talks of an experience she had when no more than fourteen years old and which occurred in 'a poor place – nothing glamorous about it, except that it was spring in the country. Suddenly everything assumed a different aspect – no, its true aspect.'[40] Pitter considered it significant that such seeing is more easily experienced in childhood, since it cannot in that case be explained as a compensating reaction to the

---

[36] From an unpublished manuscript of Alister Hardy's autobiography quoted in Hay, D. (1990), 27.

[37] Hardy, A. (1979).

[38] Quoted in Hardy, A. (1979), 85.

[39] Hay, D. (1990), 72. Hay was Director of the Alister Hardy Centre until 1990. Another former director, Edward Robinson, published work on the experiences of children in Robinson, E. (1977), 49.

[40] Taylor, J. V. (1992), 55.

disillusionments of ugly reality. Interestingly, Edward Robinson, sometime Director of the Alister Hardy Research Unit, found that over 80 per cent of a sample of over 6500 teenagers in Britain reported having had some kind of mystical experience.[41] Taylor points out that experiences such as the one described by Ruth Pitter are sometimes categorized as nature mysticism, but suggests that this is inaccurate. This can be seen, he tells us, if one compares experiences such as the above with genuine nature mysticism such as that of Richard Jefferies, a countryman-naturalist of the nineteenth century who had known moments of ecstatic communion with the physical world through its grandeur and beauty but sought to develop a religious practice of prayer which would renew this vivid awareness. It is, as Taylor puts it 'such deliberate pursuit of a philosophy and a spiritual regimen that distinguishes the so-called nature mystic from the innumerable individuals who have known some brief, unsought encounter with infinite reality shining through a transient natural object.'[42] Taylor quotes another example which typifies this unsought given-ness of such sacramental encounters (as opposed to the practice of nature mysticism) which happened to a boy aged twelve walking alone at the end of the summer holidays in the Peak District:

> It was getting towards evening, and I had climbed over a wall and was standing on a piece of rough ground covered with heather and bracken and brambles, looking for blackberries, when suddenly I stood quite still and began to think deeply, as an indescribable peace – which I have since tried to describe as a 'diamond moment of reality' came flowing into (or indeed waking up within) me; and I realised that all around me everything was lit with a kind of inner shining beauty; the rocks, the bracken, the bramble bushes, the view, the sky, even the blackberries – and also myself. And in that moment, sweeping in on that tide of light, there came also knowledge. The knowledge that though disaster was moving slowly and seemingly unavoidably towards me (and this I had known subconsciously for some time) yet in the end 'all would be well'.[43]

We should note, too, that it is not just in beautiful, wild or 'sacred' places that sacramental events of the sort we have been discussing can occur. The writer and novelist Frederick Buechner describes such an experience which happened to him during a visit to Sea World, a Disney tourist extravaganza in Florida with a main attraction in a huge tank of crystal-clear turquoise water. Suddenly, 'it was as if the whole creation – men and women and beasts and sun and water and earth and sky and, for all I know, God himself – was caught up in one great jubilant dance of unimaginable beauty. And then, right in the midst of it, I was astonished to find that my eyes were filled with tears.'[44] He interpreted this as a vision of the consummation of all things in Christ.

We can thus conclude that not only have such sacramental encounters been at the heart of some of the most important developments of the Church, they are very common among ordinary people. However, such experience has generally been

---

[41] Robinson, E. and Jackson, J. (1987), Alister Hardy Research Centre and the Christian Education Movement.

[42] Taylor, J. V. (1992), 25.

[43] Ibid., 35.

[44] Buechner, F. (1996), 126.

undervalued by the Christian community just as has place: the Church has tended to concentrate on believing and doing the right thing, with the result that the only aspect of human experience that has been thoroughly engaged with is sinfulness. This has been true across generations and traditions, with the notable exception of the Pentecostal movement. It is certainly of note that most people would not speak readily of such experiences, but the research cited above would suggest that this is not because they happen infrequently. It might, perhaps, be indicative of a prevailing rationalist culture of modernity which is inimical to such things. John V. Taylor articulates forcefully in the following passage how the devaluing of such experience has resulted in impoverishment for the Church:

> How regrettable it is, how unnatural in fact, that through the centuries the confessional stalls around the walls of many churches have received the secrets of so many sins, and have not been equally available for the confidences of men and women and children who have been overtaken by the ecstasies or insights or consolations that declare the reality of God! Had this other side of personal experience been invited, no doubt there would have been the same amount of fantasy, neurosis and self-advertisement as has always been exhibited in the confessional, and wise priests would have known how to discern and guide, as they have done hitherto. No doubt they would have found the recitals of glory just as repetitive as the catalogues of sin, for the accounts of these intensely private memories are uncannily similar. But at least it might have redressed the balance and made the churches everywhere as mindful of divine initiative as of human failure. If it could become normal for people to know that a church was the place where confidences of that sort could be shared and understood; here they would be helped to reflect upon the experience and grow by responding to it; where they could learn that, just as they have known the approach of God in a strength of a tree or the swelling of a tide of music, others have known it in a bush lapped in flame or the action of a potter at the wheel; where they could find that the church itself was living and growing by response to such experiences; then, I believe, the Christian community would present a less mummified face towards the world and, within its own life and thought, might rediscover the more dynamic exploratory view of the knowledge of God which its own scriptures display.[45]

Taylor, then, calls for the reintegration of what I have described as sacramental encounters into the life of the Church, and I would concur with that plea. However, I am not suggesting that such experience can be used as a starting point for theology. Beginning theology with experience has a noble pedigree and has produced such notable works as van der Leeuw's monumental *Religion in Essence and Manifestation*.[46] It is a tradition which continues in such people as the philosopher Erazim Kohak who, in *The Embers and the Stars*, uses the phenomenological method to argue for a recovering of the sense of human identity and meaning as being located in the natural world. He argues powerfully for the moral coherence of the natural world and makes bold claims for God's self-revelation: 'As a species, humans do know God. Of all the illusions of the world of artefacts and constructs, the most facile and the most palpably false is the claim that the awareness of God's presence – in our inept phrase, "believing in God" – is the peculiarity of certain individuals, an opinion contingently held by some members of the species. The obverse is true. It is the

---

[45] Taylor, J. V. (1992), 55.
[46] Van der Leeuw, G. (1967).

A Christian Theology of Place

blindness to God's presence that is exceptional.'[47] However, he acknowledges that: 'nature has no theology of its own to teach. Years of life close to the soil, of the dawn over Barrett Mountain and moonlit nights have not, for me, added a single proposition to what stands written in the Scriptures and the Book of Common Prayer. They add depth to what has already been written or, perhaps more accurately, they help open up the depth of what has been written. They add nothing to it. *It has all been written.*'[48]

Experience can thus enter into conversation with the scriptures, and it can lead us to look at them anew and discover fresh insights, as is the case, for example, with feminist theologians who speak of women's experience, and liberation theologians who make much of *praxis*. However, 'postliberal' theologians, among whom one of the foremost is George Lindbeck, have argued that Christians should not 'make scriptural contents into metaphors for extra-scriptural realities, but the other way around. … It is the text, so to speak, that absorbs the world, rather than the other way around.'[49] In accordance with this proposal, I am suggesting that the status of 'sacramental encounters' derives from the fact that they fit into a biblical world view, not the other way around. We start with the biblical account of a God who self-reveals, who did so to many individuals, and has done so decisively in Christ. It is through them that we are able to make sense of our experience of God in the world. Experience can and should be interpreted by Christians from the perspective of faith and understood sacramentally in the light of scripture (and in particular the incarnation) and tradition. But to rely completely upon the scriptures and tradition to the exclusion of religious experience is to ignore a large part of that to which both testify: a God who reveals. What I am proposing is that the biblical narrative leads us to expect God's self-revelation and, therefore, that the world is a possible place of sacramentality. In such moments we do not see God himself, for 'God is so great, so inexpressible, so incomprehensible, so invisible, that any disclosure of God is but a small window onto this inexpressiblility, incomprehensibility, invisibility and ungraspability of God. God is absolute freedom and cannot therefore, be limited to any single event of Sacramental *Haecceitas.*'[50] What do they reveal, then? John Taylor writes:

> They reveal this world, one might say, ablaze with his glory, but they cannot empower human eyes to look upon that tropical Sun that is the source of the illumination, and if we turn our eyes in its direction all we can perceive is darkness. These moments of cleansed vision may hint at the ultimate meaning of existence *sub specie aeternitatis* but they do not reveal the eternal; they disclose the simple coherence of all beings in an embracing unity, but Being in its oneness cannot be shown. This is the ultimate paradox of spiritual reality. It does not exist in the way all things exist, for it is totally 'other', transcending existence; yet it permeates existence, being immanent within everything. There is more to things than meets the eye, yet that 'more', which adds so vastly to their significance, adds no

---

[47] Kohak, E. (1984), 185.

[48] Ibid., 193

[49] Lindbeck, G. (1984).

[50] Osborne, K. B. (1999), 157. *Haecceitas* is a Scholastic term employed by Duns Scotus to mean 'thisness'.

measurable extra or extension to them. By being simply what they are and no more, things act as clues or symbols, pointing to what lies beyond themselves.[51]

The sacramental transfiguring nature of such events is sometimes articulated eloquently by poets. A good example is *Transfiguration* by Edwin Muir, one of the most significant poets of the twentieth century. In it he speaks of visionary experiences he had during analysis:

> So from the ground we felt that virtue branch
> Through all our veins till we were whole, our wrists
> As fresh and pure as water from a well,
> Our hands made new to handle holy things,
> The source of our seeing rinsed and cleansed
> Till earth and light and water entering there
> Gave back to us the clear unfallen world.
> We could have thrown our clothes away for lightness,
> But that even they, though sour and travel stained,
> Seemed, like our flesh, made of immortal substance,
> And the soiled flax and wool lay light upon us
> Like friendly wonders, flower and flock entwined
> As in a morning field. Was it a vision
> Or did we see that day unseeable
> One glory of the everlasting world
> Perpetually at work, though never seen
> Since Eden locked the gate that's everywhere
> And nowhere? Was the change in us alone,
> And the enormous earth still left forlorn,
> An exile or a prisoner? Yet the world
> We saw that day made this unreal, for all
> Was in its place ...
> The shepherd's hovels shone, for underneath
> The soot we saw the stone clean at the heart
> As on the starting day. The refuse heaps
> Were grained with that fine dust that made the world;
> For he had said, 'To the pure all things are pure.'
> And when we went into the town, he with us,
> The lurkers under doorways, murderers,
> With rags tied round their feet for silence, came
> Out of themselves to us and were with us,
> And those who hide within the labyrinth
> Of their own loneliness and greatness, came,
> And those entangled in their own devices,
> The silent and the garrulous liars, all
> Stepped out of their dungeons and were free.
> Reality or vision, this we have seen.
> If it lasted another moment
> It might have held for ever! But the world
> rolled back into its place and we are here. ...[52]

---

[51] Taylor, J. V. (1992), 23.

[52] Muir, E. (1960), 198.

Muir does not write that he met with God, but rather that he saw the material world transfigured. In the later Byzantine period, as we have already seen, there was a willingness to understand that God made himself known to us in his 'energies', as A. M. Allchin reminds us:

> The age of Gregory Palamas and Nicholas Cabasilas placed the mystery of our Lord's transfiguration at the very centre of its understanding of God, human nature and the world. It was an age which affirmed that while God in himself, in his essence, is wholly beyond the reach of our faculties, yet in his operations, the energies of his glory, he truly makes himself known even to our senses. Through the activity of the Holy Spirit in lives of men and women, the heart and its perceptions are so cleansed that we may see with our bodily eyes, 'the unseeable/one glory of the everlasting world,/perpetually at work though never seen,/since Eden locked the gate that's everywhere,/And nowhere.'[53]

'He makes himself truly known to our senses': the language of sacrament tells us of the wonders which lie beyond the finite, the material, but can only be reached through it. Sacramentality is not simply an affirmation of the world as it is, but of the fact that Christ is in the world to unite the broken fragments of life by making the material a vehicle for the spiritual. This is not, it should be emphasized, equivalent to proposing a dualistic approach: our experience may sometimes suggest such a duality, but religious experience understood sacramentally links the dualities under which the one world keeps appearing. Christ himself is the reintegration of God's original creation, and in Christ God has restored the sacramental nature of the universe. That union is not absolutely and transparently achieved, of course, but a sacramental view of religious experience affirms that it is, even now, being achieved, and this is what we are bidden to see glimpses of all around us in the created world in moments of transfiguration. What is broken is coming together again: this is the Christian hope. The life and person of Jesus reveal the grammar of reality to which these experiences point, which the liturgy is seeking to evoke, and which the poet is seeking to illumine. Thus, crucial to their proper understanding, and to a sacramental view of place, is the eschatological aspect of such sacramental events. This is in accord with what we concluded about the importance of the New Testament's eschatological view of place.

Michael Mayne, in a delightful book entitled *This Sunrise of Wonder*, tells us that what beguiling and unshakeable experiences suggest is a momentary lifting of the veil between a seen and an unseen world, sudden moments of illuminations which are gratuitous and unsought for, when things seem transfigured.[54] And place is central to such experiences since they are glimpses of a destination that we shall never fully know until we reach it. In the same way as the resurrection of Christ is the first fruit, as the Eucharist is a foretaste of the heavenly banquet prepared for all humankind, so these moments speak to us in a sacramental sense of our destination and of the manner in which everything will, in God's good time, be in its place. Ruth Pitter, whose experience at fourteen I quoted earlier, was emphatic that these glimpses had continued into adulthood and that they had been a foundation for her kind of poetry. So she could write that:

---

[53] Allchin, A. M. (1978), 40.

[54] Mayne, M. (1995), 40.

All was as it had ever been –
The worn familiar book
The oak behind the hawthorn seen,
The misty woodlands look:
The starling perched upon the tree
With his long tress of straw –
When suddenly heaven blazed on me
And suddenly I saw:
Saw all as it would ever be,
In bliss too great to tell;
For ever safe, for ever free,
All bright with miracle.[55]

What is asked of those who are given such experiences is that they should remain faithful to them when they 'come down from the mountain'. Mayne writes: 'You may be wondering why I have laid such stress on what might at best come to each of us a handful of times in a lifetime. ... It is because I believe such experiences are among the most valid insights we have into our transcendence.' He goes on to suggest that: 'because such moments are authentic we must, as it were, keep faith with what we have seen when (however briefly) there has been a lifting of the veil at the horizon of the known.'[56]

Belden Lane reminds us how the place of St Francis's revelation remained important to him:

St Francis found himself returning all of his life to the Portiuncula, that tiny abandoned church down the hill from Assisi. The rolling Apennines, the red poppies in the fields, the extraordinary light of Umbria itself – all these were what drew him to the place. But it was ultimately a new way of seeing more than the place seen which marked the spirituality of this thirteenth-century troubadour. He regularly discerned wonder in what others viewed with scorn. His insight would turn us back to all the places we might once have found plain and abandoned in our own experience. Indeed, such is the goal, finally, of any geography of the spirit.[57]

Others have, of course, derived much inspiration from a visit to Assisi and from it have, like St Francis, been encouraged to seek the divine elsewhere. In conclusion we can say that 'sacramental encounters' are a very important part of Christian religious experience, and they are not confined to a small minority of people. Such experiences come to many of God's people to reinforce faith and hope and love, and they come at God's initiative. The place of that revelation will be deeply significant for the person given the revelation, as I have suggested, and attention to it can help that person to be reminded of the sacredness of all places and of the certainty of the power of the Resurrection over all people and places.

---

[55] Pitter, R. (1968), 45.

[56] Mayne, M. (1995), 43.

[57] Lane, B. (1988), 8.

A Relational View of the Sacrament of Place

Holiness Determined by Event: A Relational View of Place

If we acknowledge how common are the encounters I have termed 'sacramental', and the importance of the places in which they occur, an important resulting question is: 'Has God made the world so that some places naturally evoke a sense of the divine presence?' There is certainly precedence for this view. The intrinsic holiness of place has a long history in pagan religion, as the Roman notion of *genius loci* makes clear.[58] This concept has been embraced by modern writers like D. H. Lawrence who wrote that 'every continent has its own great spirit of place ... Different places on the face of the earth have different vital effluence, different vibration, different chemical exhalation, different polarity with different stars: call it what you like. But the spirit of place is a great reality.'[59] Christian history has generally resisted the conception of there being places which are intrinsically holy, but it was certainly evident in Celtic times. A. M. Allchin recounts a delightful example in a legend concerning the monastery of Landevennec which is situated at the furthest tip of Brittany. In the early Celtic Church, Landevennec was a great centre of learning; it then went into a long period of decline, culminating with its destruction at the time of the French Revolution, but has flowered again in this generation with the establishment of a new Benedictine community there. Wrdisten, the writer of the earliest life of its founder, St Guenole, tells us that 'the spring flowers make their earliest appearance there and the autumn leaves linger there longer than anywhere else. It is a kind of paradise prepared by God for his servants, and, as it is rich in the fruits of the earth, so it is rich in heavenly fruits.' Wrdisten goes on to explain that at the time of the founder, the monks discovered, to their dismay, that they were unable to die. The reason for this was revealed in a vision in which the brethren saw an opening in heaven exactly the size of the monastery, with the angels of heaven ascending and descending from one to the other. The correspondence between earth and heaven, time and eternity had become so exact that time on earth was no longer functioning. The monks, some of whom were 'weighed down by the weight of many years' and 'longed to be released from their crumbling frame of clay', exhorted the Abbot to be allowed to pull down the buildings and move them. Permission was given, with the result that, in the new monastery, a little nearer the shore, it became possible to die – but only from old age.[60]

---

[58] Walker elucidates the meaning of the term *genius loci* as follows: 'Outside the house, to picture the character of a place, the Romans imagined a spirit who owned it, the *genius loci*. In the ancient world, when people grasped qualities, functions or principles of activity, they often represented these intangible realities in a concrete image. The *genius loci*, which first appeared in Italy as a snake and later in human form, stood for the independent reality of the place. Above all, it symbolised the place's generative energy, and it pictured a specific personal, spiritual presence who animated and protected a place. On the deepest level, the image of a guardian spirit provided a way of representing the energy, definition, unifying principle and continuity of a place' (Walker, E. V., 1988, 15). For a more contemporary literary example of a similar sentiment see Lawrence Durrell's poem *Deus Loci* in Durrell, L. (1956), 76.

[59] Lawrence, D. H. (1961), 5.

[60] Allchin, A. M. (1978), 5.

Philip Sheldrake reminds us that 'Celtic Christians had – and still have – a strong sense of living on "edges" or "boundary places" between the material world and the other world. The natural landscape was both a concrete reality where people lived and, at the same time, a doorway into another, spiritual, world.' He continues: 'Such a notion found a powerful voice in the late Dr George MacLeod, the founder of the modern Iona community and one-time Moderator of the Church of Scotland. He spoke of the Isle of Iona ... as "a thin place" where the membrane between this world and the other world, between the material and the spiritual, was very permeable.'[61] However, in the light of our discussion of sacramental encounters, I would maintain that if Iona is such a 'thin spot', it is so as a result of divine disclosure that has happened there in its Christian past as opposed to any intrinsic holiness. I would suggest that this is true for general human experience of place too, for, as the geographer Edward Relph notes, through particular encounters and experiences space is richly differentiated into places, or centres of special personal significance. This is because 'the meanings of places may be rooted in the physical setting and objects and activities, but they are not a property of them – rather they are a property of human intentions and experiences.'[62]

Certainly, place was very important in the Celtic scheme of things. Sheldrake draws our attention to one of the sermons of St Columbanus, who reminds us that the whole of the creation is satiated with the divine presence: 'Seek no farther concerning God; for those who wish to know the great deep must first review the natural world. For knowledge of the Trinity is properly likened to the depths of the sea, according to that saying of the Sage, And the great deep, who shall find it out? If then a man wishes to know the deepest ocean of divine knowledge, let him first scan that visible sea.'[63] However, one could argue that, either way, the priority lies with God's *actions*, since in the case of exemplary Christian community it is, one would suppose, the Spirit of God at work in that community which enables its holiness. As far as 'natural phenomena' are concerned, it is surely the Spirit of God, once again, which enables the believer to perceive a place as being evocative of the divine presence. It is this perception that enables what I have termed a sacramental encounter. As we shall see as we come to look at particular places which have been deemed holy in the Christian tradition, they are almost always places associated with divine revelation or with the place of dwelling of a particularly holy person to whom and in whom God has been revealed. God, people, and place cannot be separated, so what we need to emphasize in this approach to the sacramental as generating its own coordinates is the key insight of a *relational* view of place which emerged from our study of the scriptures.

So, for example, in thinking about sacramental theology and its relationship to the Eucharist, argument has often centred around the physical presence or otherwise of Christ in the sacrament. It could be argued that the relationship the believer has with Christ is as important as that presence. That is to say, if I have no real relationship with Jesus, his presence in the sacrament will not greatly impinge upon my life. To give an analogy, I can be physically very close to someone on a tube train, but that

---

[61] Sheldrake, P. (1995), 7.

[62] Relph, E. (1976), 11, 47.

[63] St Columba in Walker, G. S. M. (ed.) (1957), *Sancti Columbani Opera*, Dublin: Dublin Institute for Advanced Studies, 63, referred to in Sheldrake, P. (1995), 7.

closeness has no real significance to me unless I have a relationship with that person. That is not to say that the other person is not there unless there is a relationship, but that if there is no relationship, then his or her presence is of no effect. Osborne makes a similar point:

> If one says that a cloud is a sacrament of God, every tree is a sacrament of God or every river is a sacrament of God, these phrases have no meaning whatsoever. The world by itself is not simply sitting somewhere in space as a cosmic sacrament. Trees are not just growing in some earthly forest as a worldly sacrament. To speak in this way would be another instance of hermeneutical ease. God's creative action may be in every cloud and tree and river, but the sacramentality aspect takes place only when this action produces a subsequent reaction from some human person. One can see many trees and yet experience nothing sacramental. One can see many rivers yet see or experience nothing sacramental. Sacramental *Haecceitas* occurs when a human person or human persons begin to react to the blessing *qua blessing* of God in the tree, in the cloud or in the river. It is this action/reaction on the part of an existential person or existential persons that creates the possibility of the sacramentality of the world. There is not an objective world, unaffected by subjectivity, which one can call sacrament. Only divine action and human reaction in a concrete situation form the basis for possible sacramentality.[64]

Sacramentality must be based in action *and* in relationship. This point is reinforced by the fact that Colin Wilson writes of experiences very similar to those we have been discussing from an entirely secular perspective. After an American psychologist, Maslow, he calls them 'peak experiences', and attributes to them nothing religious at all, but describes them as 'just sudden bubbling, overwhelming moments of happiness'. Wilson's only interest is in how one might induce such an experience: 'If only there were a way in which you could push a button and induce that experience instantly – make the golden bubble burst so that you are reminded of Mozart and the stars. If only we could do it – we could even find some drug or chemical that would do it then we would have solved the basic problem of civilisation.'[65] Leaving aside any questions about Wilson's understanding of how easily 'the basic problem of civilisation' might be solved, we should note that he is clear that such experiences do not 'mean' anything except that the recipient is healthy – though he gives no convincing reason for such an assumption. He also assumes that large numbers of people enjoy such experiences. All he is interested in, though, is just that – enjoying them, rather like St Peter on the mountain wanting to prolong the experience of transfiguration by building booths. It is only faith that can provide a framework within which the significance of these experiences and the role of them in life in general can be understood. But Macquarrie asks why even believers are able to miss God who is already there in everything around them, and he answers that question as follows:

> Here, I think, we have to come back to the subject object divide. For anything to become a sacrament, something has to be contributed from both sides. There has to be a reality expressing itself in and through the object. Otherwise it is an illusion. The reality is nothing

---

[64] Osborne, K. (1999), 74.
[65] Wilson, C. (1987), 298, 303.

less that the ultimate reality, God or Holy Being, the condition that there can exist anything whatsoever, and without which there would be no bushes, no Moses, no wilderness, nothing at all. But there also has to be a subject having the capacity to see the object in depth, as it were, that is to say not just another things lying around in the world but a sign of a deeper reality.[66]

The three-way relationship of God, person, and place is of crucial importance, and there must be a response from people if such events are to be termed 'sacramental'. This is consistently the case. Only when the gracing action of God is matched by the accepting faith of a believer is sacramentality enabled and grace caused. Sacrament is not a magical imposition of grace, but a free offer of grace which can be accepted or rejected by human beings. The world in itself is not sacramental, because sacramentality is an event that involves action by God and a response by unique human beings. Sacramentality is thus historical, temporal, and singular. Susan White suggests that after the work of people like Schillebeeckx, Rahner and Lonergan, sacramentality has to be talked about as part of 'the ongoing mutual encounter between free, transcendent persons (divine and human) in which the physical, the material, becomes a mode of self-disclosure for both.'[67] We might note that this self-disclosure takes place inside *and* outside the church building. If we look at the scriptures, tradition and experience of Christians we find that they are full of such encounters – and in all cases where such an event occurs, the *place* of the happening is important and intrinsic to it. Certainly, such encounters do not lead anywhere, as I have already suggested, unless they are understood within the tradition of believers. This reinforces the importance of the relational view of a sacramental understanding of reality, for in a sacrament God has not only to reveal himself, but we must have the grace to perceive him.

However, this works both ways since, as Keenan Osborne tells us 'the possible place of sacramentality in the world at large provides a hermeneutical key, or better, an onto-hermeneutical key, for those involved in the sacramental actions of church life.'[68] This is because it is 'only if individual human beings experience the worldliness in sacramental moments will the dramatic liturgies of religion have any meaning. Only if individual human beings experience worldliness in some sacramental moments will church moments ever be meaningful sacramental moments.'[69] I feel that Osborne goes too far here since, as I have suggested above, scripture and the tradition of the Church should come first in our understanding of God's way with the world. However, there must certainly be a relationship between these and experience. Thus, there should be a two-way interaction between what is experienced in church and what is experienced in the world. There is considerable evidence from the work of social anthropologists which suggests that experience and ritual are closely related through an awareness that is developed by ritual and related to experience.[70]

---

[66] Macquarrie, J. (1997), 10.

[67] White, S. in Brown, D. and Loades, A. (1995), 40.

[68] Osborne, K. (1999), 68.

[69] Ibid., 80.

[70] Sperber, for example, contrasts 'symbolic knowledge' which is gleaned in this manner with 'encyclopaedic knowledge' (Sperber, D., 1975, 91ff).

Stephen Sykes notes that contemporary study of Paul's references to baptism are unquestionably illuminated by modern anthropological theories of rites of passage. He adds that rituals are ways in which 'frames are set around experience, and sacred boundaries established. Where the symbolic transactions inspire confidence, the social and psychological effectiveness of a ritual is strongly documented. Criticism of the tendency of ritual forms to harden into substitutes for religious experience must stop short of the destruction of ritual as a mode of religious behaviour.'[71] Indeed, and there should be a creative interplay between the two in this sense at least: that ritual relates to the transfiguration of place experienced in sacramental encounter and provides a means to understand it. Liturgy should articulate and reiterate a sense of meaning and articulate the sacred. For Christians, sacraments do this in relation to the Christ event since, as Rowan Williams tells us, for the Christian it is in these acts that 'the church makes sense of itself, as other groups may do, and as individuals do, but its "sense" is seen as depending on the creative act of God in Christ'.[72] Thus participation in the sacramental life of the church and the experiencing of grace therein will, among other things, encourage us to be aware of the world as a possible place for sacramental disclosure and to understand our experience in the light of it for in the Eucharist the reality of God is present. The Eucharist, the Christian faith teaches, is the 'locus', or place, of finding God. The world as a possible place for sacramental encounter will, in turn, enrich our appreciation of the sacramental life of the Church.

Holiness Across Time

A vital next step in our argument, already implied in some of the above, is that once divine disclosure has happened in a particular location, it remains associated with that place. Donald Allchin writes that: 'to speak of spirituality is to speak of that meeting of eternity with time, of heaven with earth; it is to recover a sense of the holiness of matter, the sacredness of this world of space and time when it is known as the place of God's epiphany.' He tells us that there is a geography of holy places which are 'places whose power persists through centuries of indifference and neglect to be revealed again when men are ready for it, places which display the potential holiness of all this earth which man has loved so much yet so much ravaged.'[73] Brown and Loades point out that baptism is the beginning of a movement of the Spirit, that in sacramental absolution there is the initiating of a process which carries a forgiven past into the promise of a transformed future. In the same way, an action on the part of God lies at the heart of those acts commonly identified as sacramental, so that 'it must be right to expect a similar pattern of movement in any wider application of the notion. Indeed, wherever such movement occurs, so far from undermining a claim to the presence of the sacramental, it is surely now more likely to enhance it.'[74] Thus:

---

[71] Sykes, S. in Hodgson, P. and King, R. (eds) (1985), 297.

[72] Williams, R. (2000), 205.

[73] Allchin, A. M. (1978), 20.

[74] Brown, D. and Loades, A. (1995), 42.

It is not just a matter of instantaneous divine action, as though we could just be there and then be pulled out of our specific context in space and time; rather God works through redefining who we are (giving us a new 'measure') and thereby initiates a process of movement towards transformation. In a similar way, then, one may argue that this is how time and space themselves operate sacramentally: not by endorsing the present universe's temporal and spatial co-ordinates nor by pulling us out into a world without either, but rather through faith generating its own distinctive medium, its own set of spatial and temporal co-ordinates. Space and time are thus given a new definition (a new 'measure'), and as a result they can now help advance us on the sacramental process towards our life's transformation. The co-ordinates we adopt are no longer our own, but those given by God, and so make it possible for us to share more deeply in a God-centred perception of the world.[75]

The inclusion of time in the equation is thus an all-important factor because the giving of new coordinates 'initiates a process of movement towards transformation' in the places of divine revelation. Susan White suggests that if a place becomes associated with 'violence, greed and injustice, pride, division, it will stop being a holy place until those things are repudiated'.[76] This seems to me to be too narrow a view of what it means for a place to be holy. This becomes apparent when we consider Jerusalem, a place which has been and still is associated with all the above evils and yet, to most people, would still be considered to be a holy place – ironically, it is exactly because it is considered to be a holy place that the evil occurs. It is a holy place which has been 'desecrated', but is still a holy place. Divine encounter initiates a process of movement which enables the location to become 'a place where prayer has been valid'.[77]

It is odd that the notion of places retaining an identity across time seems to be more readily embraced from a secular than a Christian perspective. The philosopher Edward Casey refers to time and history being so deeply inscribed in places as to be inseparable from them, and the social theorist E. V. Walker writes that place has no feelings apart from human experience there, but a place is: 'a location of experience. It evokes and organises memories, images, feelings, sentiments, meanings, and the work of the imagination. The feelings of a place are indeed the mental projections of individuals, but they come from collective experience and do not happen anywhere else. They belong to the place.' The geographer Edward Relph suggests that places are 'constructed in our memories and affections through repeated encounters and complex associations' and 'place experiences are necessarily time-deepened and

---

[75] Brown and Loades (1995), 3.

[76] White, S. in Brown, D. and Loades, A. (1995), 42.

[77] Eliot, T. S. (1969), 192. The converse is true for places with which appalling evil has been associated like Auschwitz. Interestingly, even those with a very secular world view would be willing to associate the presence of evil with such places in a manner which changes them across time. What is missing from a secular worldview is the possibility of *places being redeemed*. The possibility of the redemption of places once associated with evil has been integral to the Christian tradition. For example, the Anglican Cathedral in Zanzibar was deliberately built over the site of the slave market and the High Altar placed where the whipping post had been. As such it is a powerful symbol *precisely because* the evil past of the place remains very much part of its story. Its redemption points to the fact that all places will be redeemed in Christ. Judaism will have no truck with the redemption of places in this manner: Jewish opinion is very much against the proposed building of a convent at Auschwitz.

memory qualified'.[78] Each of these comments confirms a relational view of place that makes it inseparable from the individuals and communities associated with it and 'tells its story'. This would suggest that even Allchin's romantic notion of places waiting for their holiness to be rediscovered will only be able to have that expectation realized whilst their holiness is retained in the memory of people like Allchin himself, at the very least. A relational view of place, whilst allowing for continuity across time, does countenance the possibility of the holiness of a place to disappear if the meaning associated with it completely recedes from human memory. As Edward Relph points out, some places have died, and the world is full of the skeletons of dead places. He cites Stonehenge and Carnac as places 'which have been stripped of their original meanings and become little more than objects of casual and uncommitted observation for tourists and passers-by and other outsiders. Such withering away and modification are prevented by ritual and tradition that reinforce the sense of permanence of place.'[79] Hence the enormous importance of ritual and tradition. This character of place across time is a complicated thing, even from a human point of view. Relph elucidates the point thus:

> The individuality of places and landscapes differs in one fundamental aspect from that of people. It is accorded rather than self-created. A landscape is always an aggregation of objects and organisms arranged in a singular pattern which is the product of the interaction of physical, ecological, historical, economic and random processes. There is no single inner force directing and co-ordinating all of these. Yet it seems as though there is an individuality which lies behind the forms and appearances and maintains a coherent identity. We know that the spirit of a place can persist through countless changes in detail and structure. For instance, in a village which has existed for centuries it is quite possible that every building will have been reconstructed at least once, and they all will have been repeatedly changed in the course of maintenance and repair. There may also have been drastic changes to the fabric of the village – new churches, roads and housing estates being added to the existing ones. However, there can be little question that this is the same essential place as it has always been – grown and changed perhaps, yet as much itself as an old man is the same as the boy of seventy years ago.[80]

The force of this proposal is made clear by Relph when he contrasts the above situation with that of a reconstruction of a village as it was at some point in the past, which, even if undertaken with every possible attention to detail, is none the less a new place bearing no genuine relationship to the original and lacking historical continuity and the signs of change. He concludes that the distinctiveness of place lies not so much in its exact physical forms and arrangements, as in the meanings accorded to it by a community of concerned people. Similarly, Philip Sheldrake points out that the experience of displaced people shows that 'it is the absence of lineage and memory associated with physical place that is just as critical as separation from the landscape alone.'[81] The process being referred to here emphasizes the importance of what we have termed 'storied place'.

---

[78] Casey, E. in Feld, S. and Basso, K. (1996), 44; Walker, E. V. (1988), 21; Relph, E. in Seamon, D. and Mugerauer, R. (1989), 26.

[79] Relph, E. (1976), 32.

[80] Relph, E. (1981), 172.

[81] Sheldrake, P. (2001), 17.

There arises an associated question about the historical veracity of events associated with particular places. What is the status of a 'holy place' with which events of dubious historicity are associated? The work of Paul Ricoeur is relevant in this regard in that it attempts to overcome the absolute opposition between history as 'true' and history as 'fiction'. Philip Sheldrake points out that for Ricouer, history and fiction refer to the historicity of human existence in different ways: they share a common narrative structure. This means that although not completely wedded to the details of historical events, fiction (and thus the stories associated with particular places) may convey important truths about reality: 'In Ricoeur's sense, hagiography is a "fictive" narrative that describes an imaginative world that transgresses the constraints of "what really happened" in the positivist sense in order to give expression to what ideally ought to have happened and thus, by implication, to the promise of what may happen.'[82] The question which should be asked, therefore, is whether the stories associated with places are ones which promote Christian truth in the broadest sense.

We might note that the sense of place to which Relph refers occurs through human encounter *in a place*, just as appreciation of the world as the theatre of God's actions comes through divine encounter *in a place*. The symbolic power of place is great, but Relph is wary of any attempt to analyse it since he tells us that 'it is just not possible to draw boundaries around landscapes or to define and analyse systematically the individuality of a particular place. If someone insists on attempting these worthless pursuits it is utterly predictable that the very individuality they wish to measure will vanish beneath their methods.'[83] A strong warning. It is almost as if Relph is suggesting that places have a 'personality' as a result of people's interaction with them, and that this 'personality' will, as with a human personality, defy analysis. Tuan actually uses the word 'personality' when suggesting that geographers should take time out to concentrate on the parts of a landscape, and that 'a mood of attentive waiting (the French word 'attente' best expresses this) must follow the period of concentration before the landscape will yield to us its personality.'[84] It is striking that Tuan resorts to religious language both here and when referring to places as being entities which 'incarnate the experience and aspirations of people'. Tuan is prepared to accord an almost mystical quality to the power of place to symbolize: 'A symbolic world, resonant with meaning, does indeed provide an emotionally rewarding milieu, but only so long as we do not consciously recognise it as a world rich in symbols. Such recognition puts a distance between self and world; and we shall inevitably come to feel adrift – homeless – as fewer and fewer things are able to touch us unmediated by reflective thought.'[85]

These words from secular scholars should encourage us to remember that much of the power of a particular place, associated with its past, will not be mediated by 'conscious reflection', but by a much more integrated attention of the sort mediated by sacrament and symbol. There is, after all our attempts to clarify, a mystery associated with the power of places which is better articulated by poetry than rational

---

[82] Ibid., 40, referring to Ricoeur, P. (1984). See also Brown, D. (2001).

[83] Relph, E. (1981), 174.

[84] Tuan, Y.-F. (1972), 537.

[85] Tuan, Y.-F. (1971), 181; Tuan, Y.-.F (1984).

argument. This is partly because of the difference between 'encyclopaedic knowledge' and 'symbolic knowledge' which we have already noted. But we can be clear that when a place is sacralized, the dimension of history becomes added to personal identity and individual experience, giving it particular cultural significance. This is why people 'cling with such obstinate tenacity to the position he has once adopted; and a sacred position remains holy even when it has been long neglected. ... The consciousness of the sacred character of the locality that has once been chosen, is therefore, always retained.'[86] As T. S. Eliot expresses it:

> For the blood of Thy martyrs and saints
> Shall enrich the earth, shall create holy places.
> For wherever a saint has dwelt, wherever a martyr has given his
>   blood for the blood of Christ,
> There is holy ground, and the sanctity shall not depart from it
> Though armies trample over it, though sightseers come with
>   guide books looking over it. ...[87]

Thus, holiness is built into the story of a place so that the Christian community can be built up in faith by association with it.

From Event to Perception

In understanding place as the locus of divine revelation in sacramental encounters we have found a promising, imaginative, non-dualistic and orthodox way which to allows us to think of place as receptive to the divine. I have suggested that places are the chosen seat of God's self-revelation, and this is the sense in which we might think of them as sacramental. It is not that God can be *contained* by any particular place. Solomon declares: 'But will God indeed dwell on the earth? Behold, heaven and the highest heaven cannot contain thee; how much less this house which I have built.' (1 Kings 8:27). But just as God can be encountered in the person of Jesus Christ, the scandal of particularity, so he chooses to make himself known to humanity in and through particular places. These encounters, as all sacramental encounters, lead to a transformation of the place as well as the individuals and communities associated with them. The role of such places is to root believers in their faith and point them towards the redemption of all places in Christ.

Thus, through being associated with divine disclosure and the holiness of lives lived to God, certain places will be able to speak sacramentally of the presence and action of God elsewhere. Helen Oppenheimer makes use of the work of Oliver Quick to take an analogous approach to churchgoing: 'Sundays and churches are not nearer to God or more excellent: they are fractions, set apart to represent the truth that all time and space are God's. The part is consecrated, not instead of the whole, but on behalf of the whole.'[88] This makes sense from a phenomonological philosophical

---

[86] Van der Leeuw, G. (1967), 393.

[87] Eliot, T. S., 'Murder in the Cathedral', in Eliot, T. S. (1969), 281.

[88] Oppenheimer, H. (1988), 72; Quick proposes the principle of what he terms 'representative dedication' (see Quick, O. C., 1916).

perspective. As Casey suggests: 'Local knowledge, then, comes down to an intimate understanding of what is generally true in the locally obvious; it concerns what is true about place in general as manifested *in this place*.... That anything like this indication of place is possible exhibits place's special power to embrace and support even as it bounds and locates.'[89]

Thus, a sacramental approach can help us to navigate a middle course between place and 'placelessness', both of which are evident in the scriptures and tradition, 'placelessness' offering a critique of the tendency to locate God too specifically. The tension between these two approaches is articulated by Belden Lane: 'There is an inescapable tension here between our human need for assurances (even guarantees) of God's presence and the absolute freedom of the divine being, in whom place itself coheres. It is a tension expressed by kataphatic and apophatic traditions within the history of spirituality.'[90] Stephen Sykes amplifies the point thus:

> Though there is no place, no time or person which or who is in principle God-forsaken, though it be true that the incarnation consecrated all time, place, persons and matter, nonetheless, *hic et nunc* we need a focus of attention. Otherwise we are in danger of being unable to distinguish a defused, undifferentiated presence of God from no presence at all. (A person asked whether he did, or did not believe in the Divinity of Christ replied, 'Far be it from me to deny the divinity of any man.') Some religious people believe in the sacramental universe in such a way as to undermine the necessity of particular sacraments. Catholic Christians, by contrast, consenting to particular sacraments see them as focusing the presence of God, intensifying in a certain manner what is universally true. Thus a holy place is set aside not in order to deny the holiness of other places, but for human perception to intensify the sanctification of all places. Because the church has been set aside, the bedroom is not therefore devoid of the divine presence. Because there is a time for mass, or the angelus, it does not mean that other times are handed over to worldliness. Because a priest is set apart for holy things, it does not mean that the laity are licensed for profanity.[91]

Thus, the function of sacramental encounters and holy places that derive from them is to remind us of the presence and action of God elsewhere. It is, as John Riches reminds us, a delicate balance: 'It is too easy for the overzealous to press too quickly to the foundation of things; to scorn the sheer glory of nature or the subtle and half-perceived drawings of grace. It requires the poet's – or the mystic's – eye sensitive to the extraordinary richness of creation and the cunning of grace in history to continue to sustain a vision of the glory of the world as it is.'[92] However, having an eye sensitive to the extraordinary richness of creation makes the poet or mystic a person who can help all of us perceive that richness so that we might be led to a *sacramental* reading of reality in and through the material world we inhabit. *Through* is the sacramental preposition, and in Jesus we learn that the way to the infinite is through the finite. As Herbert puts it:

---

[89] Casey, E. in Feld, S. and Basso, K. (1996), 44.

[90] Lane, B. (1992), 10.

[91] Address given by S. Sykes at a conference, *The Holy Place: Mission and Conservation*, Keele University, 25–26 June 1996.

[92] Riches, J. (1996), 'Balthasar's Sacramental Spirituality and Hopkins' Poetry of Nature: The Sacrifice Imprinted upon Nature', in Brown and Loades (1996), 179.

A man that looks on glass
On it may stay his eye;
Or if he pleaseth, through it pass,
And then the heaven espy.[93]

Such writing suggests we might widen the notion of sacramental encounter even further, since *whenever* we are able, fortified by the tradition of which we are a part, to share more deeply in a God's centred perception of the world, we might say that God is gracing that perception in a sacramental sense. This is why Thomas Traherne tells us that we 'need only open eyes to be ravished like the Cherubims'.[94] In so doing, God is reminding us that natural things can be clothed with new meaning by relating them to Christ. So, Emily Dickinson writes:

The only news I know,
Is bulletins all day
From immortality;
The only shows I see
Tomorrow and today,
Perchance eternity.
The only one I meet
Is God, the only street
Existence; this traversed
If other news there be
Or admirabler show,
I'll tell it you.[95]

It is through these 'bulletins from immortality' given to us and to others that we should be able to relate the incarnate Christ to all things. There are poets who have consciously attempted a sacramental approach in their poetry. One such is David Jones who believed that 'a sacramental view of life could transform the brutishness of modern technological existence and the technology itself must be transformed into something more human and "creaturely", less sterile and mechanistic.'[96] Jones was protesting against all the pressures we looked at in the first chapter which have have such a disastrous effect: 'Mass production, shoddy workmanship, commercialised art, and an emphasis on utilitarian worth as opposed to traditional artistic or religious values, all encourage the public to be unreceptive to the extra-utile and, therefore, to art and sacrament.'[97] This is made explicit in Jones' *The Tutelar of The Place*, which concludes as follows: 'When the technicians manipulate the dead limbs of our culture as though it yet had life, have mercy on us. Open unto us, let us enter a second time within your stola-folds in those days – ventricle and refuge both, *hendref* for world-winter, asylum from world-storm. Womb of the Lamb the spoiler of the Ram.'[98]

---

[93] Herbert, G., 'The Elixir', Stanza 3 in Witherspoon A. and Warnke, F. (eds) (1929), *Seventeenth-century Prose and Poetry*, New York: Harcourt Brace Jovanovich, 859.

[94] Traherne, T. (1966), *Centuries of Meditation*, First Century, paragraph 37.

[95] Dickinson E. (1970), 577.

[96] Daly, C. (1981), 225.

[97] Ibid., 218.

[98] Jones, D. (1974), 63. The term 'tutelar' used in this sense derives from the pagan belief that every Roman citizen was allotted a guardian spirit or tutelary god at birth.

Similarly, von Balthasar sees Gerard Manley Hopkins' poetry as 'sacramental poetry'. Balthasar writes:

> For an understanding of the way the mystery of God takes form in the world, the conception of the sacramental is at hand, which certainly contains within itself the power of the 'symbol', while it goes far beyond it; the form of the image is a likeness to the primordial form that has the 'stress' of the latter in itself: *sacramenta continent quae significant.* ... The mystery of Christ is, on the one hand, of infinite depth, penetrating all the levels of being from flesh to spirit and beyond into the abyss of the Trinity; on the other, it is an infinitely dramatic event that in the kenotic descent into man and matter exalts and changes them, redeems and deifies them. ... The image that should interpret the mystery of Christ is, in itself, as an image of nature, utterly overtaxed, but in so far as it is grounded in Christ as the presupposition of nature, it is allowed to say by the grace of the archetype what it cannot say for itself.[99]

Here we acknowledge that a symbol participates in the reality of that for which it stands and that this is why the world, graced by God, can be the 'theatre of his glory'. The term 'theatre' is useful here since it reminds us that all sacrament, as we have continually stressed, begins with God's action. God makes known his glory in sacramental gracing. Such a view seeks to integrate creation and redemption in a manner consonant with the fact that Christ is not only the very Word of God through whom all things were created (John 1:3) but also the Lamb who was slain before the foundation of the world (Revelation 13:8, cf 1 Peter 1:20). This latter text enabled von Balthasar to write that 'the Sacrifice of the Son is God's first thought of the world',[100] and: 'Christ's cross is indeed not one historical act among others to which a natural process can be more or less arbitrarily related: it is the fundamental, ontological presupposition of all natural processes that all, knowingly or not, intrinsically signify or intend by pointing beyond themselves.'[101] Thus, creation and redemption are held in creative tension so that attention to the world around us and the places in which we find ourselves – as well as the people with whom we find ourselves – will help to restore what Thomas Traherne calls 'right sight', for places are the seat of relations, or the place of meeting and activity in the interaction between God and the world.

Conclusion

Having established that sacramentality is a concept which can be widely applied to the material world, this chapter has proposed that sacrament is best understood in relation to place by speaking in terms of 'sacramental encounters' in particular places. We have indicated that such encounters are a very important part of the Christian tradition, and suggested that they are not given only to a few, but to very many people.

The place in which such encounters occur is always important to the person who

---

[99] Von Balthasar, H. (1986), 393.

[100] Ibid., 380,

[101] Ibid., 394

has the experience, and this means that the biblical paradigm of people, place, and God which I derived from a consideration of the scriptures in the last chapter is upheld. In many instances the place can become significant to others, too. In such cases the encounter is built into the story of the place for the Christian community as well as the individual, and this is how places become designated as holy. Holy places are thus associated with holy people to whom and in whom something of the glory of God has been revealed. The existence of such holy places should facilitate a sacramental perception and serve as a reminder that all time and place belong to God in Christ – the part is set aside on behalf of, rather than instead of, the whole.

Chapter 4

Place and the Christian Tradition:
Pilgrimage and Holy Places

Pilgrimages

Pilgrimage and Place

In the last chapter we looked at the way in which a sacramental approach to reality has been expounded by many writers, and have commended it, but suggested that it is more satisfactory to begin with an appreciation of sacramental *encounters* in which the material becomes a vehicle for God's self-communication. In such events the role of place is essential. When places become associated with divine disclosure they become the defining coordinates of a sacred geography the function of which is to remind believers that they are to understand all their experience in the light of the creation of the world by God and its redemption in Jesus Christ. Sacramental encounters have also an eschatological dimension, since they reveal the reality of things as they will be. This sacramental understanding allows us to steer a middle course between ignoring the importance of the material, and its idolatrous exaltation. In this chapter I want to make clear that the significance of place thus understood has been a vital part of the Christian tradition from the earliest times, even though it may not have been articulated as such. In doing so I want, too, to expand on how a sacramental understanding of place developed in the last chapter might be related to holy places and churches.

Alongside the designation of churches as 'holy' as a result of the encounter of Christians with the living God within them, the phenomenon which has demonstrated the appreciation of place in the Christian tradition more than any other is that of pilgrimage. It is by using the model of pilgrimage that we can best understand the function that churches can play in nourishing Christian community. The landscape of the Christian world is dotted with places which have been recognized as being holy by virtue of sacramental encounter of the sort we have been discussing, and the resulting effect of such encounter on the lives of men and women. These are places into the story and fabric of which the divine human encounter has worked itelf so that they have spoken and can still speak to people of a God who makes manifest through the material and who, in Christ, hallows the material. For generations people have made their way to such places and entered into the tradition of pilgrimage, which is almost as old as the Christian faith itself:

> Christianity is not the religion of salvation *from* history, it is the religion of the salvation *of* history, of a salvation, that is, which passes through the intimately connected events and

words with which divine self-communication is made. This is why places in which the history of divine self-communication took place or became concrete at specific times, by means of specific messages are so important for the faith of Christians: they allow us to better understand what God desires to tell us about himself, helping us to enter into His language, into the 'grammar' of his actions, to taste the profundity of his words and of his silences. The stones of the Holy Places and of places made holy by certain fundamental events of grace – namely, shrines – nourish the faith of God's children ... pilgrimage to these places becomes an authentic experience of the exodic condition of the human heart and of the encounter with the Other, transcendent and divine, for which it longs.[1]

We might not only agree with this proposition, but paraphrase it to say that the Christian religion is not the religion of salvation *from* places, it is the religion of salvation *in* and *through* places.

Pilgrimage is journey to places where divine human encounter has taken place. It is journey to places where holiness has been apparent in the lives of Christian men and women who have been inspired by such an encounter and have responded to it wholeheartedly in their lives: it is travel to the dwelling places of the saints. As such, pilgrimage is, firstly, about roots: it reminds the traveller of the Christian heritage of which he or she is a part. The pilgrimage shrine speaks in many different ways of that heritage, and I shall examine these in due course. Secondly, pilgrimage is about journey. It reminds those travelling that their lives are a journey to God: the pilgrimage is symbolic of that larger journey. This aspect of journey is pregnant with biblical resonances, beginning with Abraham leaving his homeland to travel to the Promised Land and ending with the Christians travelling to their heavenly homeland, the New Jerusalem. These biblical images reveal the third ingredient of pilgrimage, an eschatological one, which is about destination and the consummation of all things in Christ.

The destination of a pilgrimage speaks of all three aspects of the phenomenon of pilgrimage: our roots in the Christian faith which give a new relationship to time and place, our Christian journey, and the consummation of all things in Christ which we await. It speaks about this world and the next. If the destination of pilgrimage is viewed in a sacramental light, it will combine the biblical themes of place and placelessness, reminding us that 'here we have no abiding city' and are continually called to journey forth. We do so with confidence in the biblical promise that we shall find rest and a place for ever. Kenneth Cragg suggests that 'sacramental' in this context is a Christian usage, which implies association. Holy places are then 'foci of meanings that are quickened by the sight (site) or feel of them but not idolatrously fused with them'.[2] The destination of pilgrimage is a foretaste of what is to come: it is not that reality, but if it is to be viewed sacramentally then it will not only point towards that new reality and speak of it but will partake of it. The sanctity of matter is affirmed in the destination of pilgrimage but its provisional nature means that it points, as do all sacramental encounters. In pilgrimage, then, we see more than anywhere else in the Christian tradition the operation of an alternative sacred geography to direct us. I shall now look at the evolution of that phenomenon and see how it should speak of these three aspects of roots, journey and destination. Since the

---

[1] Forte, B. (1999), 39.

[2] Cragg, K. (1997), 84.

supreme 'sacramental event' of divine disclosure took place in Jerusalem and the vision of the end given in the scriptures is of the New Jerusalem, it is to the history of attitudes and pilgrimage to Jerusalem and the Holy Land that we begin.

The History of Pilgrimage: Jerusalem

We have already noted in Chapter 2 how the early Christians worshipped in the temple, as did Jesus, but came to understand that Jesus had himself replaced the temple as the meeting place between God and humanity. Judaism had also developed alternative means of worship to the sacrificing cult of the temple. For different reasons, then, the destruction of the temple was something with which both Judaism and fledgling Christianity were able to come to terms. This is a development for which we must be thankful, for had it not happened we might safely conjecture that Judaism would have disappeared and Christianity would have been smothered not long after birth. However, we should not assume that the superseding of the temple by Jesus meant that Christian interest in Jerusalem and the Holy Land ceased.

Although there is not a great deal of surviving literature which speaks of how they were regarded, the relatively early work of Justin Martyr would suggest that they had great importance. His writings represent the earliest surviving ones by a Christian thinker dealing specifically with the relationship between Christianity and Judaism and it is here that the first Christian reference to 'the Holy Land' occurs. The passage concerns the person whom he sees as the forerunner of Jesus in name and deed, Joshua, who led the people into the 'holy land'. In the same way, Justin tells us, Christ will return to distribute the land to the people, though this time it will not be a temporary possession but an eternal one. In Christ, God will 'renew both the heaven and the earth; this is he who will shine an eternal light in Jerusalem'.[3] Justin wishes to show that the inheritance promised to Abraham applies not just to Jews but to all nations. Justin claims that: 'Christians, being children of Abraham, will inherit the holy land for an endless eternity. Whilst, according to Justin, Abraham's journey involves spiritual transformation, there is no hint that Justin believes Abraham's goal to have been purely spiritual. In every passage in which the term appears in *The Dialogue* it refers to the actual land. Justin can thus be seen to have a strong and literal sense of the inheritance of the land by Christians who were the spiritual descendants of Abraham. Christian hope, for him, was centred on the establishment in Jerusalem of an everlasting and imperishable kingdom. We might infer, then, that at this stage in Christian history place was very important and that, as Robert Wilken puts it, 'hopes for the future were rooted in the land promise to Abraham and in the words of the prophets about the glorification of Jerusalem'.[4]

The theme is taken up a generation later by Irenaeus, Bishop of Lyons, who, in his celebrated refutation of Gnosticism, *Adversus Haereses*, uses the Pauline term 'recapitulation' to describe the perfection by Christ of God's image and likeness in humankind.[5] Irenaeus teaches that the final act in this recapitulation will be the

---

[3] Justin Martyr, *Dialogus cum Tryphone*, 113.3–5.

[4] Wilken, R. (1992), 58.

[5] See Irenaeus, *Adversus Haereses*, Book 3, Chapter 16 and Book 3, Chapter 22. The term 'recapitulate' is a translation of *anakephalaiosis* in Ephesians 1:10.

establishment by Christ of a kingdom on earth. He quotes a whole series of passages from the prophets which speak of the promise of the land, the return of the exiles and the restoration of the temple, and in so doing he specifically rejects the notion – which he sees as Gnostic – that these texts should be interpreted spiritually. In the writings of Justin and Irenaeus, then, we see that interest in place, which had been at the centre of Judaism and in which the Christian drama of salvation had been acted out, was very much alive long before the legalization of the faith despite the disappearance of interest in the temple. These writers are the voices of orthodoxy in the second century, and their approach to the Holy Land is one which focuses on the places themselves and has much in common with Jewish restorationist hopes of the time. Attention is directed to the physical reality of the Holy Land in general, and Jerusalem in particular, and salvation is seen, literally and physically, in terms of their restoration.

This physical emphasis changed in the third century, however, and we see the force for change in the writings of Origen. He wrote that he planned to dispel the notion that writings about a good land promised by God to the righteous refer to the land of Judea. As a Christian interpreter of what he referred to as the 'Jewish scriptures', Origen sought to find spiritual significance for Christians in writings whose central theme was the relation of God to the people of Israel. He tells us that the scriptures describe how God chose a certain nation on the earth and gave them a land, Judea whose city is Jerusalem. On the prophecies which refer to these places and what is going to happen to them, Origen suggests an allegorical rather than a literal approach.[6] Origen's method here is characteristic of him. In all his work he wanted, as R. P .L. Milburn tells us, 'not so much to depreciate the events of biblical history as to proclaim that their significance was richer than an uncomprehending analysis would allow.'[7] Milburn summarizes Origen's way of proceeding thus: 'Origen declares the whole Scriptural record to be God's symphony, wherein the inexpert listener may think he perceives jarring notes whilst the man whose ear has been well trained realises the fitness and grace with which the varied notes are worked up into one harmonious composition.'[8] In Origen's interpretation we see a method similar to what we are proposing for an understanding of place as it emerges from the scriptures. He is interested in place as locus of divine disclosure and insists that its significance is richer than a literalist interpretation of passages referring to 'land' and Jerusalem will allow.

However, even if it is clear that there was interest in Jerusalem and the Holy Land from the earliest times, it is sometimes claimed that people of Origen's generation had a scholarly rather than devotional interest in the land, and that pilgrimage only began with the conversion of Constantine. So, for example, Joan Taylor tells us that: 'learned Christians of the second and third centuries were interested in the cities of Palestine in the same way that classical scholars, ever since Herodotus, had been interested in the classical cities: visiting the place helped one interpret and understand the literature.' Pilgrimage, however, is very much more than an exclusively educational journey, as Taylor herself observes: 'A pilgrim goes to a specific "holy" site in order to recall events that took place there and pray. The experience is much

---

[6] Origen, *Contra Celsum*, 7.28; Origen, *De Principiis*, 4.3.6. and 2.11.

[7] Milburn, R. (1954), 113.

[8] Ibid., quoted in Louth, A. (1983), 113.

more emotional than intellectual, and lays great store on the site's imbued aura of sanctity and importance.'[9] Contrary to what Taylor suggests, there is some evidence of this latter, as opposed to scholarly, interest from very early in Christian history. David Hunt shows that, 'individually and collectively, Christians can be demonstrated visiting places deemed to have a sacred significance for their faith long before the advent of the first Christian emperor.'[10] It might not be so easy as is sometimes suggested to pose a rigid line between the educative and spiritual functions of encounter with place sanctified by Christian history for, as Wilken puts it 'seeing was more than seeing, it was a metaphor for participation.'[11] Visiting 'holy places' has always had an impact on people much deeper than any reductionist rationalist explanation will allow.

If it was Origen who sowed the seeds for the transformation of Christian attitudes towards the Holy Land from being essentially forward-looking in literalist restorationist terms to being essentially backward-looking, by the time of Constantine's conversion the process was complete: Christians had ceased to associate salvation with the land in a physical sense. The forward-looking momentum required in faith was now to be found in the notion of pilgrimage. Hence, fully fledged Christian pilgrimage began to develop: by making a journey to either the Holy Land or the place where a saint had dwelt, people were able to enter into the history of their salvation, to travel to their roots, as well as be involved in something which was symbolic of their journey towards their heavenly home, the new Jerusalem, the 'spiritual city' above. This backward-looking literalist dimension and forward-looking eschatological dimension which are linked by a dynamic of journey meant that pilgrimage captured the imagination of generations to follow.

As the popularity of pilgrimages gathered momentum after the conversion of Constantine, Cyril of Jerusalem was the one who did more than any other to establish pilgrimage to the Holy Land in general, and Jerusalem in particular, as being of central importance to Christian piety. He believed in the intrinsic sanctity of material parts of Palestine, the 'holy places'. They were witnesses which proved the truth of gospel, and a pilgrim, by seeing and touching places once touched by Christ, could step closer to the divine.[12] Cyril enjoyed help from the Emperor himself, who had encouraged pilgrimage to the 'holy sites' and used the 'holy city' of Jerusalem as a symbolic focus of his new Christian empire. In the year 326 AD Constantine's mother, Helena, went on her celebrated pilgrimage, and within a short period of time countless pilgrims had come to Jerusalem – including one in 333 from Bordeaux, whose diary gives a fascinating view of these early years of Christian pilgrimage after 325.[13] The power of pilgrimage to Jerusalem to renew and rekindle faith in succeeding generations has been immense and makes clear the manner in which Christian memory is inescapably bound to place.

---

[9] Taylor, J. E. (1993), 311.

[10] Hunt, D. in Brown, D. and Loades, A. (1995), 60. See also Hunt's contribution 'Were There Christian Pilgrims before Constantine?' to Stopford, J. (ed.) (1999), *Pilgrimage Explored*, Woodbridge, Suffolk: York Medieval Press.

[11] Wilken, R. (1992), 116.

[12] Cyril of Jerusalem, *Catecheses*, i.1; iv.10; v.10. x.19; xiii.22, 38–39, x.19, xiv.22–3.

[13] See Stewart, A. (1887).

Jerusalem was, then, from the very earliest times, a focus of Christian interest and devotion. Although it would never have been articulated in this manner in the early church, we might say that the divine disclosure which took place in Christ, the ultimate sacramental event, was one which hallowed Jerusalem and the Holy Land more than any other place. The holy places and the tombs of the patriarchs as well as the sites in Jerusalem and Bethlehem became witnesses to the truth of biblical history and of the Christian religion.

The imagery of Jerusalem, as J. G. Davies points out, is multilayered: 'Literally or historically it denotes the city of the Jews; allegorically or typologically it can be referred to the church; tropologically or morally it stands for the human soul; analogically or eschatologically it indicates the heavenly city of God.'[14] Although the marring of Christian history by the Crusades and the present sad tension in the Holy Land make many nervous about its status, it continues to draw people. Jerusalem has an unrivalled position in Christian psychology and, as we have seen, the psychological importance of place should not be underestimated, as demonstrated by the work of people like Bachelard, whom we considered in Chapter 1. It combines to potent effect a backward momentum to the incarnation itself and a forward momentum to the heavenly Jerusalem, and continues to allow Christians to immerse themselves in their own sacred geography better than anywhere. Interestingly, the fact that there are very few if any Christians who would want to advocate the 'possession' of Jerusalem as a consequence of their interest in it might suggest that such a sacramental approach is implicitly present in the attitude of most Christians who have an interest in the Holy Land even though it might not be expressed as such. What pilgrims understand intuitively is what Kenneth Cragg articulates, that they are holy by association:

> Land or place are not, then, as in Judaic dogma, inherently 'holy', but can be regarded so by virtue of what has happened in them. The holy aura they then possess is governed by the drama they served to stage or locate. Such, broadly, is the associationism that underlies Christian pilgrimage and its accompanying sense of the sacrament of geography. If the land is held holy it is by dint of divine dramas, not divine donation. The significance of a drama may be carried without essential loss across endless territories, none having exclusive prerogative even if one has the sole honour of incidence. Events, in that sense, will not engender a kind of idolatry to which places are vulnerable.[15]

A Sacred Geography Emerges

Cragg refers to the 'accompanying sense of the sacrament of geography'. The importance of places other than Jerusalem which had been sanctified by 'divine drama' was important in the early Church, as is evidenced in the emergence of *martyria*, the development of which is explained by Robert Wilken:

> From early times Christians gathered for worship to the places where the faithful departed had been buried. Like Greeks and Romans who built shrines to mark the place where they buried their famous dead or celebrated the exploits of mythical heroes, Christians

---

[14] Davies, J. G. (1988), 29.
[15] Cragg, K. (1997), 84.

constructed memorials to their dead. Called *martyria* (places that bear witness), these rooms were erected over the site where the martyr had been buried.[16]

In implying that the place itself bears witness, the term *martyria* is instructive. Acknowledgement is given to the involvement of the place itself in devotion being real and meaningful. The earliest testimony we have to this practice is a letter from the community at Smyrna to that at Philomelium describing the martydom of its bishop, Polycarp, sometime between 155 and 160 AD,[17] and the writing gives the impression that this was nothing new. Thus, the notion of holiness being associated with a place and that holiness enduring across time has been a part of the Christian tradition from at least the second century. Christians gathered at the anniversary of the saint's martyrdom and visited graves for prayer at other times. In the late second century Gaius of Rome writes to the Phyrgian Proclus that if he were to visit Rome he would be able to see the monuments (*tropia*) of the Roman Church's founding apostles.[18] The graves of Peter and Paul were known and venerated by early Christians: excavations below the high altar of St Peter's basilica have uncovered a large number of graffiti, some of which date from the second century, invoking the apostles' prayers. The importance of the material as a result of the incarnation was recognized very early, as was the association of holy places with people, living or dead, and we see operating the equation of God, people, and place.

As with Jerusalem and other sites in the Holy Land, the conversion of Constantine gave great impetus to pilgrimage, in particular to Rome. The poems of Prudentius whose *Peristephanon*, published in 405, celebrates a host of martyrs associated with the city. In the fourth century Damasus had opened up the catacombs and restored the tombs of the martyrs so that they became more pilgrimage shrines than cemeteries – a practice to which Gregory the Great (560–604) had lent his authority.[19] For Gregory, the most precious relics were the chains of St Peter: he would send filings enclosed in crosses to his friends. St John Chrysostom speaks of his desire to enter St Paul's cell, 'consecrated by this prisoner' and behold his fetters.[20]

Gradually, centres of pilgrimage emerged all over Europe: there were, among many others, shrines to St Martin and St Denys in France, St Francis in Italy and St James in Spain. Their multiplication was given huge impetus in the eleventh and twelfth centuries by the loss of the Holy Land: the inaccessibility of the latter gave rise to a whole sacred landscape in Europe. It is difficult for us to overestimate the importance which relics, holy places, the cult of the saints and pilgrimage had in medieval Christianity. We might note, too, that this association of holy places with the cult of the saints mean that the approach to place in medieval pilgrimage was relational. As Peter Brown puts it, pilgrims were 'not merely going to a place; they were going to a place to meet a person'.[21]

---

[16] Wilken, R. (1992), 91.

[17] *The Martrydom of Polycarp*, 18.2–3 in Staniforth, M. (1968), *Early Christian Writings*, Harmondsworth: Penguin.

[18] Although the *Dialogue against Proclus*, written in the late second century, is lost, this passage is quoted by Eusebius. See Eusebius (1965).

[19] Dudden, F. H. (1915), 278.

[20] John Chrysostom, *Homiliae in Epistolam ad Ephesios*, 8.2.

[21] Brown, P. (1981), 88.

Shrines were associated with the life and witness of holy men and women, but with their popularity and the inevitable incentive for financial gain which it presented, it is not surprising that there was abuse. The growth of the system of indulgences whereby a pious act such as a pilgrimage received a reward in the form of remission of time in purgatory, was an aberration which helped spark the Reformation. It was a system which was very much bound up with pilgrimage, and it helped to reinforce the idea of a pilgrimage as a transaction (as Urban II realized in granting indulgences to crusaders, it was also useful as an incentive). There was also straightforward dishonesty: Thomas More wrote of fraud at shrines in England and Germany.[22] Despite such abuse, the development of *martyria*, and from it the cult of saints and relics, allowed what Hunt has referred to as 'the dislocation of space and time'. Gathering at the place where the body of the saint lay as opposed to the site of martyrdom where he or she had been 'born' (martyred) was 'an assertion of identity which transplanted them not only spatially outwards from the centres of secular life, but also temporally backwards into the history of their community – actually, so it was firmly held, into the presence of the sainted martyr'.[23] This meant that the holy place was the spot which bridged the gulf between past and present, between living and dead.

Pilgrimage to sites which speak by their history, their story, of divine human encounter have thus served, across the generations, to root the Christian community in its identity. This understanding fits well with the sacramental notion of certain places being given different coordinates, as discussed above. In the UK, the Venerable Bede, who died in 735, mentions visits to the graves of Alban, Oswald, Chad and Cuthbert, among others. English consciousness of many of the holy sites of the Middle Ages remains: from Canterbury, where the shrine of St Thomas was located, to Durham, where St Cuthbert lay; from St Albans, place of the death of the protomartyr, to Ely and the shrine of St Etheldreda; from St Edward's resting place in Westminster Abbey to St Swithun in Winchester. These shrines constitute the coordinates of a sacred geography which was very powerful and still has meaning, despite centuries of repression. It has the power to speak of a God who revealed himself in the incarnation, and does so still in the lives of those who live in the faith of that incarnation.

An Authentic Christian Phenomenon?

There are many today who are suspicious of the notion of pilgrimage. Why is this? Some claim that it has been opposed by many from the earliest times. Gregory of Nyssa is often cited in this regard. After the experience of going to Jerusalem in the year 379, he argued that change from one place to another does not draw one any closer to God and that the altars of his native Cappadocia are no less holy than those in Jerusalem. He writes: 'What advantage, moreover, is reaped by him who reaches those celebrated spots themselves? He cannot imagine that his Lord is living, in the body, there at the present day, but has gone away from us (who are not there); or that

---

[22] More, Thomas (1557).
[23] Hunt, D. in Brown, D. and Loades, A. (1995), 63.

the Holy Spirit is in abundance in Jerusalem but unable to travel as far as us.'[24] What is not quoted is the fact that in another letter Gregory refers to the 'holy places' as 'saving symbols'.[25] Early criticism of pilgrimage is often simply protest against abuse. Gregory, for instance, bewails the fact that Jerusalem was full of 'evil, adultery, stealing and idolatry, and that in no other city were people 'so ready to kill each other'.[26] Modern critics like Peter Walker suggest that such abuse was in stark contrast to the growing Christian belief in Jerusalem as the holy city: 'The myth thus needed to be maintained in the face of unobliging reality. A "holy city" was one thing, a true renewal of Christian commitment within the city was quite another.'[27]

Do such aberrations mean that the holiness of Jerusalem is rendered null and void, and that pilgrimage is to be discouraged? Surely not. Walker's remarks show that, like Susan White whom I quoted above, he is only prepared to ground holiness in people, and is looking for support for this position from whomever he can find it. His is a common Protestant interpretation of the Christian tradition, but it is not the only one and, as I have tried to show, the scriptures and the Christian tradition can be construed to support the notion of holiness being associated with places of divine disclosure and, further, that abuse cannot eradicate the effects of that having happened. Walker himself acknowledges that 'theological thinking can rarely, if ever, be done in a vacuum; a theologian's context invariably results in certain theological truths receiving greater emphasis than others.'[28] With this in mind, we should remember that Gregory of Nyssa had his own axes to grind which coloured his interpretation: he was determined to bring every argument possible to bear in order to demonstrate that his own see of Cappadocia was just as good as that of Jerusalem. He was not against the material as such: Hunt points us to a sermon of his in which the saint honours the relics of the martyr Theodore in lavish terms: 'Those who behold them embrace them as though the actual body, applying all their senses, eyes, mouth and ears; then they pour forth tears for his piety and suffering, and bring forth their supplications to the martyr as if he were present.'[29]

In fact, comment on pilgrimage by the Church Fathers was generally encouraging, except for the fact that they sometimes saw the need to redress a balance and encourage people to see that it was possible to seek holiness away from holy sites as well as at them. Jerome, writing in the fourth century, was one of those most in favour of pilgrimage but he wrote: 'access to the court of heaven is as easy from Britain as it is from Jerusalem.'[30] Similarly, St Augustine wrote: 'God is everywhere, it is true, and that He that made all things is not contained or confined to dwell in any place' – but this did not stop him from sending a priest accused of sexual scandal to the shrine of St Felix of Nola, which he characterized as: 'a holy place, where the more awe

---

[24] Gregory of Nyssa, *Second Epistle*, 85, in Gregory of Nyssa, Saint, *Gregorii Nysseni Epistulae* (Leiden: E. J. Brill, 1952), 13, quoted in Walker, P. W. L. (ed.) (1992).

[25] Ibid., 20.

[26] Ibid., 13.

[27] Walker, P. (1992), 85.

[28] Ibid., 87.

[29] Davies, J. G. (1988), 29.

[30] Jerome, *Epistolae*, 47.2

inspiring works of God might more readily make manifest the evil of which either of them was conscious.' So far as God's wisdom is concerned in this, Augustine asks: 'Who can search out His reason for appointing some places rather than others to be the scene of miraculous interpositions?'[31]

Some modern scholars who are opposed to pilgrimage have sought to show that pilgrimage is a syncretistic phenomenon. So, at the end of an investigation into Christians and holy places, Joan Taylor concludes:

> The concept of the intrinsically holy place was basically pagan, and was not in essence a Christian idea.... The idea of sanctified places, to which pilgrims might come to pray, cannot, however, be found in Christian teaching prior to Constantine, and certainly not in any Jewish Christian 'theology' that might be traced back to the very origins of the church. It would appear rather that the idea of the holy place is dangerously close to idolatry.[32]

I have sought to show that Taylor's analysis is incorrect. The notion of the holiness of place can be seen to derive directly from the scriptures, and was an essential part of the Christian tradition from the beginning of Christian history. It is clear, from both the scriptures and the tradition, that God chooses some places for self-revelation to people, just as God chose one place for the incarnation. It cannot be otherwise since, as we have seen, places are the seat of meeting and interaction between God and the world. It is not that some places are intrinsically holy, but that this self-revelation on the part of God is then built into their story, and this makes such places worthy of pilgrimage. It puts people in touch with their Christian story, their roots. There then develops a three-way relationship between people, place, and God which endures across time. In other words, it is not that God has chosen some places in preference to others, but rather that holy places point to the redemption of all places in Christ. Places have a story, and sacred places are those places whose story is associated with God's self-revelation and with the lives of the holy. These, then, are places which attract pilgrimage. Pilgrimage is a very powerful model which links people, places, and God together in a way which has great potential because it is dynamic and yet it also *roots* people. Philip Sheldrake tells us: 'The importance of pilgrimage and journey in the Celtic tradition, balanced with a strong sense of place, are sentiments that are very much in tune with the experience and temper of our own age. We seek both firm roots and yet a capacity to deal with continuous change.'[33]

It would be foolish to pretend that attachment to the Holy Land has not led to some pretty ugly episodes in the Church's history. The crusades, beginning with Pope Urban II's preaching a holy war against Islam, were an attempt to 'rescue' the Holy Land from several centuries of Muslim rule. By advocating a crusade, he united 'the paradigm of pilgrimage to Jerusalem ... with the chivalrous ideals and opportunist potential of war. Not only was this a pious war, a war fought to rescue the holy city of Jerusalem, but it was a war sanctioned, blessed and advocated by the apostolic successor to St Peter himself.'[34] The pull of the crusades was immense, and the

---

[31] Augustine, Letter 78.
[32] Taylor, J. E. (1993), 341.
[33] Sheldrake, P. (1995), 3.
[34] Coleman, S. and Elsner, J. (1995), 32.

effects of war disastrous. But this, as well as the abuses which developed prior to the Reformation, is just that – abuse – and should not be seen to detract from the legitimacy of pilgrimage as a Christian phenomenon. We might ask whether much modern criticism of pilgrimage is not yet another manifestation of the prejudice against place that has arisen in the Church and the world during the period of modernity.

There has been, in the recent past, a great resurgence in books of popular piety encouraging pilgrimage in the Reformed tradition. Though they make much of the notion of journey as a model for understanding the Christian life, they make little mention of the importance of the destination. In a book entitled *Pilgrims*, Stephen Platten reminds us that the image of pilgrimage was used for the life of the individual in medieval times when actual pilgrimage was an integral part of Christian life and commitment, and tells us: 'the lines remain interesting since they show how the theme of the spiritual journey had taken root in the soul of humankind.' He goes on to argue that 'pilgrimage has remained both a practical expression of religious faith and also an image applied down the ages to the journey of human life and existence', and that 'the reformers sought to drive out idolatry; the writers of the Enlightenment effectively undermined what they believed to be superstition. The broader understanding of pilgrimage, however, which used the term as a way of understanding one's life, remained an image rich in its resonances.'[35] Although one might quarrel with the fact that concentration is sometimes too exclusively on journey and too little on destination – something which arises, perhaps, as a result of sensitivity to the criticisms of people like Joan Taylor – it is true that the symbolic nature of the journey made is a vital ingredient of the whole. J. G. Davies points out that when making pilgrimage, people are embodying in a journey what is related to the experimental, ritualistic and social dimensions of religion. Thus, a pilgrimage centre is 'universally regarded as a place of intersection between everyday life and the life of God. It is a geographical location that is worthy of reverence because it has been the scene of a manifestation of divine power or has association with a holy person'.[36]

The anthropologists Victor and Edith Turner characterize pilgrimage as a liminoid phenomenon. A limen is, literally, a threshold, and a pilgrimage provides a highly valued route to a liminal world where the ideal is felt to be real, where people can feel cleansed and renewed. Both the journey and the place have great symbolic significance. Pilgrimage, they suggest:

> has some of the attributes of liminality in passage rites: release from mundane structure; homogenization of status; simplicity of dress and behavior; communitas; ordeal; reflection on the meaning of basic religious and cultural values; ritualized enactment of correspondences between religious paradigms and shared human experiences; emergence of the integral person from multiple personae; movement from a mundane center to a sacred periphery which suddenly, transiently, becomes central for the individual, an axis mundi of his faith; movement itself, a symbol of communitas, which changes with time, as

---

[35] Platten, S. (1996), 12, 14.
[36] Davies, J. G. (1988), 1.

against stasis, which represents structure; individuality posed against the institutionalised milieu.[37]

The place becomes, for those who visit it, a limen, and so symbolic of journey to the divine. Thus what people experience is very similar to what I have described, after Brown and Loades, as alternative coordinates.

But the impetus is human as well as divine. The geographer Yi-Fu Tuan speaks of the way in which pilgrimage can combine the need for human beings to be 'in place' with the opportunity to transcend place and so be 'out of place' to break up the dreariness of routine, expand horizons and allow us to achieve a balance between attachment to place and the realization that it is but a 'temporary abode'.[38] Eamon Duffy takes a similar line in his reassessment of the meaning of the cult of the saints in the Late Middle Ages from a modern Catholic perspective. He argues that pilgrimage had important symbolic and integrative functions in 'helping the believer to place the religious routine of the closed and concentric worlds of household, parish, or guild in a broader and more complex perception of the sacred, which transcended while affirming local allegiances'.[39]

It should be said that pilgrimage is universal in its appeal to humanity, and that our designation of a pilgrimage site as one with which the manifestation of the divine to human beings is associated is by no means confined to Christian sites. This might be seen by some as lending weight to the assertion of people like Taylor, quoted above, that it is 'not a Christian idea', and that it is therefore dangerously close to idolatry. Against this, however, we could argue that the phenomenon of pilgrimage speaks to a need deep within the human heart to which the incarnational character of the Christian faith has a decisive answer. The fact that anthropologists and others can analyse ritual from their own perspective should make us more confident about it, rather than less. Christian pilgrimage is, at any rate, always distinct as a result of its Christocentric character, as Davies reminds us:

> He who is believed to be the beginning and the end, the door and the way, summons his disciples to take up their crosses and follow him, as he himself walked the *via crucis* and thereby voluntarily submitted himself to the will of his heavenly Father. Even when the destination is the tomb of a saint, the Christo-centric nature of the devotion is not lost because all the saints are only of importance as so many examples of different ways to imitate their Master.[40]

It may be that the contemporary increase in interest in pilgrimage is an example of grassroots protest against the loss of place imposed on Christians by modernism and reformed Christianity. The growth is marked. This may be because pilgrimage offers us a dynamic model to link people, place, and God, and if we miss place out of the equation we shall not be making good use of that model. Neither shall we be true to human and Christian experience. In an age when people feel disorientated and cut off

---

[37] Turner V. and Turner E. (1978), 34.

[38] Tuan, Y.-F. (1984), 3–10.

[39] Duffy, E. (1992), 197.

[40] Davies, J. G. (1988), 2.

from their roots, a Christian approach to combating such a sense of alienation is to plug into sacred landscapes. So, as Davies puts it, pilgrimage may help people to overcome a sense of separation:

> Hence while there are few grounds, if any, for linking pilgrimage in the twentieth century with all the penitential aspects of the Middle Ages, there is no reason why a repentant sinner should not take the road with the same hope and intention as those who wrote the psalms so many centuries ago. The Bible in fact does provide examples and interpretations that are directly relevant to a contemporary theory of pilgrimage. This does not require the adoption of a medieval literalism as when the pilgrims of that epoch adopted the very garb of the Israelites on the first night of the first Passover. This is not the essence of pilgrimage, but if the biblical teaching is to be taken seriously it is not to be forgotten that the image combines two aspects. The first aspect of pilgrimage is the one mentioned just above, i.e. the sense of alienation but felt as a distance from one's true country; the second aspect is a sense of belonging, belonging to heaven which is one's true homeland. These dimensions of Christian discipleship find expression in the imagery of a journey from earth to heaven and in the practical exercise of travelling through space from here to there. In this way, as F.C. Gardiner has pointed out, there emerges an emotional landscape that provides us with a framework of ultimate destiny so that pilgrims are stimulated to hope and to seek for the transcendent promised at the end of their journey.[41]

Davies' words remind us that if pilgrimage is a journey, it is a journey to a particular place, and that the destination is seen as being symbolic of a heavenly one. Having established that pilgrimage is an authentic Christian phenomenon, I now look at how we might understand the nature of the destination of a pilgrimage.

Shrines

In what follows I shall argue that the best term to describe the destination of a pilgrimage is a *shrine*, which John V. Taylor characterizes as: 'a permanent and much needed reminder that this is not a human-centred universe: it revolves round God and for God'.[42] It is, in other words, a place which witnesses (like *martyria*) to the fact that God *has* acted in history in Christ and in those who have followed him faithfully in the past; that God *is* acting in the world in and through the lives of those who dedicate themselves to his will and whose witness is encouraged by sacramental encounters and the witness of holy places; and that God *will* act in history to consummate all places in Christ. It represents, in one place, all three aspects of the phenomenon of pilgrimage and the Christian commitment which it symbolizes. This was clear to the medieval pilgrim, since at that time the importance of buildings and not just journeys as symbols was recognized. The very shape of great medieval shrines spoke of journey – from west to east, from fallenness towards redemption and sanctification. James Jones illustrates this with respect to Chartres:

---

[41] Ibid., 212. The reference is to Gardiner, F. C. (1971), 11.

[42] J. V. Taylor, unpublished lecture, Heritage and Renewal', commemorating the 25th anniversary of the founding of the Guild of Guides of Winchester Cathedral, 14 September 1995.

Christianity is a progressive religion in which man moves from a state of original sin towards a greater understanding of God. Every pilgrim accepts a hierarchy of ideas when he comes to the cathedral, like the west being more mundane, from which he enters to look towards the altar and the rising sun at the east. His place is the nave, and he prays towards the choir. Within that lay the altar, and beyond that the invisible eastern doors that led to paradise. Like the Heavenly Jerusalem, the church had twelve gates facing the four directions, and though the eastern ones were real, they were not of this world and therefore not visible. This axis represents man's understanding of the divine, and could therefore be called the axis of Understanding.[43]

The Past: The Shrine as Memorial

Shrines root people in their sacred past and the history of the Christian community of which they are a part. Shrines are 'permanent antennae of the Good news linked to decisive events of evangelisation or of the life of faith of peoples and of communities. Every shrine can be considered a bearer of a specific message, in as much as today it represents the founding event of the past, which continues to speak to the heart of pilgrims.'[44] These words come from a document entitled *The Shrine: Memorial, Presence and Prophecy of the Living God*, distributed by the Pontifical Council for the Pastoral Care of Migrants and Itinerant People in Rome in 1999, which contains some valuable insights into the operation of a Christian shrine to which I shall make critical reference. The document speaks imaginatively of shrines functioning like milestones that guide the journey of the children of God on earth. We might add that these milestones operate on the alternative coordinates to which I have made reference in order to guide the people of God on their earthly journey according to a sacred geography. As such, the shrine has a universal and a local dimension. As a 'permanent antenna of the good news', it points to Christian salvation history wrought for all peoples everywhere in Christ. However, it has a local dimension – that of the particular impact of that good news upon the 'life of faith' of the people and community in which it is set. On this account, then, the efficacy of the shrine as a place which can speak to the heart of pilgrims results from the Christian history of salvation and the manifestation of that history in a particular place. It is not that the shrine is somewhere which is intrinsically holy.

An alternative view is expressed by Angela Tilby in arguing for the role of cathedrals as 'monuments of cosmic religion'. She draws parallels between a cathedral understood as a shrine and a Hindu temple, points out that it has often been suggested that some of our ancient cathedrals are built on the site of pre-Christian shrines, and goes on: 'I suppose it is conceivable that there may be some continuous memory of the sacredness of certain places, of a religion more ancient than Christianity associated with them, for which the use of the word "temple", with its pagan as well as Jewish overtones, might be a kind of verbal relic.'[45] In support of this speculation, she goes on to cite the findings of Kathleen Basford whose work on the strange phenomenon of carved foliate heads in the stonework of a number of

---

[43] James, J. (1982), 85.

[44] *The Shrine: Memorial, Presence and Prophecy of the Living God*, distributed by the Pontifical Council for the Pastoral Care of Migrants and Itinerant People (1999), 2.

[45] Tilby, A. in Platten, S. and Lewis, C. (1998), 159, 163.

medieval cathedrals has led her to believe that 'it was not simply that things could be used as symbols, or be invested with symbolic meaning by human beings. They were symbols, and the task was to discover their intrinsic significance as such.'[46] Without entering into a discussion about whether some existing places of worship are sited on pre-Christian worship sites, we should reiterate what is being proposed in this book: that only what has happened in them as Christian places of worship has any significance for the Christian. They are places where God has revealed himself and where 'prayer has been valid'.

The Vatican document *The Shrine* suggests that, as a place of memorial of the powerful action of God in history, the shrine is, in biblical tradition, not simply 'the fruit of human work, filled with cosmological or anthropological symbolism, but gives witness to God's initiative in communicating himself to human persons to stipulate with them the pact of salvation. The significant meaning of every shrine is to be a reminder in the faith of the salvific work of the Lord.'[47] It goes on to argue that in the same way as the shrines of the people of Israel (Shechem, Bethel, Beersheba, Silo) were all linked to stories of the Patriarchs and were memorials of the encounter of the living God, so the shrines of the Church must be memorials to encounter with that same living God who remains faithful.

The document acknowledges that the Son of God has become the new temple, the dwelling of the eternal with us, the alliance in person. But it argues that there is continuity, for just as the people of Israel looked at the temple with the eyes of faith and saw the initiative of love of the living God for humankind, Christians look in the same way at Christ, the new temple, and at the shrines that, from the edict of Constantine, they themselves built as a sign of the living Christ among us, and see that same initiative. So the shrine is the 'place of the permanent actualisation of the love of God who has planted his tent among us (cf Jn 1,14)'.[48] As an effective sign, the shrine rekindles Christian hope. The stories told in it and about it speak of the God who has made himself known to us in Christ and who comes to us still in the midst of our materiality. This potential is one that can be recognized from the perspective of social theory as articulated by Parker-Pearson and Richards:

> Our environment exists in terms of our actions and meanings: it is an existential space which is neither external object nor internal experience. Architectural space may be defined as a concretisation of this existential space. Space is perceived only as places. The environment is categorised and named. Through the cultural artefact of a name, undifferentiated space is transformed into marked and delimited place. Stories and tales may be attached to such places, making them resonate with history and experience. The culturally constructed elements of a landscape are thus transformed into material and permanent markers and authentications of history, experience, and values. Although the stories change in the retelling, the place provides an anchor of stability and credibility.[49]

The Present: The Shrine as Prophetic Presence

I spoke in the last chapter of sacramental encounter in particular places as the means

---

[46] Ibid., 161.

[47] *The Shrine: Memorial, Presence and Prophecy of the Living God* (1999), 5.

[48] Ibid., 7.

[49] Parker Pearson, M. and Richards, C. (1994), 4.

by which such places can be deemed holy and of the manner in which sacramental encounter should relate to sacramental encounter at the Eucharist. The shrine is, of course, a place of Eucharistic celebration and therefore a place of repeated sacramental encounter which can be deemed holy as a result of that encounter. Thus, holiness having been incorporated into the place as a result of sacramental event in the manner suggested in the last chapter, it is then reinforced by Eucharistic celebration. The holiness of the place does not *depend* upon current Eucharistic celebration, but there can be no doubt that the shrine is most itself when it is a place of Eucharistic celebration, just as the people of God is most characteristically the people of God when at Eucharist. If the Eucharist is not frequently celebrated in the shrine in the here and now, it will have been in the past, and it will only become most fully itself again when such celebration resumes. That is not to say that its 'holy' character will change immediately and irrevocably if such celebration ceases for, as I have argued, its status is not derivative of ethics in the here and now, but of association with the divine in the past. It is, however, to suggest that the *fullness* of its witness requires it. In Eucharistic worship, a connection is made between our embodied condition, the flesh and blood of Christ, the Eucharist, and the new creation of the end times. As Irenaeus puts it:

> Since, then, the cup and the bread receive the Word of God and become the Eucharist of the body and blood of Christ, and from them the substance of our flesh grows and subsists: how can they (the Gnostics) deny that the flesh is capable of the gift of God which is eternal life, that flesh which is fed by the body of the Lord and is a member of him? For blessed Paul says in his letter to the Ephesians: 'We are members of his body, of his flesh and of his bones.' He does not say of this a spiritual and invisible sort of man (for a spirit has no flesh and bones), but of man in his real constitution of flesh and nerves and blood. It is this man which receives nourishment form the cup which is his blood, and growth from the bread which is his body. And as the wood of the vine planted into the ground bears fruit in its season, and the grain of wheat falls into the ground and moulders and is raised manifold by the Spirit of God who upholds all things; and afterwards through the wisdom of God they come to be used by men, and having received the word of God become the Eucharist which is the body and blood of Christ: so also our bodies, nourished by the Eucharist, and put into the ground and dissolved therein, will rise in their season, the word of God giving them resurrection to the glory of God the Father.[50]

The Eucharist is concerned with the past, in that it takes us back to sacred history; it is linked to the present, in that it incorporates those who celebrate it into the body of Christ, and it looks to the future in that it witnesses to the consummation of all things in Christ. It is, at the same time, particular and material. All these can be said to be true of the shrine. I have already noted how a shrine has a backward-looking dimension and a material power in the present. Like the Eucharist, which, as commended by Irenaeus, has both of these, the shrine itself should not only make clear the same connection between materiality and the body of Christ, it should also point towards the end-time. I shall consider this aspect of its witness shortly. Before doing so, we should look more carefully at what both the Eucharist and the shrine can do for the people of God in the present.

---

[50] Irenaeus, *Against the Heresies*, IV.17.5.

Gerard Loughlin points out that the narrative of the last supper, which is intrinsic to the Eucharist, gives, first and quite simply, the story of a meal: 'At a certain time and in a certain place – on the night he was betrayed – a group of friends gather for a meal. Not once upon a time, but at a certain time. Not anywhere or somewhere, but there in Jerusalem.'[51] The Eucharist is bound to place and, by its very particularity, can be a potent prophetic symbol. As an example of such prophetic potential, William Cavanaugh has argued that the Eucharist offers a counter-narrative to that of globalization which, as I noted in Chapter 1, produces some of the negative and dehumanizing effects of the loss of place. He contends that although the Eucharist is done from east to west, the true catholicity of the Church does not depend on the mapping of global space since, as he reminds us, the Church gathered in the catacombs was as catholic as the Church that would 'ride Constantine's chariots to the ends of the known world'.[52] Although the Church is catholic in its missionary imperative to spread the gospel, catholicity is not dependent on extension through space. However, the Eucharist celebrated in the scattered local communities is, nevertheless, gathered up into one. This was demonstrated in the early Church, he reminds us, by the practice of setting aside a particle of the host from a Papal mass and sending out other fragments to priests celebrating masses in various other places: 'In such practices the Body of Christ is not partitioned, for the whole body of Christ is present in each fraction of the elements: the world in a wafer.' By the same liturgical action, not part but the whole Body of Christ is present in each local assembly: 'In Romans 6:23 Paul refers to the local community as *hole he ecclesia*, the whole church. Indeed, in the first three centuries the term "catholic church" is most commonly used to identify the local church gathered around the Eucharist.'[53]

Cavanaugh suggests that Catholic space is not a simple, universal space uniting individuals directly to a whole since the Eucharist 'refracts space in such a way that one becomes more united to the whole the more tied one becomes to the local. ... The transcendence of spatial and temporal barriers does not depend on a global mapping, therefore, but rather on a collapsing of the world into the local assembly.'[54] Beyond what Cavanaugh proposes, I would want to suggest that the shrine in which the Eucharist is celebrated is caught up in this transcendence that enables people to become more united to the whole the more they are united to the local. Shrines manifest an alternative geography to that of globalization and are symbols, too, of the alternative ethic and *telos* that accompany that geography.

Cavanaugh goes on to express the importance of the fact that, in the early Church, what distinguished the Christian Eucharistic community was the way it transcended natural and social divisions. In Christ there is neither Jew nor Greek, slave or free, male or female (Galatians 2:28) and it is the remarkable collapsing of spatial barriers that makes the local community truly catholic. So, too, within the shrine, there should be no social boundaries. However, Cavanaugh is aware that his description of the manner in which the Eucharist breaks down the dichotomy of the universal and the local may provoke the suspicion that the Eucharist as antidote to globalism is simply

---

[51] Loughlin, G. (1996) in Brown, D. and Loades, A. (1996), 125.
[52] Cavanaugh, W. (1999), 189.
[53] Ibid., 190.
[54] Ibid., 190.

a retreat into place-bound theocracy or sect. He points out that the Eucharist – as in some medieval Corpus Christi rites – can be used to reinforce a fixed social hierarchy within a certain location, and to exclude others, especially the Jews. Are not all Christian attempts to privilege the local, he asks: 'similarly subject to the fascist temptation, or the temptation of "sectarianism", the very antithesis of a catholicity which seeks to unify rather than divide?'[55]

Cavanaugh seeks to answer this charge by arguing that the Eucharist is not a place as such, but a story which performs certain spatial operations on places. In doing so he draws on de Certeau's distinction between maps and itineraries, which I noted in Chapter 1, and argues that stories organize and link spaces on a narrative sequence: 'They not only move from one space to another, but more accurately construct spaces through the practices of characters who trace an itinerary through the story. As such, the spatial story is not simply descriptive but prescriptive. Stories give us a way to walk.' Thus:

> The spatial story is an act of resistance to the dominant overcoding of the map. And yet it does not depend on establishing its own place, its own territory to defend. Instead it moves through the places defined by the map and transforms them to alternative spaces through its practices. The City of God makes use of this world as it moves through it on its pilgrimage to its heavenly home. But this pilgrimage is not the detachment from any and all spaces, the sheer mobility of globalism. The Eucharist journeys by telling a story of cosmic proportions within the particular face to face encounter of neighbours and strangers in the local Eucharistic gathering. In an economy of hypermobility, we resist not by fleeing but by abiding. The community may journey without leaving its particular location, because the entire world and more comes to it in the Eucharist.[56]

Following this approach, I want to argue that shrines in which the Eucharist is celebrated participate in this witness of 'telling a story of cosmic proportions', and thus to such an alternative geography by their abiding. It remains static, but embodies journey in itself, as we have seen. Cavanaugh reminds us that in the Eucharist the particular is of the utmost importance, for this particular piece of bread at this particular place and time is the body of Christ. Thus the importance of the particular, which postmodernism theology asserts against modernism, is there in the Eucharist, just as it is there (and because it is there) in the Incarnation. In the same way, the shrine is caught up with the reality of which it is symbolic. There has been much work in the recent past on the relationship between a sacrament and a symbol. Joseph Nolan, 'summing up many, many, arguments and explorations', points out that a sacrament is symbolic in that a symbol contains a reality to which it still points and is clear that to speak of something as 'only symbolic' is inaccurate. He reminds us that 'symbol' does not mean everything, but it does mean a thing on its way to becoming much more: 'For instance, in the communion of the Mass there is certainly the reality of God present. There is an enlarging of myself with my brother, with life, and with mystery that my tradition tells me is the "locus", or place, of finding God.'[57] So, too,

---

[55] Ibid., 191.

[56] Ibid., 191

[57] Nolan, J. (1981). Cf. Tillich, who, as we observed above, states that 'the symbol participates in the reality of that for which it stands' (Tillich, P., 1951, 265).

the shrine cannot be understood as 'only symbolic'. This is something the medievals understood well. James Jones, writing of Chartres again, speaks of the medieval conception of what they were building:

> Since the cathedral was to be the most divine thing on earth, as the symbol – and therefore at one with the reality itself – of Paradise, it had to incorporate every possible attribute of that spiritual reality. In our day we call the church the House of God, for his presence occupies it. But the thirteenth century was less circumspect. They had the audacity to believe they were constructing a slice of eternity itself, and the simplicity to trust that God's Essence would be made manifest in something they had built from the materials found on the earth.[58]

We might disagree with Jones' use of the term 'essence' but the substantive point remains. Cavanaugh tells us that 'the Eucharist not only tells but performs a narrative of cosmic proportions, from the death and resurrection of Christ, to the new covenant formed in his blood, to the future destiny of all creation. The consumer of the Eucharist is no longer the schizophrenic subject of global capitalism, awash in a sea of unrelated presents, but walks into a story with a past present, and future.'[59] It is this story, of course, that the pilgrim is acting out dramatically when on pilgrimage. It is from this perspective, operating on these new coordinates, that the shrine develops, like the Eucharist, a prophetic dimension.

The prophetic role for the shrine is that it should become a 'constant reminder to criticise the myopia of all human realisations, that would like to dominate as if they were absolute'. From it there should blossom the vocation of the faithful to be, in history, 'the evangelically critical conscience of human proposals, that reminds men and women of their greater destiny, that impedes them from growing wretched in the myopia of what is being done, and obliges them to unceasingly be like leaven (cf Matthew 13:33) for a more just and more humane society.'[60] So, too, the shrine should be: 'a protest against every worldly presumption, against every political dictatorship, against every ideology that wishes to say everything regarding the human being, because the shrine reminds us that there is another dimension, that of the kingdom of God that must come fully. In the shrine, the *Magnificat* resounds constantly.'[61] This ethical dimension of what happens in the shrine is vital. Louis-Marie Chauvet writes that

> the element '*Sacrament*' is thus *the symbolic place of the ongoing transition between scripture and ethics, from the letter to the body*. The liturgy is *the powerful pedagogy where we learn to consent to the presence of the absence of God who obliges us to give him a body in the world*, thereby giving the sacraments their plenitude in the 'liturgy of the neighbour' and giving ritual memory of Jesus Christ its plenitude in our existential memory.[62]

---

[58] James, J. (1982), 85.

[59] Cavanaugh, W. (1999), 192.

[60] *The Shrine: Memorial, Presence and Prophecy of the Living God* (1999), 20. See also Green, L. (2001), esp. 32ff.

[61] Ibid., 20.

[62] Chauvet, L.-M. (1997), 265, his italics.

We note that there is a very clear connection between scripture, sacrament (and therefore shrine) and ethics, but ethics do not come first. They derive from scripture and sacramental encounter, both of which are nourished by the sacrament of the shrine. Chauvet elaborates on this insight as follows:

> It is precisely because the ritual memory sends us to the existential memory that the sacraments in general, and the Eucharist in particular, constitute a *'dangerous memory'*, in the words of Metz. It is dangerous for the church and for each believer, not only because the *sequela Christi* (following of Christ) leads everyone onto the crucifying path of liberation (as much economic as spiritual, collective as personal), but because this 'following of Christ' is sacramentally the location where Christ himself continues to carry out through those who invoke him the liberation for which he gave his life. The ritual story told at each Eucharist, retelling why Jesus handed over his life, sends all Christians back to their own responsibility to take charge of history in his name; and so they become his living memory in the world because he himself is 'sacramentally' engaged in the body of humanity they work at building for him.[63]

Sacramental memory sends us out into our existential memory both in terms of developing a God-centred perception of the world and in terms of living for the ethic of the gospel. Meeting Christ in the shrine should be inseparable from meeting him in the world and living his life in the world so as to 'take charge of history in his name'. Bauerschmidt suggests that 'Christians need places precisely for the sake of resistance.'[64] What we are talking about here is the fostering of what have been termed 'communities of virtue'. Interestingly, virtue ethicists have been criticized for an emphasis upon particularity, as is evident from Cavanaugh's worry, cited above, about Christian attempts to privilege the local (being) subject to the fascist temptation, or the temptation of sectarianism. I would suggest that the development of Christian communities of virtue is profoundly connected with place, and that we should not apologize for it.

In a study of the theological ethics of Stanley Hauerwas, Samuel Wells uses the story of Le Chambon-sur-Lignon to illumine the themes of Hauerwas' work. Le Chambon is a village in the south of France where the community set about harbouring very many Jews and others under the noses of Nazi occupation at great risk to themselves during the Second World War, the story of which is well documented in papers edited by Pierre Bolle. Wells shows how Hauerwas' themes of community, narrative, virtue, habit, imagination and politics are exemplified in it *par excellence*. Having narrated the story, Wells himself says that 'Le Chambon is a geographically isolated community made up largely of one oppressed denomination. Once again, it proves very difficult to avoid spatial conceptions in describing the community of character.'[65] Certainly, the people of Le Chambon had a long history of living out a particular Protestant Christian tradition in a country which is overwhelmingly Catholic. That history could not have emerged independent of the Christian story, devotion to which was what impelled the inhabitants of le Chambon on their way. But it was also associated with a particular place and one might

---

[63] Ibid., 261.

[64] Bauerschmidt, F. (1996), 513.

[65] Wells, S. (1998), 140.

reasonably ask whether the habits of virtue which Hauerwas proposes could develop without place being taken very seriously. I would suggest that we should not be afraid to acknowledge the role of many particularities of place, including perhaps more than anything else places of worship, in encouraging habits of virtue in the manner commended by virtue ethicists. The link between churches and the communities in which they stand is a complex one. Wells is sensitive to the charge articulated above by Cavanaugh that virtue ethics might be 'simply a retreat into place-bound theocracy or sect' – a charge often levelled against the approach of Hauerwas. But if we are to talk of church buildings as being the focus of the place identity of Christian communities, there is no need for them to be any more exclusivist than the Eucharist is, according to Cavanaugh's description.

The shrine can, with the help of the narrative of the Eucharist celebrated within it, be a powerful aid to generating and sustaining Christian virtue over and against secular pressures. In this way the shrine should witness not only against the dehumanizing ignoring of place (represented by globalization) which has character-ized modernity but also against all dehumanizing aspects of a broken world. Cavanaugh tells us that in its organization of space:

> the Eucharist does not simply tell the story of a united human race, but brings to light barriers where they actually exist. When Paul discovers that the Corinthians are unworthily partaking of the Lord's supper because of the humiliation of the poor by the rich, Paul tells them, 'Indeed, there have been faction among you, for only so will it become clear who among you are genuine' (1Cor.11.9). This verse is puzzling unless we consider that the Eucharist can be falsely told as that which unites Christians around the globe while in fact some live off the hunger of others. Theologians of the Southern hemisphere remind us that the imperative of 'church unity' is often a cover for exploitation of the worst kind. In the North American context, many of our Eucharistic celebrations too have been colonised by a banal consumerism and sentimentality. The logic of globalization infects the liturgical life of the church itself; Christ is betrayed again at every Eucharist. Where the body is not discerned, Paul reminds the Corinthians, consumption of the Eucharist can make you sick or kill you (1Cor.11.30). This might explain the condition of some of our churches.[66]

Whilst acknowledging the force of Cavanaugh's words, perhaps it would be more encouraging to approach the problem from the other direction. For example, when I was incumbent of the parish in the heart of inner-city Tyneside to which I made reference in Chapter 1, and occasionally felt depressed that our church community was not as effective a sign of the kingdom as I would have liked it to have been, I would comfort myself by trying to imagining what the community at the heart of which it was set would have been like without it. I could not help but come to the conclusion that it would have been very greatly impoverished. The church was a sign of the Kingdom of God not only by virtue of the good things done corporately by its members in the way of facilities for the elderly, young children and others in need, not only by virtue of the witness of individuals in their daily lives and their worship, it was a symbol of the Kingdom simply by being there as a building which would speak to those outside it as well as those inside it, of the conviction of those who worshipped in it that this world is not a system closed unto itself, but that it is the

---

[66] Cavanaugh, W. (1999), 193.

creation of a loving God revealed in Christ. Susan Hill makes a similar point about English cathedrals:

> Durham. Westminster. Wells. Norwich. Exeter. Salisbury. Canterbury. St Paul's. Picture them. Click. Picture them gone. The idea of their absence is an absence in the heart, not an airy emptiness, a leaden one. It is a deadness. To think of the world without these cathedrals, without all cathedrals, is like a bereavement. It is painful. The loss of the buildings themselves, the grandeur, the beauty, is unimaginable – the mind veers away from it. But think of the world without the great palaces. Surely that is the same? We know, deeply, instinctively, that it is not. Destroy all the churches then. Is not that the same? We know that it is more. And that it is not merely a question of thunderbolts.[67]

Why is it not merely a question of thunderbolts? Surely because these buildings continue to witness in varying degrees against the dehumanizing effects of secularism in all its aspects, including the downgrading of the importance of place. There are, in fact, many ways in which they can be considered to act prophetically, as well as in a witness against globalization. One of these Susan Hill reflects upon when she asks: 'Where else in the heart of a city is such a place, where the sense of all past, all present, is distilled into the eternal moment 'at the still point of the turning world?'[68] She asks another rhetorical question which amplifies the point:

> But surely there are other places that will serve the purpose? To which people may come freely, to be alone among others? To pray, to reflect, to plead, gather strength, rest, summon up courage, to listen to solemn words. What are these other places? To which the pilgrim or the traveller, the seeker, the refugee, the petitioner or the thanksgiver may quietly come, anonymously, perhaps, without fear of comment or remark, question or disturbance.[69]

Earlier in this book we mentioned the approach of Christopher Rowland who is suspicious of cathedrals because, in part, of his perception of their lack of prophetic edge. I would suggest that there is more prophetic potential in shrines than he is prepared to recognize, and that if we were able to understand our churches and cathedrals in the manner I have been attempting to elucidate there would be no question of them being anything but a challenge to the mores of secular modernism. However, there should, at the same time, be no doubt about the need for continual penitence:

> The shrine makes us recognise, on the one hand, the holiness of those to whom they are dedicated and, on the other hand, our condition as sinners who must begin the pilgrimage towards grace anew each day. In this way, they help discover that the church 'is at the same time holy and always in need of being purified' because its members are sinners.... Continuous conversion is inseparable for the proclamation of the horizon towards which theological hope stretches out. Each time the community of the faithful gathers together in the shrine, it does so to remind itself of the other shrine, the future city, the dwelling of God that we want to start building already in this world and that we, full of hope and aware of our limits, committed to the preparation, as much as possible, of the advent of the Kingdom,

---

[67] Hill, S. (1998), in Platten, S. and Lewis, C. (1998), 8.

[68] Ibid., 13.

[69] Ibid., 4.

cannot help desiring. The mystery of the shrine thus reminds the church, pilgrim on earth, of her condition of temporariness, the fact that she is walking towards a greater aim, the future homeland, that fills the heart with hope and peace.[70]

The above words from *The Shrine* make clear the need for penitence, and draw our attention to the fact that the shrine speaks not just of roots and current discipleship in the manner I have been articulating, but also of destination. For our current discipleship needs to be seen in the light not just of our Christian past and our Christian present, but of our Christian future.

The Future: The Shrine as Eschatological Sign

I have already made reference to Samuel Wells' study of the work of Stanley Hauerwas. In seeking to free Hauerwas from the criticisms that he is a 'sectarian, that he is a fideist and that he lacks a doctrine of creation', Wells suggests that greater attention should be paid to the eschatological dimensions of his ethics. At one point Wells tells us: 'Once one is committed to an ahistorical salvation, an ahistorical eschatology comes close behind. The heresy involved in both is docetism. God is so other that he could not stoop to be involved in time. The moral consequence is that Christ has no decisive relevance for ethics.'[71] Our argument here is that exactly the same applies to place, since places are the seat of relations or the place of meeting and activity in the interaction between God and the world. I have suggested that new coordinates of time *and place* are given in Christ, and that both are important. Wells goes on to suggest that 'salvation creates a new people, the eschatological people: and a characteristic of this new people is that they live in a new time – an eschatological time. In this new time the priorities of existence are transformed: activities are significant to the extent that they proclaim and accord with the new time.'[72]

Similar considerations apply to place since, as I have suggested, the New Covenant gives us new coordinates not just of time, but of space. Sacramental encounter, I argued in Chapter 3, can show place transfigured and give us a glimpse of the consummation of all things in Christ. So, too, the shrine directs us to the new coordinates of time and place, and Christians, who await Christ's return, have the conviction that all time and all places have been redeemed in him. As such they can have a cosmic symbolism, for it is the whole cosmos which has been redeemed in Christ. This was made especially clear in early Eastern churches. Here *Christus Pantocrator*, Christ in majesty, is portrayed in the main dome and surrounding vaults as ruler of the cosmos which the church represents. Below him angels pay him homage, and yet lower still we see the saints and martyrs. It is a clear vision of heaven as described in the Book of Revelation and, as Harold Turner notes: 'No pagan temple ever had a more coherent and explicit manifestation of its function as a microcosm of the universe than is to be found in the combined horizontal and vertical hierarchies of a Byzantine church'.[73]

---

[70] *The Shrine: Memorial, Presence and Prophecy of the Living God* (1999), 19.

[71] Wells, S. (1998), 147.

[72] Ibid., 147.

[73] Turner, H. (1979), 187.

This eschatological element should be reinforced by the celebration of the Eucharist within the shrine. Patristic writers emphasized the eschatological aspect of the Eucharist as foretaste of the heavenly banquet prepared for all mankind.[74] This dimension is one which is beginning to be recovered and the shrine should be able to assist this process:

> The shrine does not only remind us from where we come and who we are, but also opens our eyes to discern where we are going, towards what aim our pilgrimage in life and in history is directed. The shrine, as a work of human hands, points to the heavenly Jerusalem, our Mother, the city that comes down from God, all adorned as a bride (cf Rev 21.2), perfect eschatological shrine where the glorious divine presence is direct and personal ... in the contradictions of life, the shrine, an edifice of stones, becomes an indicator of the foreseen Homeland, although not yet possessed. Its expectation, full of faith and hope, sustains the journey of the disciples of Christ.[75]

The shrine should thus enable worshippers to live in this in-between time, and be symbolic to them of it. This the medievals understood well – it was a conscious part of their vision. In conclusion, then, we can say that the pilgrimage shrine speaks to the past, the present and the future and in so doing roots the Christian community associated with it in the Divine scheme of things as revealed in Christ.

Churches as Shrines

What I have been saying so far pertains to shrines, which are the destination of pilgrims. How, though, do we delineate between a shrine and other Christian places of worship? Gianfranco Ravasi cites Mary Lee Nolan's calculation that there are about 6000 churches that belong to the category 'shrine', which he then defines as 'that place towards which an itinerary of faith converges, almost like a halo, to celebrate a holy Christian presence and a memorial.'[76] John V. Taylor tells us that there are four categories of religious buildings world-wide: the wayside shrine, the school of religion (such as the Koranic schools or the early Wesleyan chapels), the local congregation-church and the major temple-shrine.[77] By reducing most of its churches to either 'local congregation' or 'school of religion' the Church has not done itself or the Christian faith a service. Would not the potential of all church buildings be increased if we were to think of them as shrines? They should be there not just to act as a centre for the worshipping community, but as a sign to them and to all people that God is not to be forgotten.

J. G. Taylor makes clear that the influence of a shrine is essentially centripetal, ingathering. Shrines gather in a particular manner. They gather the experiences, languages and thoughts of Christian communities and put them in touch with their sacred history so that they might truly become the body of Christ in the present and look with faith, hope and love towards the end of their journey. In thinking of places

---

[74] See Wainwright, G. (1981).

[75] *The Shrine: Memorial, Presence and Prophecy of the Living God* (1999), 17.

[76] Ravasi, G. (1999), 37.

[77] Taylor, J. V.(1993), 2.

of pilgrimage, Ravasi speaks of a centripetal movement from the outside towards that central point 'where one experiences an encounter with God, with Christ, with the history of salvation, with Mary, with the martyrs, with the saints'.[78] All churches should gather the communities in which they stand to the Christian faith as it engages with the story of that community and the world. All churches should stand in their communities as the celebration of a holy Christian presence, and a memorial – a memorial to the faithfulness of the worshipping community in that place in the past and of lives transformed and redeemed in that faithfulness.

David Harvey tells us from a discipline other than theology: 'I think that it is correct to argue that the social preservation of religion as a major institution within secular societies has been in part won through the successful creation, protection and nurturing of symbolic places.'[79] This has not been widely recognized. Many Christians became impatient with church buildings in the late twentieth century when the period of modernity reached its apotheosis. It was not just those whose Reformed theology made them suspicious of attention given to anything material which might encourage idolatry. Although the importance of holy places had been upheld by the catholic tradition throughout the times of downgrading of place by Western thought and practice, Harold Turner quotes the comment of a prominent Roman Catholic Professor of Dogmatics (whom he does not name): 'If there is one simple method of saving the church's mission it is probably the decision to abandon church buildings.'[80] I would suggest that viewing all our churches as shrines and using them as such would have a profoundly positive effect upon the witness of the Christian Church. Should not all churches be places wherein there is a history of divine self-communication, of 'sacramental encounters' with the worshipping community that inhabits them? Should not their presence in the midst of that community nourish the faith of that community? Should they not proclaim to the secular world in which they stand that God is present and active in this world? Cannot each journey made to such a church be thought of as a 'mini-pilgrimage'? In short, should not every church be understood as a shrine? This is a much richer way of looking at the potential of our buildings to lead us on in faith than is prevalent today. In operating sacramentally buildings should help focus the Christian community's attention on its prophetic task. But in order to put this contention in perspective, we must look briefly at the history of church buildings in the tradition.

In the earliest times the Christian community met in the homes of its members. The names of some of those in whose houses the community met have been recorded: Aquila and Prisca at Ephesus (Romans 16:3, 5), Nympha at Laodicea (Colossians 4:15 and Philemon) and Apphia and Archippus at Colossae (Philemon 1–2). At this stage one particular space in Christian homes was of deep significance, as Dillistone reminds us:

> It was, in the Gospel phrase, 'an upper room', large enough to contain a substantial gathering, but always within the semi-privacy of an ordinary dwelling-house. It was a room into which the faithful temporarily withdrew, in which the Lord's presence was specially

---

[78] Ravasi, G. (1999), 39.

[79] Harvey, D. (1993), 23.

[80] Turner, H. (1979), 323.

manifested, and from which there was a going-forth constantly into situations of stress and even danger. For the moment it was small in dimension but it could aptly symbolise either the growing body or the expanding temple, terms applied to the church as a whole by the apostle Paul.[81]

The assertion that 'the Lord's presence was specially manifested' in such rooms and that they could 'symbolise' the body should make us pause before suggesting that they were 'mere' meeting rooms. The Christian tradition from the earliest times has, as we have seen, been reverent towards places of divine disclosure and, according to Dillistone's definition, this is what such rooms were. Neither should it be assumed that there was no desire for something more visible. As H. W. Turner points out: 'The reason why no special buildings appeared are obvious enough: the Christians in any one place were usually not numerous and belonged on the whole to the poorer classes; local hostility was common and outbreaks of violence or of official persecution occurred from time to time until the fourth century, so that there was every incentive to maintain inconspicuous existence.'[82]

Turner goes on to say that this approach also fitted with the teaching of Jesus and with the community's understanding of itself as a new spiritual temple that abrogated the Jerusalem temple and all such sacred places. We might respond that the phenomenon of *martyria* could be seen to question this latter assumption, and that if it is true that the early Christians were opposed to buildings for theological reasons, it would be just as likely to be as a result of the fact that they expected the *parousia* imminently. The truth is that we do not know what the attitude of the early Christians to churches understood as sacred places was, even though there exist interesting remains of 'house churches' which are set aside for worship; one of the most complete examples dating from the early third century is at Dura-Europolis in Syria. What we do know is that house churches were gradually replaced by the erection of the first specifically Christian buildings, and that by the third century there must have been many of these buildings, for we know that they existed in widely flung corners of the different parts of the empire. By the turn of the century there were over forty in Rome itself.

After the legalization of the faith, there was enormous building activity. The first church buildings of this time had a form which was suggested by the secular basilica used in the legal world – St John Lateran and St Maria Maggiore in Rome are examples of this type. The word 'basilica' derives from *basileus*, an Oriental monarch in the Greek tradition after the conquests of Alexander the Great. The basilica was originally the throne room in which the *basileus* showed himself to the people. The line of pillars down the building drew the eye to the end which the people faced, and where the apse-like structure focused attention on those who stood in front of it. The Bishop would have taken the place of the *basileus* in the Christian's basilicas. Richard Giles decries the choice of basilica as model, rather than temple or synagogue or house, for in so doing the Church thereby: 'aligned itself with secular authority in an extremely high profile manner, the basilica was an imposing civic building redolent with the power and the glory of the Roman Empire. The type of

---

[81] Dillistone, F. (1973), 89.
[82] Turner, H. W. (1979), 158.

building previously associated in every town with the dispensation of law and order now became synonymous with Christian assembly.'[83] He sees the move from 'house' to 'palace', from property to privilege, echoing precisely the Jewish movement from tent to temple between Abraham and Solomon. Presumably, in view of how he describes the building of the temple in Jerusalem as an act of apostasy, he feels that the construction of such buildings was the same. He contends, however, that although the Church may have been disobedient in littering the face of the earth with so many sanctuaries: 'it has been gloriously disobedient, erecting in every corner of the world countless buildings, all of which have a special character all of their own, most of which enable their users to glimpse the glory of the Kingdom, and many of which bring people to their knees in wonder and thanksgiving to God.'[84] In other words, although he goes on to suggest many wonderfully innovative ways in which the Church can make use of its buildings, he feels that this is really just making use of the mammon of unrighteousness.

Against Giles, we might say that it is perhaps understandable that Christians in Constantine's time, after generations of enforced secrecy, vulnerability and humiliation, wanted their churches to symbolize other strands in the Christian narrative: of the authority, the grandeur and the glory of God. My own conviction, flowing from my proposition that both scripture and tradition bid us hold a trinity of God, people and place in creative tension, is that church buildings can and should operate sacramentally as shrines. In fact, I would go so far as to suggest that buildings do symbolize in a very powerful fashion the faith that they represent, whether we like it or not. Giles more or less accepts this when he says:

> When it comes to the environment of worship, we should never underestimate the influence of our building upon the way we think about God, about each other, and about the relative importance of the activity we have come together to engage in. ... All Christians (even those whose dogmatic formulations tell them otherwise!) are fully aware in daily life of the power of sacramental signs. Exactly why the bunch of flowers should nearly always do the trick, why we can almost hear them speak the words 'I am sorry' or 'I love you', is a total mystery, but it works.[85]

Giles implies that church buildings operate 'sacramentally', but invokes the term 'mystery' too soon. There will always remain a mysterious element to sacraments, but sacramentality is a category that flows directly from scripture and tradition, and is not just something we observe to be true to our experience, as Giles suggests. There is a straightforward aspect, too, of course: the function of the sign, in part, is to teach the faith. St Gregory the Great in the sixth century observed that 'the image is to the illiterate what scripture is to those who can read, for in the image even the illiterate can see what they have to.'[86] Thus great churches have a sacred purpose of educating the faithful – but not *just* in terms of learning facts about the faith. Education operates at deeper levels than the didactic.

---

[83] Giles, R. (1995), 37.

[84] Ibid., 28.

[85] Ibid., 57.

[86] Gregory the Great, *Epistle*, 2.13.

Until the Reformation, sacred place was valued very highly in Christendom, and the practice of pilgrimage which we have examined had a huge impact upon church building, reinforcing a concentration upon the sacramental power of the material. P. T. Forsyth speaks of the intentional power to lift the soul which gripped the medieval designers. The Gothic church, he says, was thrust like a fine question heavenward.[87] Interestingly, in Renaissance design the vertical thrust is cut off by the more dominant horizontal. Might it be that whereas Gothic buildings were intended to be a *sursum corda* in stone – their effect being to lift the heart to God – Renaissance buildings were more about a celebration of humanity? The effect of great Gothic buildings must have been all the more remarkable when the majority of those visiting a cathedral or great church came from small wattle-and-daub dwellings. The architectural skill, sheer size, vivid colour, graceful architecture and surpassing beauty of these buildings will have had a great impact. There was in this architecture and the theology that lay behind it a tremendous embracing of the physical as a vehicle for the spiritual. The artist Rodin wrote of Gothic architecture in the fateful year 1914 in ecstatic terms:

> Built in anticipation of the multitude and designed for the multitude, speaks the grand and simple language of masterpieces. I should like to inspire a love for this great art, to come to the rescue of as much of it as still remains intact; to save for our children the great lesson of this past which the present misunderstands. In this desire I strive to awaken intellects and hearts to understanding and to love. ... For we no longer understand them, idle despite our agitation, blind in the midst of splendours. If we could but understand Gothic art, we should irresistibly be led back to truth.[88]

The Reformation marked a huge break for much of Western Christendom. The Reformers were determined that churches would become simply meeting houses, and in the process destroyed a great deal of fine religious art. However, those buildings that were defaced rather than destroyed retained the power of a sign, even though what was being signalled had changed. So, in thinking about Eucharistic presence, Denys Turner meditates upon the once medieval Catholic, now Calvinist, cathedral at Berne in Switzerland. He observes that in altars stripped, niches empty, walls whitewashed, glass plain and orientation reversed, one is confronted by a visibly Calvinist architectural revision which is all the more striking because of our knowledge of architectural history and therefore of what is missing:

> Its former ornateness of iconography, lurid colour schemes, its architectural orientation towards a high-altar; for the overwhelming sense of 'absence' is reinforced by the more

---

[87] He elaborates: 'The pointed arch, reproduced in great and small throughout the fabric, the upright line instead of the classic horizontal, the vast height of the pillars prolonged into the roof, the effect produced by bundles of small pillars rolled into one column, and carrying the eye upward along their small light shafts, the judicious use of external carving, so as to add to the effect of height instead of reducing it, the pinnacles and finials which run up everywhere on the outside, the tower, and still more the spire, placed above all these – the total effect was to make the spirit travel upwards with the eye and lose itself in the infinity of space' (Forsyth, P. T., 1911), *Christ on Parnassus*, London: Hodder and Stoughton, quoted in Turner, H. (1979), 192.

[88] Rodin, A. (1965), 8.

absolute and architecturally organic effect of the gothic style itself which, I suppose, could be said to give priority to the engineering and organisation of space rather than to the articulation of solid mass. Berne cathedral is, one might say, a place of absence, a place fit for a community witnessing to absence. It 'speaks' absence as a theological – and still to some degree as a theological-polemical – and liturgical statement.[89]

Turner contrasts this with the richness of the cathedral in 1500, which he characterizes as: 'a statement of holy presence, a fullness of theological affirmation, a space filled with presence and with a community *in* that presence.' I catalogued in Chapter 1 the demise of place in Western thought, and noted that it is surely no coincidence that a theology which downgraded particularity arose in conjunction with a science which looked to infinity, and a cartography which replaced the 'itinerary' with the 'map' and so homogenized space. If religious buildings in the Protestant era still acted as a sign, they were, as Turner points out above, signs of absence, reinforcing the belief that God was not to be identified with any particular place. The danger, surely, is that in refusing to identify God with the particular, the Reformed tradition has fuelled the rise of a secular conviction that God is not just absent, but non-existent.

Holding out against this development, the Roman Catholic Church continued to value place in popular piety until the mid-twentieth century. In speaking of the Church before 1965, Lawrence Cunningham recalls:

> Over the arch of the main door of our parish church which led from the vestibule was the Latin phrase *Haec est porta Caeli* – 'This is the gate of heaven'. To step through that portal was to leave the world of the profane (*profanum* means 'outside the temple') for the world of the sacred. The boundary of vestibule/nave was further circumscribed by the communion rail beyond which priests and acolytes entered for the weekday celebration of the liturgy. … If there was any doubt about the sacred nature of that space deduced from the architecture, the elaborate courtesy demanded of those who entered provided a forceful reminder of where they were. The holy water stoops, the covered heads of the women and the bareness of the men (save for the various chapeaus of the clergy), the complex gestures of reverence (genuflections when the Blessed Sacrament was present; bows when it was not), the requirement of silence, and the orchestrations of sitting, standing, and kneeling all contributed to the sacred atmosphere of the church.[90]

However, all this was to change in the wake of the Second Vatican Council which welcomed into Catholic theology and practice the assumptions of modernity that had long been assimilated by the Reformed tradition. Cunningham goes on to characterize the changes of Vatican II as a shift from emphasis on sacred space to sacred time, meaning an emphasis on the church not so much as a place where God dwells, but as a locus for those times when the faithful gather to hear the word of God and make sacramentally present Jesus who is the Christ.

I have noted the way in which time became a dominant preoccupation in late modernity and the developments of Vatican II are perhaps better understood in that light. There was also, in accord with our observation that the Vatican Council laid

---

[89] Turner, D. (1999), 155.
[90] Cunningham, L. (1988), 237.

great stress on the church as sacrament, an accompanying stress on people. The ecclesiastical and liturgical consequences of Vatican II have served to concentrate attention upon people and community, and although this has resulted in many good things, there has been an accompanying shift away from the appreciation of the significance of place which speaks in its symbolic language to tell us that:

> You are not here to verify
> Instruct yourself, or inform curiosity
> Or carry report. You are here to kneel
> Where prayer has been valid.[91]

This does not seem to be the case in modern Roman Catholic churches. One can still go into Westminster Cathedral and find more than a few people engaged in prayer in its dark, cavernous and shrine-like atmosphere. This would have once been so in many Roman Catholic churches, but the latter are now treated simply as 'worship spaces' which are closed except for the celebration of the liturgy on Sunday (or, for most people, Saturday evening). In the Church of England, the increasing influence of those with a suspicion of sacrament and the notion of holiness being associated with place has meant a move away from the sense of churches being 'holy places' which had, to some extent at least, been recaptured in the wake of the Oxford Movement. The way in which most Anglicans and Roman Catholics now treat their churches is similar to that which has always pertained in Methodist, Presbyterian and other Churches of the Reformed tradition, and this has been a great impoverishment. The irony about all this is that supporters of these developments would see them as a return to gospel roots whereas, in the light of our study, we would perhaps better characterize them as a final capitulation to modernity.

Despite all this, there has remained appreciation of the sanctity of place in the most unlikely areas: even meeting places which, unlike the Reformed cathedral described by Denys Turner above, were built to be nothing more, develop a sacred power. Harold Turner quotes an article from *The Friend*, the journal of the Religious Society of Friends, which reads:

> Places and things do not hallow people but the enduring faith of people may hallow places. Where you are sitting in that calm cool place there has been unbroken prayer and worship generation after generation. In the outward and inner silences there … you may realise that … 'we are surrounded by a great cloud of witnesses' … you cannot but 'be the better for coming here'.[92]

Thus a building, even when empty, speaks of its use, which will prompt us to regard it as more-than-ordinary. However, much of the force of Reformed theology and practice was to militate against such re-emergence of a sense of holy place.

The force of all that I have been saying in the previous chapters is that the Christian faith cannot and should not, if it is to remain true to its roots rather than become enslaved to secular modernity, surrender to this lack of awareness of the significance

---

[91] Eliot, T .S., 'The Four Quartets' in Eliot, T. S. (1969), 192.
[92] Nicholson, F. J. (1979), 327.

of place. Churches viewed as shrines should witness to this importance. It should surely be true that if God makes himself known anywhere, it will be in the place where his people worship together. This is something that should be focused in the theology of religious buildings since, as the sentiment from the Society of Friends above suggests, such buildings will develop a power in the piety of their worshippers whether or not it is theologically acknowledged. Whether we like it or not, all our buildings tell a story – they are storied places. The story they tell will be a complex mixture of at least two different factors. First, the Christian faith – depicted by various architectural means, including in some cases the cruciform shape of the building, the font, altar and other artefacts within the building and, in the case of the cathedral in Berne, as in many re-ordered churches, different theological emphases that have prevailed upon the building during its history. Second, they will tell the story of the community which uses the building, its character and history. I have attempted to show elsewhere how I believe that the complex interplay between these is what should characterize a Church community,[93] and it is right and proper that the church building should display this. Richard Giles makes a similar plea for what church buildings can do:

> A church building can tell the story of creation, of the self-inflicted pain of disobedience; of slavery, exile, and estrangement; of wandering and helplessness; of waiting and longing; of rescue in the person of Jesus, showing us for the first time what it means to be truly human. It can go on to tell the story of that particular group of people who meet regularly within its walls to encounter the living Lord and to grow in faith and love. It can leave the visitor with something to chew on, something to make them think that perhaps there is something in this Christianity lark after all, if this particular group of people can tell their story with such pride and vigour and delight.[94]

The building is not the Church, but it speaks of the character and reality of the Church in a profound and vital way. It helps to root the community in its faith, nurture its prophetic witness, and draw it to its destination. In this manner a proper relationship between God, people, and place is maintained, and when it is, the church will speak as an effective sign. To be sure, any acceptance of the importance of place remains a danger, so clearly perceived by the reformers, that an idolatrous attitude might develop. As Dillistone reminds us:

> The sense of place can enrich and deepen human sensibilities. The symbol celebrating a particular place can bring together past and present in living relationship and strengthen hope for the future. It can stir the hearts of all kinds and conditions of people to realise that the living God has made himself known to men in judgement and in grace. At the same time, unhappily, the symbol can be made to turn in upon itself, to become defined and concentrated within its original limits. The symbol then becomes a monument. It may still provoke admiration. It in no way leads to the worship of the living God.[95]

If we are to avoid churches becoming museums, they must be allowed to live and

---

[93] Inge, J. G. (1995), 122–7.

[94] Giles, R. (1995), 64.

[95] Dillistone, F. (1973), 87.

breathe by being re-ordered, adapted and changed to reflect the life of the contemporary Christian community. This is the way to avoid Dillistone's warning. Sadly, the conservationist movement makes this difficult in the case of some of the Church's must eloquent symbols. However, it should be admitted that sometimes when churches become museums they do accurately reflect the state of the Christian community in that place. This is when buildings can become idolatrous – attachment is to building as building, rather than building as sign and sacrament – but this is merely derivative of the fact that the Christian community has lost its way and is taking its building with it into the wilderness. If churches were to operate as shrines in the manner I have suggested, their witness could be transformed and renewed.

I would suggest that one of the best ways in which Christians can witness to the importance of place in all aspects of human experience is by cherishing their holy places. I believe that this could have a significant impact upon the lives of professing Christians in terms of strengthening their witness whilst at the same time speaking to a society which has lost all sense of roots, place and destination. I take it as axiomatic that if places are important in God's relationship with us, then they will also be important in our relations with one another, for the place of our encounter with God will also, as a local church, be the place of our communal habitation. Churches, we have seen, should root Christians, guide them on their journey, and speak of their destination. In fact, in a country like England, the Church has the resources, in the buildings of which it has custody, to bring very substantial renewal. Church buildings can speak of a sacred geography which roots the people of God in their story, reinforces and strengthens their witness in the present and beckons them to their destination.

Conclusion

In this chapter we have examined the history of pilgrimage and shown how it fits with the biblical understanding of place in relationship to both God and people which I proposed in Chapter 2. A consideration of pilgrimage shrines has shown how they can operate sacramentally in order to root the Christian community to its past, enable its prophetic witness in the present, and encourage it to look towards its future in Christ.

It has been suggested that all churches could operate as a shrine. This would mean that church buildings would enhance the capability of the Christian community to live out their prophetic and priestly ministry to the secular world. But if they were to be valued and cherished, instead of being viewed as a liability, they would not only help the worshipping community to speak, they would themselves speak as sacramental signs, for that is what they are. They would be able to increase the sense in which those from outside the tradition are able to question the dominant secular assumptions of late modernity and find openings to faith. It is to dialogue with those who are willing to ask such questions that I now turn in the final chapter.

Chapter 5

A Renewed Appreciation of Place:
An Offering to the World

Place and Humanity

Theology and Other Disciplines

Christian theology should always begin with God and God's relationship with the world in Christ. So, in attempting to establish a Christian theology of place, I have begun with a consideration of the scriptures and religious experience within Christian tradition, and from them constructed a theology of holy places. It is from this perspective that we can now look again at the importance of place in general to human experience. If we look again at some of the writings of those of other disciplines who are protesting against the 'loss of place', we shall want to seek points of convergence, for, as Rowan Williams argues, Christians in general and theologians in particular must be 'involved as best they can in those enterprises in their culture that seek to create or recover a sense of shared discourse and common purpose in human society.'[1] It might seem, at first glance, that this will be an uphill struggle. What will geographers, for instance, want with churchpeople or theologians? Jamie Scott and Paul Simpson-Housley point out that 'the study of religion has not been a major domain of human geography, even though the manifestations of religious experience express themselves with spatial variety on the landscape.'[2] Their volume, which is an interdisciplinary project in the study of religion and geography, attempts to redress the balance in shedding light on what they term 'the geographics of religion'. But such studies are in their infancy. Chris Park attempts an analysis of why this is the case:

> Post-Enlightenment geography, with its emphasis on the observable, countable and measurable properties of phenomena, has no place for spirituality. After all, geography in the Middle Ages and Reformation demonstrated the dangers of putting faith before reason, of allowing evangelical zeal to overshadow objective reality, and of allowing geography to be the handmaiden of theology. The pendulum seems to have swung too far the other way, and so called 'modern geography' is founded upon a set of assumptions about people and what motivates them that gives no credit to the supernatural, the apparently irrational, or the normative influence of belief systems. There are some signs of attempts to redress the balance. If these are even partially successful, we might expect to see spirituality back on the geographical agenda again in the future.[3]

---

[1] Williams, R. (2000), 37.

[2] Scott J. and Simpson-Housley, P. (1991), xii.

[3] Park, C. C. (1994), 26.

Park attempts to bring the study of geography and religion back onto the geographical agenda in his own work. Scott and Simpson-Housley point to the potential benefit of concentration upon the geographics of religion to interdisciplinary study in revealing the imaginative roles of geographical phenomena in the development of religious self-understanding. Despite an unpromising past, these efforts suggest that the valuing of place is one area where a sense of shared discourse might be possible. There are certainly signs that some scholars would welcome such a sharing. Anne Buttimer, whose work we looked at in Chapter 1, is one:

> What does it mean to dwell? Civilisations have varied greatly in their modes of understanding and dealing with the rest of the biosphere. In each civilisation, the human spirit has sought to discern the meaning of earth reality in mythopoetic as well as rational terms. The criteria of rationality and truth in every culture have always been derived from foundational myths. Each civilisation has its story to tell. The unfolding patterns of the earth around us invite a sharing of these stories as one essential step toward discovering mutually acceptable bases for rational discourse and wiser ways of dwelling.[4]

Buttimer wants a 'renaissance of humanism', which calls for 'an ecumenical rather than a separatist spirit; it calls for excellence in special fields as well as a concern for the whole picture. It encourages sensitivity to what the barbarism of our times might be, and it challenges all to seek ways to heal or overcome it in responsible action fully as much as elegant rhetoric.'[5] We may not all want to march under the banner of humanism but we can surely help our contemporaries to discover that one of the barbarisms of today's world is a devaluing of place which is dehumanizing – and help find ways to heal or overcome it. Our study of the Christian scriptures and tradition has led us to the conclusion that a relational view of place emerges from them. I have argued that holy places are those that are associated with divine disclosure or what I have termed 'sacramental encounters'. We might therefore expect that the nature of places other than those designated as holy should be approached from this same relational standpoint as the setting for human encounter. But we have already seen from the work of people like Giddens that if we understand places in this light it will not simply be as an environment, but as something which enters into the very meaning of such encounters. The geographer Michael Godkin insists that 'the places in a person's world are more than entities which provide the physical stage for life's drama. Some are profound centres of meanings and symbols of experience. As such, they lie at the core of human existence.'[6]

Places then develop their own story as a result of human experience in them, just as do holy places as a result of Divine experience in them, and I have already looked in Chapter 3 at the work of humanistic geographers like Relph and Tuan, who argue that they develop something akin to a 'personality' which, though not static, is recognizably the same over time. Thus, a religious view of place from within the Christian tradition, as I have articulated it, accords very well with what academics from other disciplines who are recognizing the value of place have to say about it. To

---

[4] Buttimer, A.(1993), 3.

[5] Ibid., 221.

[6] Relph, E. (1981), 174.

take this point of view will lead us to the inevitable conclusion that places are inextricably bound up with the communities associated with them, just as churches are inextricably bound up with the Christian communities associated with them. Places, then, are intrinsic and essential to the building up of human community just as I have argued that churches understood as shrines are intrinsic and essential to the building up of Christian community.

Place and Community

As soon as we use the word 'community' in this manner, however, we touch upon a very heated argument raging particularly fiercely in the United States concerning what has become known as 'communitarianism'. Those who write on this subject have in common their espousal of community, but there is a fault line running between two distinctive groups. On the one side are those who propose an extensive view of community which embraces the nation state as a tool for engendering equality in a situation in which the market economy is the real villain. So for instance, Robert Bellah and his co-authors in *The Good Society* write:

> We feel that the word communitarian runs the risk of being misunderstood if one imagines that only face-to-face groups – families, congregations, neighbourhoods – are communities and that communitarians are opposed to the state, the economy and all the larger structures that so dominate our life today. Indeed, it is our sense that only greater citizen participation in the large structures of the economy and the state will enable us to surmount the deepening problems of contemporary social life.[7]

Against them are ranged 'conservatives' whose inclination is to view the state as the villain, the market economy as essentially benign, and the locus of community as small face-to-face groups as distinct from (and sometimes opposed to) the state. These include people such as Charles Murray and Michael Novak.[8] The latter see the demise of intermediate groups, associations and affiliations and the rise of the 'nanny state' as having undermined the structure of society. Although complicated by distinctly American features (for example, the espousal of States' rights against the Federal is one important undercurrent of these discussions), we can see these alignments as being essentially left- and right-wing. Witness the contrast between the assertion of Bellah and his co-authors, who state in *Habits of the Heart* that 'poverty breeds drugs, violence and unstable families',[9] and the contrasting view of Stone, 'the evidence does not show that poverty or any other structural factor produces unstable families. Rather, it is unstable families that produce poverty, in addition to producing drug use, violence and other forms of social pathology.'[10] Elsewhere Bellah states that 'most of our problems in America come from the market

---

[7] Bellah, R. et al. (1991), 6. See also Beiner, R. (1992); Etzioni, A. (1993); Unger, R. (1984); Bellah, R., Madsen, R., Sullivan, W., Swidler A. and Tipton, S. (1991).

[8] Murray, C. (1988) and Novak, M. (1989).

[9] Bellah, R., Madsen, R., Sullivan, W,. Swidler, A. and Tipton, S. (1985 and 1991), Preface to 1991 edition, xiv.

[10] Stone, B. (1998), 136.

economy',[11] whereas Stone contends that 'all the available evidence shows that it is not material circumstances that shape culture. It is culture that determines material circumstances.'[12] In other words: don't blame the market.

For a Christian, an uncritical espousal of both the nation state and the market should be treated with suspicion. My interest in this book is with place and I have already noted in previous chapters the adverse effects of globalisation on an appreciation of place and similar considerations apply to the state. William Cavanaugh quotes a classic text by William Nisbet which, interestingly, is used by the 'conservatives' above. Nisbet holds that 'the history of the Western state has been characterised by the gradual absorption of powers and responsibilities formerly resident in the associations and by an increasing directness of relation between the sovereign authority of the State and the individual citizen.'[13] Cavanaugh suggests that the modern state has become but a false copy of the body of Christ, which promised peace but brought violence, whilst Hauerwas characterizes the nation state as a sect.[14] Alastair Macintyre, often considered the leading exponent of communitarianism, states that:

> modern nation states which masquerade as embodiments of community are always to be resisted. The modern nation state, in whatever guise, is a dangerous and unmanageable institution, presenting itself on the one hand as a bureaucratic supplier of goods and services, which is always about to, and never does, give its clients value for money, and on the other as a repository of sacred values, which from time to time invites one to lay down one's life on its behalf. As I have remarked elsewhere ... it is like being asked to die for the telephone company.[15]

The danger of uncritical devotion to the nation state to Christians is also shown by an accompanying espousal of 'civil religion' by some communitarians in the tradition of Durkheim and Rousseau. Bellah, for instance, has been accused of reducing religion to the 'social, temporal and instrumental – it is simply yoked to political ends'.[16] Bellah's eschatological hope is for this civil religion to be exported to the world. As he says: 'A world civil religion could be accepted as a fulfilment and not as a denial of American civil religion. Indeed, such an outcome has been the eschatological hope of American civil religion from the beginning.'[17]

There is much truth in the notion that most Western societies function in what has been characterized as the individual–state–market grid. This situation, designated by Grasso as 'liberalism', represents a combination of two evils:

> The relentless pressures generated by the market will act to reinforce the atomising effects of liberal culture. Specifically, these forces will weaken intermediary institutions both by depriving them of the social environment they require to flourish and by refashioning them

---

[11] Bellah, R. (1990), 236.

[12] Stone, B. in Carey, G. and Frohen, B. (1998), 133.

[13] Nisbet, R., quoted by Cavanaugh, W. (1999), 192.

[14] Cavanaugh, W. (1999), 194; Hauerwas, S. (1987), 87.

[15] MacIntyre, A. (1994), 303.

[16] Stone, B. in Carey, G. and Frohen, B. (1998), 133.

[17] Bellah, R. (1970), 186.

in a way that brings them into conformity with market models of social relations. The welfare state of egalitarian liberalism exacts its own cost on the institutions of civil society. In essence, reform liberalism undermines these institutions in two ways. On the one hand, the internal dynamic of the liberal model of man and society drives it to attempt to remake these institutions in accordance with liberal values. Liberalism's true goal is not limited government per se but rather the maximisation of individual autonomy. Driven by the internal logic of this commitment, the liberal welfare state will aggressively intervene in the internal affairs of intermediary institutions to remake them in accordance with its individualistic and egalitarian ethos.[18]

Rowan Williams suggests that Christians should develop some sort of critical identification with 'whatever political groupings speak for a serious and humane resistance to consumer pluralism and the administered society. These days, such groupings are less likely than ever to be found within historic mainstream political parties, though there are some countries happily, where moral imagination has not been so completely privatised.'[19] As far as community and place are concerned, Williams is quite right in suggesting that the historic mainstream parties will be of no use: socialism, liberalism and conservatism will all tend to put too much faith in either the state or the market, or both. For our purposes, it is of great interest to note that those few people who want to look for a different way forward emphasize the importance of *place* and the notion of *inhabiting* as being vital in the formation and nurture of community – and it is worth pointing out that the converse is also true: namely that the proponents of what we might term 'mainstream communitarianism' pay scant attention, if any, to the importance of place. One of the most notable among the former group is the Christian American poet, novelist and essayist Wendell Berry. Berry has a passionate commitment to communities in the country, and writes that: 'I am a member, by choice, of a local community. I believe that healthy communities are indispensable, and I know that our communities are disintegrating under the influence of economic assumptions that are accepted without question by both parties – despite their lip service to various non-economic "values".' Later, Berry states that:

> the great centralised economic entities of our time do not come into rural places in order to improve them by 'creating jobs'. They come to take as much of value as they can take, as cheaply and quickly as they can take it. They are interested in 'job creation' only so long as the jobs can be done more cheaply by humans than by machines. They are not interested in the good health – economic or natural or human – of any place on this earth.[20]

He is clear that the old political alignments are virtually useless, because 'communists and capitalists are alike in their contempt for country people, country life and country places … the dialogue of Democrats and Republicans or liberals is likewise useless to us … the leaders of these parties are equally subservient to the supranational corporations'.[21] The evil here, for Berry, is globalization, for:

---

[18] Grasso, K. in Carey, G. and Frohen, B. (1998), 35.

[19] Williams, R. (2000), 37.

[20] Berry, W. (1995), x, 11.

[21] Ibid., 15.

> The promoters of the so-called global economy are following a set of principles that can be
> stated as follows. They believe that a frame or a forest is or ought to be the same as a
> factory; that care is only minimally necessary in the use of the land; that affection is not
> necessary at all; that for all practical purposes a machine is as good as a human; that the
> industrial standards of production, efficiency, and profitability are the only standards that
> are necessary; that the topsoil is lifeless and inert; that soil biology is safely replaceable by
> soil chemistry; that the nature or ecology of any given place is irrelevant to the use of it; that
> there is no value in human community or neighbourhood and that technical innovation will
> produce only benign results.[22]

The argument is articulated with passion, and illuminates well the ecological as well
as the human cost of the principle of globalization. Berry gives an example of the
manner in which a local independent bank in Kentucky was taken over. The result
was that local farmers and small business people who had good credit records
stretching back twenty years were refused credit: 'Old and once-valued characters
now find that they are known by category rather than character. The directors and
officers of the large bank clearly have reduced their economic thinking to one very
simple question: "Would we rather make one big loan or many small ones?" or, to put
it only a little differently: "Would we rather support one large enterprise or many
small ones?" And they have chosen the large over the small.'[23] This represents
another dehumanizing effect of the downgrading of place as it is worked out in the
economics of our time. Another example is a recent decision by Barclay's Bank to
close hundreds of country branches in England. And we might add that bound up with
all this is the fact that in the large-scale economy, money has now accrued to itself
many of the attributes of an idol as it is understood in biblical terms, as Peter Selby
has shown.[24] Berry is convinced that globalization dehumanizes since 'the voter is no
longer understood as an intelligent citizen to be persuaded, but rather as a benighted
consumer requiring only to be distracted or deceived.'[25]

What is the way forward in this situation? Surely not to pine after the past. The
rapid change in which we find ourselves can lead to an idealization of the past which
cannot be a solution to present problems, not simply because we cannot return to the
past, but because community in the past had its drawbacks, as Schaffer and Anundsen
clearly remind us:

> As tightly knit and stable as most old-style communities were, they were also
> homogeneous, suspicious of outsiders, socially and economically stratified, emotionally
> stifling, and limited in opportunities for personal and professional development. So long as
> members belonged to the right ethnic, religious or racial groups – or stayed in their place if
> they did not – and behaved within a narrowly defined set of parameters, they could count on
> strong communal support. But if they strayed too far outside their fellow community
> members might well shun or harass them.[26]

Christopher Lasch suggests that to opponents of communitarianism, who include

---

[22] Ibid., 13.

[23] Ibid., 10.

[24] Selby, P. (1998).

[25] Berry, W. (1995), xi.

[26] Schaffer, C. and Anundsen, K. (1993), 6.

right-wing libertarians as well as left-leaning liberals: 'The word community sounds like a prescription for bigotry and parochialism. From this point of view, communitarianism appears to threaten everything the modern world has achieved in its progress from provincialism to cosmopolitanism, including the respect for "diversity" that has become the hallmark (we are told) of civilised societies'.[27] So, too, David Harvey cites Edward Relph's plea that if places are a source of security and identity for individuals and for groups of people, then it is important that the means of experiencing, creating and maintaining significant places is not lost. Harvey believes that the problem is that 'such sentiments easily lend themselves to an interpretation and a politics that is both exclusionary and parochialist, communitarian if not intensely nationalist (hence Heidegger's respect for Nazism).'[28]

But how can this dehumanizing situation be confronted if not through an emphasis on place? Even when we have diagnosed the problem, the answer to it might still be very elusive. One of the first to identify it was Heidegger, as we noted in Chapter 1, but in invoking the romantic ideal Black Forest farmhouse as an example of the integration that is possible and suggesting that it illustrates that dwelling is the basic character of Being in keeping with which mortals exist, David Harvey does not find him very helpful. Harvey is critical of Heidegger on several counts. First, he accuses Heidegger of being, like most great philosophers, extraordinarily vague in his prescriptions, and wonders what 'dwelling' might mean in the modern world. He acknowledges that Heidegger does not advocate a return to the Black Forest idyll but asks what it is that we might turn to. He accuses Heidegger of 'simply wanting to withdraw from the world of the market and attempt to find methods of recovering authentic human existence by meditation and contemplation.'[29]

Practical Proposals

Despite all these difficulties, constructive practical propositions have been mooted. Wendell Berry advocates the development of a 'community economy' which stands against the modern national and global economies – the latter having been formed, he believes, in almost perfect disregard of community and ecological interests. The community economy, he proposes, will 'always ask how local needs might be supplied from local sources, including the mutual support of neighbours.'[30] His suggestions are radical, and are not, alas, likely to make much of an impression until people grow tired of the illusion promoted by our consumer society that greater and greater wealth and possession produce greater and greater happiness. It is not just those who promote the global economy who perpetuate such a state of affairs: an eager consuming public is equally part of the problem. Daniel Kemmis, a writer who is not so completely dismissive of the corporate sector as Berry, acknowledges that the hurdles are very substantial and very deeply rooted, but suggests that it is a

---

[27] Lasch, C. (1995), 109.

[28] Harvey, D. (1993), 14.

[29] Ibid., 12, 14. David Seamon also speaks of Heidegger's presentation of dwelling as having a 'vague, philosophical character which often seem romantic and nostalgic' (Seamon, M., 1984, 46).

[30] Berry, W. (1995), 19, 21.

mistake to assume that all of those problems derive from the nature of the corporation itself, and that they are therefore beyond public control. He feels that a large part of the corporate problem in public life is the public's problem, stemming from the latter's own lack of clear identity, and tells us that this overall lack of identity, in turn, stems from our overall failure to demand of ourselves an active practice of citizenship and that 'until corporations are presented with a public which understands and practices citizenship, their own capacity for citizenship will never be fully brought into play.'[31]

However great the hurdles, if it is identity that is at the root of the problem, then there can be no escape from the necessity of a revitalized sense of place, since identity, as we have seen, is formed, nurtured and fostered by place. If places are the geography of our imagination, it is also true to say that how we are affected by them will be a function not only of the place, but of the people we find in it, as the poet Jeremy Hooker articulates:

> Entering a place that is new to us, or seeing a familiar place anew, we move from part to part, simultaneously perceiving individual persons and things and discovering their relationships, so that, with time, place reveals itself as particular identities belonging to a network, which continually extends with our perception, and beyond it. And by this process we find ourselves, not as observers only, but as inhabitants, citizens, neighbours, and locate ourselves in a space dense with images.[32]

Thus, we are driven back, once again, to a relational view of place. Places exert a profound effect as a result of our encounter with them *and* with their inhabitants. Lawrence Durrell suggests, somewhat impishly, that if you were to exterminate the French at a blow and settle France with Tartars, you would, within two generations, 'discover, to your astonishment, that the national characteristics were back to norm – the restless metaphysical curiosity, the tenderness for good living and the passionate individualism: even though their noses are now flat.'[33] Here the concept of *genius loci* reasserts itself, but Durrell weakens his own argument by adding that: 'this is the invisible constant in a place with which the ordinary tourist can get in touch just by sitting quietly over a glass of wine in a Paris *bistro*.'[34] Surely the great complexity of urban Paris and French culture within it cannot be reduced to being a function of a particular spot on the banks of the Seine? No, places and people are irrevocably linked, and just as an appreciation of holy places is a result of divine encounter, so, in our ordinary human experience, places exert themselves on us by human encounter and culture that derives from it. This encounter – or repeated encounter – will deepen our perception of the place and appreciation of it as time goes on. In this context, much of what I have said about Christian churches understood as shrines fostering the identity of Christians will be true, too, of a sense of place fostering the identity of local communities, and vice versa.

---

[31] Kemmis, D. (1990), 137.

[32] Hooker, J. (1998), 15. Frederick Turner has conducted an impressive study of the importance of place in literature. See Turner, F. (1989); also Hiss, T. (1990); Gillian Tindall has explored the significance of place to writers in Tindall, G. (1991); see also Lutwack, L. (1984).

[33] Durrell, L. (1969), 157.

[34] Ibid., 157.

Kemmis recognizes the importance of place, and argues for a 'politics of inhabitation' which would depend less on procedures and bureaucracies and more upon human virtues and patterns of relationship in which people learn to listen to each other and to work effectively on the project of inhabitation. He suggests that we have ignored the fact that 'the kinds of values which might form the basis for a genuinely public life ... arise out of a context which is concrete in at least two ways. It is concrete in the actual things or events – the barns, the barn dances – which the practices of co-operation produce. But it is also concrete in the actual, specific places within which those practices and that co-operation take place.'[35] These words emphasize once again that there is an indissoluble link between healthy communities and place. Similarly, in reflecting on Emerson's *The American Scholar*, Berry notes that action implies place and community: 'There can be disembodied thought, but not disembodied action. Action – embodied thought – requires local and communal reference. To act, in short, is to live ... and one does not live alone. Living is a communal act, whether or not its communality is acknowledged.' He asserts that 'neighbourhood is a given condition, not a contrived one', and that 'this leads us, probably, to as good a definition of the beloved community as we can hope for: common experience and common effort on a common ground to which one willingly belongs'.[36] Here we see the deep significance that place-in-community will have on the way in which we lead our lives. It is this common experience and common effort on a common ground that leads to inhabitation properly understood. As Kemmis suggests:

> To in*habit* a place is to dwell there in a practised way, in a way which relies upon certain regular, trusted, habits of behaviour. Our prevailing, individualistic frame of mind has led us to forget this root sense of the concept of 'inhabitation.' We take it for granted that the way we live in a place is a matter of individual choice (more or less regulated by bureaucratic regulations). We have largely lost the sense that our capacity to live well in a place might depend upon our ability to relate to neighbours (especially neighbours with a different life-style) on the basis of shared habits of behaviour. ... In fact, no real public life is possible except among people who are engaged in the project of inhabiting a place.[37]

The implications of Kemmis' approach go far. He identifies with those who are suspicious of the nation state, and laments the fact that, as he sees things, people continue to believe, against mounting evidence to the contrary, that the nation is the vehicle by which we must move to a humane future. He suggests that a frame better suited to humankind's challenges and its potential is the biblical measure 'that they might have life and have it abundantly', and that if this becomes our focus, 'we have already begun to view the human situation in a framework that has everything to do with life and very little to do with nationhood'.[38] But it will have everything to do with place. Consonant with this suggestion, Berry believes that devotion should thin as it widens: 'I care more for my household than I do for the town of Port Royal, more for the town of Port Royal than for the County of Henry, more for the County of

---

[35] Kemmis, D. (1990), 79, 138.

[36] Berry, W. (1990), 85.

[37] Kemmis, D. (1990), 79.

[38] Kemmis, D. (1995), xv, xvi.

Henry than I do for the State of Kentucky, more for the State of Kentucky than I do for the United States of America. But I *do not* care more for the United States of America than for the world.'[39] This is analagous with how, after Cavanaugh, I have suggested that Christian community should understand itself in view of Eucharistic theology. The Catholic Church is complete in the local Eucharistic community *and* in the church universal – the body of Christ is fully present in both. And what the local church is to the Catholic Church, the local human community is to the entire human community – not the nation state. Thus, the church can witness to the fact that stressing the importance of the local does not mean a disregard for the universal, but can set it, rather, in a proper context.

Although both Berry and Kemmis are suspicious of the nation state, Kemmis' priorities, as the mayor of a city, lie with cities much more than with the countryside, the latter being Berry's first concern. However, the two are linked: Kemmis advocates that neighbourliness should stretch from city to the surrounding rural community, especially now, when rural life is threatened more and more severely by international markets, by technological dislocations and corporate domination: 'It may be time for a reassessment of the relationship between cities and their rural environs. It may well be that neither towns nor farms can thrive in the way they would prefer until they turn their attention more directly to each other, realising that they are mutually complementary parts of the enterprise of inhabiting a place.'[40] Kemmis makes much reference to the notion of 'citizenship', and observes that 'we are so accustomed to seeking personal wholeness through various forms of self-development, counselling, or therapy that it would occur to very few people to think of citizenship as a path to greater individual wholeness.'[41] Citizenship, he tells us, means more than 'community', since it implies responsibility for making community happen in a particular place.

Kemmis makes this proposition less abstract by reference to the 'Healthy Cities Movement', which has been transported from the United States to the United Kingdom as 'Common Purpose'. This movement brings together people from the corporate, public and voluntary sectors in order to encourage them to work together for the good of the city. It is a movement which, when I was part of it in Newcastle-upon-Tyne in the early 1990s, was doing very good things to build up the fabric of the city. Kemmis notes:

> The healthy cities movement only makes sense if we are prepared to acknowledge that cities are enough like organisms that we can actually speak of them as healthy or unhealthy. But the essence of organisms is that their wholeness cannot be captured by adding together all their parts. When individual cells evolve into an organism, something new emerges that cannot be described simply by adding together all the cells. This is precisely what is meant by the synergy of cities. The very concept of synergy is an affront to sharp analytical minds, because synergy cannot be located in any of the parts of what is being analysed. But, of course, synergy means that something beyond the mere collection of individual activities has suddenly entered the picture. To say that a city is organic, then, and that healthy cities

---

[39]Berry, W. (1969), 77.

[40] Kemmis, D. (1990), 124.

[41] Kemmis, D. (1995), 198.

produce various kinds of synergy, is to say the same thing in different ways. If the city is organic, (and indeed we can see that any good city is) it does have a life force of its own.

Thus, the relationship between community and place is indeed a very powerful one in which each reinforces the identity of the other. What is important from a practical perspective is that this relationship should be recognized and cherished – and the encouragement of good citizenship is one way in which that can be done. Good citizenship viewed in this manner will entail witnessing against those media which encourage what we spoke of in Chapter 1 as an 'inauthentic' attitude to place, which arises as a result of mass communications, mass culture, big business, powerful central authority, and the economic system which embraces all of these. Implied in this is the necessity to refuse to submit to the tyranny of either the market or the nation state – two of the most conspicuous developments of modernity. It will also be necessary to be suspicious of the phenomenon of postmodernism. Stanley Hauerwas believes that if modernism is a rejection of the Christian God in the interest of a kind of divinization of the human, postmodernists, seeking to be thorough in their atheism, deny such humanism. He suggests: 'It is hard to imagine an intellectual alternative better suited for the elites of a global Capitalism than postmodernism. Capitalism is, after all, the ultimate form of deconstruction.'[42]

The witness of neighbourliness in pursuit of proper inhabitation is not only important for the recovery of psychological health. The places, city and country with which we develop a very complex and deep relationship are our very lifeblood in a very *physical* as well as psychological sense, and a recovery of the importance of place would do much to encourage a more responsible attitude to the environment. Roger Hart, who has studied the importance of place in the early experience of children, makes important recommendations to educationalists and others. For example:

> A radical reorganisation of schools is required. They should recognise children's competent engagements with the environment as crucial to the definition of, and development of, intelligence. A future-oriented philosophy would see education as the process by which children learn to interact with, and intelligently transform, the environment and themselves. 'Environmental competence' in such an educational system would involve more than the effective construction and modification of environments. Children would learn to see a range of outcomes from their environmental manipulations.[43]

I am not aware of these recommendations being taken up anywhere. In fact, it has been suggested that 'modern educational theory has all but ignored questions of space, of geography, of architecture'.[44] This may be one reason why the undervaluing of place continues to be a crucial factor in the abuse of the natural environment. We

---

[42] Hauerwas, S. (2000), *A Better Hope*, Grand Rapids, Michigan: Brazos Press, 40, 223. Cf. David Harvey's observation that capitalism 'builds and rebuilds a geography in its own image' (Harvey, D., 2000, 54). John Milbank criticizes modern Catholic social teaching as being in thrall to what he terms 'enlightenment simple space' as opposed to his preferred 'gothic complex space', and thus being in danger of 'engendering a kind of soft fascism' (Milbank, J., 1997, 268–92).

[43] Hart, C. (1979), 347.

[44] Peters, M. (1996), 93.

must, though, beware of the word 'environment' for reasons articulated well by Berry, who protests against what we might see as the 'container' view of place seen as environment: 'The concept of country, homeland, dwelling place becomes simplified as "the environment" – that is, what surrounds us. Once we see our place, our part of the world, as surrounding us, we have already made a profound division between it and ourselves.'[45] We might add that a Christian perspective, as we have argued throughout this book, will want to see the material world as a theatre for God's activity, and that just as we can make no firm division between our environment and ourselves, we cannot, either, leave God out of the picture. If Hart is right in his conclusion that children's relationship to their environment is so important to them, then they will have a respect for it which will be eroded by an education which takes no account of its importance. Christian insights could make an important contribution to reinforcing this process. As John Habgood observes:

> If our culture and our history convey to us a purely secular vision of the world, emptied of divine meaning, the likelihood is that we shall think of it as mere material, available for manipulation and exploitation. If, on the other hand, in trying to make sense of it, we begin with the presupposition that material things are capable of bearing the image of the divine, then we are likely to be more respectful. And we are more likely too to be receptive to the energy and grace released through encounter with God, whether through church-based sacraments or through those aspects of nature which most readily lend themselves to a sacramental interpretation.[46]

There has, as I noted in the last chapter, been a great movement in 'virtue ethics' among Christians in recent years, led by people like Stanley Hauerwas, though the latter is critical of mainstream communitarianism.[47] Christian virtue ethicists do not generally, I would suggest, give adequate attention to the importance of place in fostering ethics and community. One theologian who has touched briefly upon such importance is Belden Lane. He follows the definition of the French sociologist Pierre Bordieu in speaking of a community's *habitus* as the manner in which accepted modes of behaviour are unconsciously imbibed from one generation to another, since a *habitus* 'ensures the active presence of past experiences which ... tend to guarantee the "correctness" of practices and their constancy over time, more reliably than all formal rules and explicit norms.'[48] In modern Western society, however, *habitus* is reduced to 'a nonsacramental, individualistic quest for transcendent experience. We lose any sense of being formed in a community, participating in a tradition that allows us to act unconsciously, with ease and delight, out of a deep sense of what is natural to us and to our milieu. We are, in short, a people without "habit", with no common

---

[45] He goes on: 'We have given up the understanding – dropped it out of our language and so out of our thought – that we and our country create one another; that our land passes in and out of our bodies just as our bodies pass in and out of our land; that as we and our land are part of one another, so all who are living as neighbours here, human and plant and animal, are part of one another, and so cannot possibly flourish alone; that, therefore, our culture and our place are images of each other and inseparable from each other, and so neither can be better than the other' (Berry, W., 1977, 22).

[46] Habgood, J. in Brown, D. and Loades, A. (1995), 22.

[47] See Hauerwas, S. (1994).

[48] Bourdieu, P. (1990), quoted in Lane, B. (1998), 235.

custom, place, or dress to lend us a shared meaning.'[49] The key to a way out of this impoverished state of affairs is surely a recovery of the dormant virtue of neighbourliness. Understood in the Judaeo-Christian sense of the word it is this which is vital to a recovery of community-in-place and what Kemmis terms 'inhabitation':

> Deep-seated attachment to the virtue of neighbourliness is an important but largely ignored civic asset. It is in being good neighbours that people very often engage in those simple, homely practices which are the last and best hope for a revival of a genuine public life. In valuing neighbourliness, people value that upon which citizenship most essentially depends. It is our good fortune that this value persists. So it is that places may play a role in the revival of citizenship. Places have a way of claiming people. When they claim very diverse kinds of people, those people must eventually learn to live with each other; they must learn to inhabit their place together, which they can only do through the development of certain practices of inhabitation which both rely upon and nurture the old fashioned civic virtues of trust, honesty, justice, tolerance, cooperation, hope, and remembrance. It is through the nurturing of such virtues (and in no other way) that we might begin to reclaim that competency upon which democratic citizenship depends.[50]

Neighbourliness of this sort is something which is central to what being Christian is all about, and as such Christians should be able to give a lead in its recovery in order to assist what Kemmis terms 'inhabitation'. But neighbourliness of this sort is something that the Christian community needs to recover for, as O'Donovan points out, although there are some societies in which rebuke of the parable of the Good Samaritan 'strikes like a meteor against the complacency of racial or class self-love ... in the Western world at large there is probably more danger of our taking the parable complacently as an endorsement of our own characteristic universalism'.[51] He suggests that the universalist claim of every human being upon every other is, after all, more a critical principle than a substantial one, since to love everybody in the world is to love nobody very much. On the other hand, as far as the Good Samaritan is concerned, 'far from denying the significance of proximate relations, the parable discovers them where they are not looked for, nearer to us, not further away, under our very noses.'[52] As it does so, the parable calls into question our current forms of Western universalism, and 'challenges us not to ignore that which is nearest to us, not to let the place where we are become neutralised into a mere passage that excludes neighbourly encounter. In Western society nothing could be more striking, in fact, than its tendency to dissolve all places into communications

---

[49] Lane, B. (1998), 10. He says further: 'The intimate connection between spirit and place is hard to grasp for those of us living in a post-Enlightenment technological society. Landscape and spirituality are not, for us, inevitably interwoven. We experience no inescapable linkage between our "place" and our way of conceiving the holy, between habitat and *habitus*, where one lives and how one practices a habit of being. Our concern is simply to move as quickly (and freely) as possible from one place to another. We are bereft of rituals of entry that allow us to participate fully in the places we inhabit. ... We have realised, in the end, the "free individual" at the expense of a network of interrelated meanings' (Lane, B., 1998, 10).

[50] Kemmis, D. (1990), 119.

[51] O'Donovan, O. (1989), 53.

[52] Ibid., 53.

networks, surrendering a sense of place (being in) into a mere sense of space (passing through).'[53] At this stage we find ourselves brought back both to the loss of place which I charted in Chapter 1, and on to a fruitful tool for the recovery of its loss which comes from the Christian tradition. If members of Christian communities could learn to be good neighbours to one another and to the larger communities of which they are a part, they would have something infinitely worthwhile to offer to the world. And it would be the very best form of evangelization.

As an aspect of such neighbourliness, Leonard Jason concentrates his attention on what he terms 'psychological community', and identifies symbolic practices as the thread for weaving community:

> To attain a psychological sense of community, we should develop traditions, norms, and values that are tied to the settings or communities in which we live. The notion of a supportive community represents a comprehensive way of thinking about health and healing. Such an approach combines strategies that strengthen inner resources by instilling hope, confidence, enthusiasm, and the will to live with strategies that provide a place for people to live that is protected and nourishing.[54]

Such a description is, of course, exactly what many would believe the Church should be about. Jason gives examples of therapeutic communities, including l'Arche and Bonaventure House, a residential facility for those infected with HIV in Chicago. He accepts that most of his examples have operated on a small scale, and feels that it is unclear whether they could be effectively implemented on a larger scale. He suggests that, instead, the proliferation of small-scale projects could lead to a transformation of the larger society.[55]

The Distinctive Role of Christians

As far as the Christian community is concerned, I would contend that the above is a question which must be left open. It is not up to the Church to prescribe, but to *live out* a witness in the service of God and humanity. This will mean concentrating upon both community and place. Large-scale strategies are not appropriate. Referring to the manner in which John Milbank has shown how particularity is central to Christian witness (a theme at the heart of this book), Samuel Wells points out that since Christian moral judgements are related to regeneration, to forgiveness, to the Church, to Christian hope: 'They cannot simply be moralized into a blueprint for a non-Christian society. Because the church claims no special insight into the general form of society, its witness will always be expressed in specific criticisms and suggestions, addressing particular injustices at a given time and place.'[56] The community of faith, then, has a specific task in worshipping and following the God who is revealed in Jesus Christ, and it is in being faithful to that task that it will resist the inhumanities of our day and witness to the gospel. Stanley Hauerwas, in speaking of resistance to postmodernism, writes the following:

---

[53] Ibid., 54.

[54] Jason, L. A. (1997).

[55] Ibid., 86.

[56] Wells, S. (1998), 103. The work by Milbank to which Wells is referring is Milbank, J. (1990).

To survive will require us to develop practices and habits that make our worship of God an unavoidable witness to the world. By unavoidable I mean that we must help the world to discover that it is unintelligible just to the extent that it does not acknowledge the God we worship. That God 'is whoever raised Jesus from the dead, having before raised Israel from Egypt.'[57] That is the God, who having created all that is, can be known only by way of analogy. Analogy is but the way we name the metaphysical implications that God wills to care for his creation through calling into existence a faithful people.[58]

It is the contention of this book that attention to place by the Christian community will afford great nourishment and sustenance to it. Rowan Williams tells us that 'the doctrine of the incarnation is recovered and revitalised so often as we recover our authority as a *Christian* community to challenge and resist what holds back *human* community.'[59] In allowing a sense of holy place to strengthen not only their own faith but their sense of the importance of place in human experience, Christians can witness to the biblical truth that our 'placement' is much more important than is generally imagined. It is no mere backdrop to actions and thoughts. This needs to be part of the 'unavoidable witness' of the Christian community.

The Western world, which was once rooted in the Christian story, has lost those roots and, at the same time, lost any rootage in place. Simone Weil points out the importance of rootage:

To be rooted is perhaps the most important need of the human soul. It is one of the hardest to define. A human being has roots by virtue of his real, active, and natural participation in the life of a community, which preserves in living shape certain particular treasures of the past and certain particular expectations of the future. This participation is a natural one, in the sense that it is naturally brought about by place, conditions of birth, profession, and social surroundings. Every human being needs to have multiple roots. It is necessary for him to draw well-nigh the whole of his moral, intellectual, and spiritual life by way of the environment of which he form a natural part.[60]

It is no accident that Weil talks about human beings having roots by virtue of 'natural participation in the life of a community', and that she designates place the first determinant of that participation. Roots are markedly lacking from Western society, and Christians have the resources to witness to their importance by re-emphasizing how crucial is place in human experience. But it is not only roots that are lacking. This has been poignantly expressed by Zygmunt Bauman, who characterizes the self in postmodernity as a vagabond: 'a pilgrim without a destination; a nomad without an itinerary.'[61] The Christian community can witness to the fact that roots, place and destination are all important to human existence. It needs to help the rest of the world

---

[57] Jenson, R. (1997).

[58] Hauerwas, S. (2000), 43.

[59] Williams, R. (2000), 238.

[60] Weil, S. (1952), *The Need for Roots*, New York: G. P. Puttnam's Sons, 43.

[61] Bauman writes: 'The vagabond journeys through unstructured space; like a wanderer in the desert, who only knows of such trails as are marked with his own footprints, and blown off again by the wind the moment he passes, the vagabond structures the site he happens to occupy at the moment, only to dismantle the structure again as he leaves. Each successive spacing is local and temporary – episodic' (Bauman, Z., 1993, 240).

to recover some imagination about what place can be, for how we imagine communities and places of the future becomes part of the of what our future is. It can do this by quietly revitalizing a sense of place in the shrines in which it worships and the places that surround them. It is the practice of Christian communities which will be important in witnessing to the truth that places are profound centres of human existence.

In so witnessing, the Church must, however, whilst working for the appreciation of place in this world and community-in-place, stand out against false eschatological hopes like Bellah's 'world civic religion' and the proposal from secular sources that it is possible to construct a perfect community in place in this world of the sort Harvey describes in the following passage:

> The long historical geography of capitalism has so liberated us from specula constraints that we can imagine communities independently of existing places and set about the construction of new places to house such communities in ways that were impossible before. The history of utopian thinking, from Thomas More and Francis Bacon onwards, is illustrative of the discursive point: the penchant for constructing and developing new towns from Welwyn Garden City to Chandigarh, Brazilia or the much talked about Japanese plan for Multifunctionopolis in Australia testifies to the frequent attempt to materialise such ideas through actual place construction.[62]

Harvey suggests that there are difficulties here in reconciling such transformative practices with the desire to retain familiarity, security and the deep sense of belonging that attachment to place can generate. However, the difficulties run much deeper than those adumbrated by Harvey for, as our analysis of the importance of place in terms of sacramental encounter has shown, that gift of the perfect place will only be given in God's good time. This world cannot hold all the hopes which secularized humanity demands of it. One perceptive analysis of the extraordinary outpouring of grief that took place in the United Kingdom and beyond following the death of Diana, Princess of Wales, was given by Stephen Sykes. He suggested that it was a result of the fact that the present generation had invested huge hopes in this life in a way that had never happened before, and that this life simply could not hold those hopes. Consequently, when the life of an individual who held within her own person many of those hopes, being, as she was, young, rich, beautiful, elegant, famous – and a princess – was cruelly cut short, these hopes were symbolically dashed. The fact is that this life cannot hold all those hopes. They are for the future, for God's future.[63]

If we are to mourn concerning the fact that here we shall find no abiding city, that all our experience of place in this world will be tainted, we are also called to have hope. We are to have hope that, just as sacramental encounter in the world and sacramental presence in the Eucharist come to us as pure gift, so too the eschatological gift of a place which Jesus has promised to prepare for his disciples will come to us in his good time. But the biblical sacraments of Baptism and the Eucharist speak of new life coming *only through death*, and thus we must be prepared to relinquish our hold on the places of this world, die to them, if they are to be restored to us in transfigured and glorious state. This is the ultimate sense in which we are to

---

[62] Harvey, D. (1993), 17.

[63] Personal conversation with Stephen Sykes.

understand the biblical tradition, which, as well as stands valuing place, warns us not to become too attached to it and limit God to it. For all our proper attachment to life, to community and to place, ultimate hope lies in life, community and place, which come only through death, separation and detachment. That ultimate hope must not be abandoned, for that would be to betray what sacramental encounter in the church and the world points us toward.

Ultimate Hope for an Ultimate Place

How are we to understand the relation of place to ultimate hope? Place certainly has a role in apocalyptic writing. In his essay *Mapping an Apocalyptic World*, Leonard Thompson urges that the spatial aspects of apocalyptic writings are as important as their temporal features.[64] What are we to make of this? Can it be that place has permanent significance? I take as my starting point the statement of Jesus: 'There are many rooms in my Father's house; if there were not I would have told you. I am going now to prepare a place for you' (John 14:4). These words give a further eschatological dimension to the importance of place, and remind us of our conclusion that the ultimate biblical promise is of implacement. But what is the nature of this place?

We read in Revelation that John was permitted to see 'a door open in heaven' (Revelation 4:1) which he enters on being invited to do so by an angel. There he sees a vision which is in the tradition of that experienced by Ezekiel, except that, while earlier visionaries saw God surrounded by angels and spirits, John recognizes human beings in proximity to the divine presence. These, John is told, are the martyrs who have washed their robes in the blood of the Lamb, and in heaven they join the angels in partaking in a great liturgy: there is shouting and singing and burning of incense (Revelation 4 and 5). Here, once again, place is presented as relational, and we see the consummation of that threefold union of people, place, and God which was first suggested to us by our examination of the Old Testament material.

This picture derives from our roots. Susan Niditch argues that the picture of the promised new reality as it emerges from Paul's letters and certain portions of the gospels makes sense only in the light of Eden and the return to paradise, while expanding and building on earlier visions in the tradition. This vision of what she terms 'communitas', which evens out hierarchies such as those between men and women to emphasize all persons' commonality, unity and equality 'was the ideal of the early church maintainable even with difficulty as long as the full establishment of God's kingdom is believed to be imminent ... once this fulfilment becomes clearly delayed, man's tendency to order, to structure, to compartmentalise, to make law takes over.'[65] She ends her study by suggesting that the creation myths of Genesis 1–11 provide a means of self-renewal even while preparing us to live the world of structures and reality. They prepare us for who we are as human beings, but also remind us of who we might be.

Resonances with the description of the Garden of Eden reach very deep into our psyche and our own early experience of community-in-place:

---

[64] Thompson, L. in Scott J., and Simpson-Housley P. (1991), 115.

[65] Niditch, S. (1985), 98, 103.

What is the connection between the home we knew and the home we dream? I believe that what we long for most in the home we knew is the peace and charity that, if we were lucky, we experienced there, and I believe that it is the same peace and charity we dream of finding once again that the tide of time draws us toward. The first home foreshadows the final home, and the final home hallows and fulfills what was most precious in the first. That, at least, is my prayer for us all.[66]

Thus speaks Frederick Buechner at the beginning of a beautiful book entitled *The Longing for Home*. Quoting the letter to the Hebrews and its talk of 'being strangers and exiles on the earth' and 'seeking a homeland' (Hebrews 11:13–14), he writes eloquently of the connection between heaven and home. He understands that people and place are vitally entwined. He writes of how the word '*longing*' 'comes from the same route as the word *long* in the sense of length in either time or space and also the word *belong*, so that in its full richness the word to long suggests to yearn for a long time for something that is a long way off and something that we feel we belong to and that belongs to us.'[67] He articulates how his career as a writer was energized by the search for home, touches on the way in which the longing for home is bound up with all our deep longings and a sense of homesickness, and suggests that this homesickness will be consumed in the heaven which is the ultimate place of promise.

Notions of heaven, in the scriptures and elsewhere, are bound up with God, place, and people. Which of these dominates varies, as McDannell and Lang articulate in an impressive study entitled *The History of Heaven*. They characterize two major images of heaven dominating theology, pious literature, art and popular ideas down the centuries. One, which they term the 'theocentric view', conceives of heaven as 'eternal solitude with God alone', and the other, the 'anthropocentric view', conceives of heaven as focusing on the human:

Although social and religious expectations combine and balance in various ways to produce a variety of heavens, a certain emphasis on the divine or a clear preference for the human appears in each heaven. These two concepts do not depend on the level of sophistication of those presenting the image (theologians versus lay people), or time frame (early versus contemporary), or theological preference (Protestant versus Catholic). Rather, we have found that throughout Christian history anthropocentric and theocentric models emerge, become prominent, and weaken.[68]

If our contention about the relationship between people, place, and God is correct, we would expect to see this sort of vacillation. And in an age when the importance of place has been downgraded, their finding that by far the most persuasive element of the modern heaven for many contemporary Christians is the hope of meeting family again is not surprising – the emphasis is on people, rather than place. However, there are a good many Christians who find it hard to believe in a place called heaven at all: 'Life after death, for many Christians, means existing only in the memory of their families and of God. Scientific, philosophical, and theological scepticism has

---

[66] Buechner, F. (1996), 3. For further secular reflections on the psychological importance of home see Relph, E. (1976), esp. 39ff.

[67] Ibid., 18.

[68] McDannell, C. and Lang, B. (1988), 353.

nullified the modern heaven and replaced it with teachings that are minimalist, meagre and dry.'[69]

But to abandon such a belief is to abandon the creed in which we speak of the resurrection of the body. Such terminology implies that our ultimate destiny is to be embodied – that bodies are no temporary delight or encumbrance. If we are to have bodies, we must, as now, have places in which to put them. The ultimate importance of the material that the Christian faith declares is something to which sacramental encounters in the church and the world point. They point towards our ultimate destiny which is to be *implaced*, where the nature of the places in which we will find ourselves will be a transfigured version of the places of the here and now. In God's grace, our occasionally transfigured experience of them now gives us a foretaste of the glory that is to be revealed to us in which the nature of these places, like our own, will be changed and not taken away.

The ultimate significance of matter articulated by a belief in the resurrection of the body is something which is skipped over as a matter of some embarrassment by most modern Christians, but support for an insistence that it might not be so untenable in the twenty-first century comes from the distinguished scientist and theologian John Polkinghorne. Polkinghorne points out that, although there is some discussion about whether the expansion of the universe as a result of the 'Big Bang', or gravity, will win out, either way modern science predicts that the universe will come to an end. If expansion prevails, galaxies will continue to move away from each other, and within each galaxy everything will eventually decay into low-grade radiation. If gravity wins, what began as a 'Big Bang' will conclude as a 'Big Chruch'. So, although these alternative scenarios lie tens of billions of years into the future: 'it's as certain as can be that humanity, and all life, will only be a transient episode in the history of the universe.'[70]

The Christian faith, however, has always been clear about resurrection. In reinforcing his commitment to this, Polkinghorne recounts the story of the Sadducees' attempt to catch Jesus out with the conundrum about a woman who had been married to a succession of brothers, and Jesus' comment concerning God as the God of Abraham, Isaac and Jacob: 'He is the God not of the dead but of the living' (Matthew 22:32). Polkinghorne tells us that the point of the story is as follows: 'If Abraham, Isaac and Jacob mattered to God once – and they certainly did – they matter to him for ever. The same is true of you and me. God does not just cast us off as discarded broken pots, thrown onto the rubbish heap of the universe when we die. Our belief in a destiny beyond death rests in the faithfulness of the eternal God.'[71] Polkinghorne goes on to ask whether this makes sense. He rejects a dualistic notion of soul and body, and suggests, in accordance with Hebrew thinking and modern insights, that we appear to be animated bodies rather than embodied souls. Observing that the material of our bodies is changing all the time and that there are very few atoms of our bodies left from among those that were there a few years ago since wear and tear mean that they are continually being replaced, he suggests that:

---

[69] Ibid., 352.

[70] Polkinghorne, J. (1994), 90.

[71] Ibid., 92.

the real me is an immensely complicated 'pattern' in which these ever-changing atoms are organised. It seems to me to be an intelligible and coherent hope that God will remember the pattern that is me and recreate it in a new environment of his choosing, by his great act of resurrection. Christian belief in a destiny beyond death has always centred on resurrection, not survival. Christ's Resurrection is the foretaste and guarantee, within history, of our resurrection, which awaits us beyond history.[72]

Polkinghorne reminds us that we are talking of resurrection into a new world and that this is different from resuscitation into the old one, since the scriptures talk of a new heaven and a new earth. It is, he tells us, the pattern that signifies, not the matter that makes it up, but he is clear that this new 'world' will be a material one:

Where will this new 'matter' of this new world come from? I suppose that it will come from the transformed matter of this present world, for God cares for all of his creation and he must have a destiny for the universe beyond its death, just as he has a destiny for us beyond ours. This is why the empty tomb is so important. Jesus' risen body is the transmuted and glorified form of his dead body. This tells us that in Christ there is a destiny for matter as well as for humanity, In fact, our destinies belong together, precisely because humans are embodied beings.[73]

Although Polkinghorne's thoughts are, by his own admission, speculative, they are significant, coming as they do from a distinguished scientist. Those who would want to dismiss them as romanticism should remember that until recently the idea that human beings were made from stardust would have been treated in the same way. We now know that it is fact.

Polkinghorne's insights are highly relevant to the argument of this book because, just as to have a body is necessarily to have a place for that body in the here and now, they imply that the material nature of the resurrection world and our embodiment within it will necessitate place, too. It will not consist of the same places as this world in a material sense, but if the 'pattern' of our material human identities can be remembered and recreated, so can the places of this world. If place is of such final significance, it should surely be treated with more respect in the here and now. Elsewhere, Polkinghorne writes:

The old creation was a creation *ex nihilo*. The new creation will be something different; it is a creatio *ex vetere*, for it is the transmutation of the old consequent upon its free return to its Creator. I struggle to grasp that deeply mysterious notion, but I am convinced that it is central to a consistent and convincing eschatology ... there are hints of this in scripture: in Paul's amazing vision in Romans 8 of a creation 'subjected to futility' that will 'obtain the glorious liberty of the children of God' (vv 20–21). There are also hints in experience, particularly in the Real Presence in the sacrament. The ultimate destiny of the whole universe is sacramental. What is known locally and occasionally will then be known globally and forever.[74]

So, places are not only of importance, they are of *ultimate* importance and

---

[72] Ibid., 92.

[73] Ibid., 93.

[74] Polkinghorne, J. (1995), 108.

Polkinghorne's final comment reinforces the central theme of this book – that the most constructive manner in which we can view them as Christians is sacramentally. But there will, finally, be resolution, too, of the themes of time, space and place which have been woven into our study, for the resurrection of the flesh and the accomplishment of a new earth will resolve the temporary opposition of history and eschatology, of matter and spirit. So, at the conclusion of our ultimate journey, the end of all our exploring really will be 'to arrive where we started and know the place for the first time.'[75]

---

[75] Eliot, T. S., 'The Four Quartets' in Eliot, T. S. (1971), 197.

Bibliography

Agnew, J. and Duncan, J. (eds) (1989), *The Power of Place: Bringing together the Geographical and Sociological Imaginations*, London: Unwin Hyman.

Allchin, A. M. (1978), *The World is a Wedding*, London: DLT.

Andrewes, L. (1841), *Ninety Six Sermons*, Oxford: John Henry Parker, 1.

Augé, M. (1997), *Non-places: Introduction to an Anthropology of Super-Modernity*, London: Verso.

Augustine, *The Works of Aurelius Augustine, Bishop of Hippo* (ET), Edinburgh: T. & T. Clark, 1872.

Bachelard, G. (1964), *The Poetics of Space*, New York: Orion.

Barrett, C. K. (1985), *Church, Ministry and Sacraments in the New Testament*, Grand Rapids, Michigan: W. B. Eerdmans.

Barrie, T. (1996), *Spiritual Path, Sacred Place: Myth, Ritual and Meaning in Architecture*, Boston, Massachusetts: Shambhala.

Barrow, J. (1990), *Theories of Everything*, London: Vintage.

Bauerschmidt, F. C. (1996), 'Walking in the Pilgrim City', *New Blackfriars*, Issue **77**.

Bauman, Z. (1993), *Postmodern Ethics*, Oxford: Blackwell.

Beguerie, P. and Decheschau, C. (1991), *How to Understand the Sacraments*, London: SCM.

Beiner, R. (1992), *What's the Matter with Liberalism?*, Berkeley, California: University of California Press.

Bellah, R. (1970), *Beyond Belief: Essays on Religion in a Post-Traditional World*, New York: Harper and Row.

——— (1990), 'The Invasion of the Money World', in Blankenthorne D., Bayme S. and Elshtain, J. (eds), *Rebuilding the Nest: A New Commitment to the American Family*, Milwaukee: Family Service America.

Bellah, R., Madsen, R., Sullivan, W., Swidler, A. and Tipton, S. (1985 and 1991), *Habits of the Heart: Individualism and Commitment in American Life*, New York: Harper and Row.

Bellah, R., Madsen, R., Sullivan, W., Swidler, A. and Tipton, S. (1991), *The Good Society*, New York: A. A. Knopf.

Benko, G. (1997), 'Introduction: Modernity and Postmodernity and the Social Sciences', in Benko, G. and Strohmayer, U. (eds), *Space, and Social Theory: Interpreting Modernity and Postmodernity*, Oxford: Blackwell.

Bennett, V. (1997), *Sacred Space and Structural Style: The Embodiment of Socio-religious Ideology*, Ottawa: University of Ottawa Press.

Berry, W. (1969), *The Long-Legged House*, New York: Brace and World.

——— (1977), *The Unsettling of America*, New York: Avon Books.

——— (1990), *What Are People For?*, San Francisco, California: North Point Press.

——— (1995), *Another Turn of the Crank*, Washington DC: Counterpoint.

Blunt, A. and Rose, G. (eds) (1994), *Writing Women and Space: Colonial and Postcolonial Geographies*, New York: Guildford Press.

Bokser, B. M. (1985), 'Approaching Sacred Space', *Harvard Theological Review*, **78**.

Bourdieu, P. (1990), *The Logic of Practice*, Stanford, California: Stanford University Press.

Brown, D. (2001), 'The Annunciation as True Fiction', in *Theology* CIV.

Brown, D. and Loades, A. (eds) (1995), *The Sense of the Sacramental*, London: SPCK.

Brown, D. and Loades, A. (eds) (1996), *Christ: The Sacramental Word*, London: SPCK.

Brown, P. (1981), *The Cult of the Saints: Its Rise and Function in Latin Christianity*, Chicago, Illinois: Chicago University Press.

Brueggemann, W. (1978), *The Land: Place as Gift, Promise and Challenge in Biblical Faith*, London: SPCK.

Buechner, F. (1996), *The Longing for Home: Recollections and Reflections*, San Fransisco, California: Harper.

Buttimer, A. and Seamon, D. (eds) (1980), *The Human Experience of Space and Place*, London: Croom Helm.

Buttimer, A. (1993), *Geography and the Human Spirit*, Baltimore, Maryland: John Hopkins Press.

Calvin, J. (1986), T. Lane and H. Osborne (ed.), *The Institutes of Christian Religion*, London: Harper and Collins.

Canter, D. (1997), *The Psychology of Place*, London: Architectural Press.

Carey, G. and Frohen, B. (eds) (1988), *Community and Tradition: Conservative Perpectives on the American Experience*, Lanham, Maryland: Rowman and Littlefield.

Casey, E. (1993), *Getting Back into Place: Toward a Renewed Understanding of the Place World*, Bloomington, Indianapolis: Indiana University Press.

——— (1997), *The Fate of Place: A Philosophical History*, Berkeley, California: University of California Press.

Cassell, P. (ed.) (1993), *The Giddens Reader*, London: Macmillan.

Cavanaugh, W. (1999), 'The World in a Wafer: a Geography of the Eucharist as Resistance to Globalization', *Modern Theology*, Issue **15**.

Chauvet, L.-M. (1997), *Symbol and Sacrament: A Sacramental Reinterpretation of Christian Existence* (ET), Collegeville, Minnesota: The Liturgical Press.

Coleman, S. and Elsner, J. (1995), *Pilgrimage Past and Present*, London: British Museum Press.

Conzelmann, H. (1960), *The Theology of St Luke*, London: Faber and Faber.

Cragg, K. (1997), *Palestine: The Prize and Price of Zion*, London: Cassell.

Cunningham, L. (1988), 'Sacred Space and Sacred Time: Reflections on Contemporary Catholicism', in Shafer, I. (ed.), *Essays in Theology, The Arts and Social Sciences in Honor of Andrew Greely: A Feschrift*, Bowling Green, Ohio: Bowling Green State University Popular Press.

Cyril, Saint, Bishop of Jerusalem, *The Works of St Cyril of Jerusalem*, trans. L. P. McCauley and A. A. Stephenson, Washington: Catholic University of America Press, 1969.

Daly, C. (1981), 'Transubstantiation and Technology in David Jones', *Notre Dame English Journal* **14**.

Davies, J. G. (1988), *Pilgrimage Yesterday and Today: Why? Where? How?*, London: SCM Press.

Davies, W .D. (1974), *The Gospel and the Land: Early Christianity and Jewish Territorial Doctrine*, Berkeley, California: University of California Press.

―――― (1991), *The Territorial Dimension of Judaism*, Minneapolis, Minnesota: Fortress Press.

Day, C. (1990), *Places of the Soul: Architecture and Environmental Design as a Healing Art*, Wellingborough: Aquarian Press.

de Certeau, M. (1984), *The Practice of Everyday Life* (ET), Berkeley, California: University of California Press.

Dickinson, E. (1970), *The Complete Poems*, London: Faber and Faber.

Di Santo, R. (1999), 'The Threat of Commodity Consciousness to Human Dignity', in Duffy, R. and Gambatese, A. (eds), *Made in God's Image: The Catholic Vision of Human Dignity*, New York: Paulist Press.

Dudden, F. H. (1915), *Gregory the Great: His Place in History and Thought*, London: Longman.

Duffy, E. (1992), *The Stripping of the Altars*, London: Yale University Press.

Duncan, J. and Ley, D. (eds) (1993), *Place/Culture/Representation*, London: Routledge.

Durrell, L. (1956), *Selected Poems*, New York: Grove Press.

―――― (1969), *The Spirit of Place: Letters and Essays on Travel*, New York: E. P. Dutton.

Eade, J. and Sallnow, M. (eds) (1991), *Contesting the Sacred: the Anthropology of Christian Pilgrimage*, London: Routledge.

Edwards, R. and Usher, R. (2000), *Globalisation and Pedagogy: Space, Place and Identity*, London: Routledge.

Eliot, T. S. (1969), *The Complete Poems and Plays of T.S. Eliot*, London: Faber and Faber.

Elizondo, V. and Frayne, S. (eds) (1996), *Pilgrimage*, London: SCM Press.

Entriken, J. N. (1991), *The Betweenness of Place: Toward a Geography of Modernity*, Baltimore, Maryland: John Hopkins University Press.

Etzioni, A. (1993), *The Spirit of Community*, New York: Simon & Schuster.

Eusebius, *Ecclesiastical History* (ET), Harmondsworth: Penguin, 1965, II(25).

Eusebius, *Vita Constantini*, English translation, with introduction and commentary by A. Cameron and S. G. Hill, *The Life of Constantine*, Oxford: Clarendon Press, 1999.

Eyles, J. (1985), *Senses of Place*, Warrington: Silverbrook Press.

Feld, S. and Basso, K. H. (eds) (1996), *Senses of Place*, Santa Fe, New Mexico: School of American Research Press.

Flannery, A. (ed.) (1975), *Vatican II: the Conciliar and Post Conciliar Documents*, Leominster, England: Fowler Wright Books.

Forte, B. (1999), 'The Shrine: "Cipher" of the Encounter with the Other', in *The Shrine a Privileged Place for a Meeting between God and His People, a Pilgrim in Time*, Proceedings of the XIV Plenary Meeting of the Pontifical Council for the Care of Migrants and Itinerant People, The Vatican, 23–25 June 1999.

Foucault, M. (1980), 'The Eye of Power', in Gordon, C. (ed.), *Power Knowledge: Selected Interviews and other Writings* (1972–77), New York: Pantheon.

────── (1986),'Of Other Spaces', *Diacritics*, Spring.

Fry, T. (1981), *RB80: The Rule of St Benedict in Latin and English with Notes*, Collegeville, Minnesota: The Liturgical Press.

Funkenstein, A. (1986), *Theology and the Scientific Imagination from the Middle Ages to the Seventeenth Century*, Princeton: Princeton University Press, 1986.

Gardiner, F. C. (1971), *The Pilgrimage of Desire: A Study of Theme and Genre in Medieval Literature*, Lieden: E. J. Brill.

Giddens, A. (1979), *Central Problems in Social Theory*, Cambridge: Polity Press.

────── (1985), *The Nation State and Violence*, Berkeley, California: University of California Press.

────── (1990), *The Consequences of Modernity*, Cambridge: Polity Press.

Giles, R. (1995), *Re-Pitching the Tent: Re-ordering the Church Building for Worship and Mission in the New Millennium*, Norwich: The Canterbury Press.

Green, L. (2001), *The Impact of The Global: An Urban Theology*, London: The Anglican Urban Network.

Gorringe, T. (1989), 'Sacraments', in Morgan, R. (ed.), *The Religion of the Incarnation: Anglican Essays in Commemoration of Lux Mundi*, Bristol: Bristol Classical Press.

Gregory of Nyssa, Saint, *Gregorii Nysseni Epistulae*, Leiden: E. J. Brill, 1952.

Gregory, D. and Urry, J. (1985), *Social Relations and Social Structures*, London: Macmillan.

Gupta, A. and Ferguson, J. (1992), 'Beyond "Culture": Space, Identity and the Politics of Difference', *Cultural Anthropology* 7.

────── (1999), *Culture, Power, Place: Explorations in Critical Anthropology*, Durham, North Carolina: Duke University Press.

Gutierrez, G. (1983), *We Drink from Our Own Wells: The Spiritual Journey of a People*, London: SCM Press.

Habel, Norman C. (1995), *The Land is Mine*, Minneapolis: Fortress Press.

Hall, E. (1969), *The Hidden Dimension*, Garden City, New York: Anchor Books.

Hardy, A. (1979), *The Spiritual Nature of Man*, Oxford: Clarendon Press.

Harvey, D. (1990), *The Condition of Postmodernity*, Oxford: Blackwell.

────── (1993), 'From Space to Place and Back Again: Reflections on the Condition of Postmodernity' in Bird, J. et al (eds), *Mapping the Futures: Local Cultures, Global Change*, London: Routledge.

────── (2000), *Spaces of Hope*, Berkeley, California: University of California Press.

Hauerwas, S. (1987), 'Will the Real Sectarian Stand Up?', *Theology Today* **44**(1).

────── (1994), *Despatches from the Front:. Theological Engagements with the Secular*, Durham, North Carolina: Duke University Press.

────── (2000), *A Better Hope*, Grand Rapids, Michigan: Brazos Press.

Hay, D. (1990), *Religious Experience Today: Studying the Facts*, London: Mowbray.

Heidegger, M. (1958), *The Question of Being* (ET), New York: Twayne Publishers.

────── (1971), *Poetry, Language, Thought*, London: Harper Colophon.

Heyden, D. (1995), *The Power of Place*, Cambridge, Massachusetts: MIT Press.

Hiebert, T. (1996), *The Yahwist's Landscape: Nature and Religion in Early Israel*, Oxford: Oxford University Press.

Hiss, T. (1990), *The Experience of Place*, New York: Knopf.

Hodgson, P. and King, R. (eds) (1985) (eds), *Christian Theology: An Introduction to its Traditions and Tasks*, Philadelphia: Fortess.

Holm J and Bowker J. (1994), *Sacred Place*, London: Pinter Publishers.

Hooker, J. (1998), 'One is Trying to Make a Shape', in *David Jones Journal*, **15**.

Horne, B. (1993), 'The Sacramental Use of Material Things', in Rowell, G. and Dudley, M., *The Oil of Gladness: Anointing in the Christian Tradition*, London: SPCK.

Inge, J. G. (1995), 'It's a Pantomime: Reflections on Parish Ministry', in *Theology* **XCVIII**.

Inge, J. (1999), 'Towards a theology of Place', in *Modern Believing*, **40**.

Irenaeus, *Adversus Haereses* (ET), Unger, D. (ed.), in *St Irenaeus of Lyons Against the Heresies*, New York: Paulist Press, 1992.

Isaacs, M. (1992), *Sacred Space: An Approach to the Epistle to the Hebrews*, Journal For the Study of the New Testament Supplement Series, **73**.

Jackson, J. B. (1994), *A Sense of Place, a Sense of Time*, New Haven, Connecticut: Yale University Press.

Jackson, P. (1989), *Maps of Meaning*, London: Routledge.

James, J. (1982), Chartres: *The Masons who built a Legend*, London: Routledge & Kegan Paul.

Jammer, M. (1969), *Concepts of Space*, Cambridge, Massachusetts: Harvard University Press.

Jarvis, B. (1998), *Postmodern Cartographies: The Geographical Imagination in Contemporary American Culture*, New York: St Martin's Press.

Jason, L. A. (1997), *Community Building: Values for a Sustainable Future*, London: Praeger.

Jenkins, T. (1999), *Religion in English Everyday Life: An Ethnographic Approach*, Oxford: Berghahn Books.

Jenson, R. (1997), *Systematic Theology: The Triune God*, Oxford; Oxford University Press.

Jerome, Saint, *The Letters of St. Jerome*, trans. C. C. Mierow, introduction and notes by T. C. Lawler, Westminster, Maryland: Newland Press, 1963.

John Chrysostom, *Saint Chrysostom: Commentary on the Epistle to the Galations, and Homilies on the Epistle to the Ephesians, of S. John Chrysostom* (ET), Oxford: Parker, 1840.

Johnstone, R. J. (1991), *A Question of Place: Exploring the Practice of Human Geography*, Oxford: Blackwell.

Jones, D. (1974), *The Sleeping Lord and Other Fragments*, London: Faber and Faber.

Justin Martyr, *The Writings of Justin Martyr and Athenagoras* (ET), trans. M. Dods, G. Reith, and B. P. Pratten, Edinburgh: T. & T. Clark, 1867.

Keith, M. and Pile, S. (1993), *Place and the Politics of Identity*, London: Routledge.

Kemmis, D. (1990), *Community and the Politics of Place*, Norman, Oklahoma: University of Oklahoma Press.

——— (1995), *The Good City and the Good Life*, Boston, Massachusetts: Houghton Mifflin.

Kohak, E. (1984), *The Embers and the Stars*, Chicago, Illinois: University of Chicago Press.

Kuhn, T. (1962), *The Structure of Scientific Revolutions*, Chicago, Illinois: University of Chicago Press.

Lacoste, J.-Y. (1994), *Expérience et Absolu*, Paris: Press Universitaires de France.

Lane, B. (1998), *The Solace of Fierce Landscapes: Exploring Desert and Mountain Spirituality*, Oxford: Oxford University Press.

Lane, B. L. (1988), *Landscapes of the Sacred: Geography and Narrative in American Spirituality*, Mahweh, New Jersey: The Paulist Press.

────── (1992), 'Landscape and Spirituality: A Tension between Place and Placelessness in Christian Thought', *The Way* Supplement, **73**.

Langer, S. (1953), *Feeling and Form*, New York: Charles Scribner's Sons.

Lasch, C. (1995), *The Revolt of the Elites and the Betrayal of Democracy*, New York and London: W. W. Norton.

Lash, S. and Freidman, J. (eds) (1992), *Modernity and Identity*, Oxford: Blackwell.

Lash, S. and Robertson, R. (eds) (1995), *Global Modernities*, London: Sage.

Lawrence, D. H. (1961), *Studies in Classic American Literature*, New York: Viking Press.

LeFebvre, H. (1991a), *The Production of Space*, Oxford; Blackwell.

────── (1991b), *Critique of Everyday Life – Volume I: Introduction*, London: Verso.

Lilburne, G. R. (1989), *A Sense of Place: A Christian Theology of the Land*, Nashville, Tennessee: Abingdon Press.

Lindbeck, G. (1984), *The Nature of Doctrine: Religion and Theology in a Postliberal Age*, Philadelphia, Pennsylvania: Westminster.

Loades, A. (2000), in Hastings, A. Mason, A. and Pyper, H. (eds), *Oxford Companion to Christian Thought*, Oxford: Oxford University Press.

Louth, A. (1983), *Discerning the Mystery*, Oxford; Clarendon Press.

────── (1991), *The Wilderness God*, London: Darton, Longman and Todd.

Luther, M., *Luthers's Works* (ET), Concordia, Missouri: Concordia Publishing House, 1961.

Lutwack, L. (1984), *The Role of Place in Literature*, Syracuse, New York: Syracuse University Press.

Mackenzie, I. (1995), *The Dynamism of Space: A Theological Study into the Nature of Space*, Norwich: The Canterbury Press.

MacIntyre, A. (1994), 'A Partial Response to My Critics', in Horton J. and Mendus, S. (eds), *After MacIntyre: Critical Perspectives on the Work of Alasdair MacIntyre*, Notre Dame, Indiana: University of Notre Dame Press.

Macquarrie, J. (1997), *A Guide to the Sacraments*, New York: Continuum.

McDannell, C. and Lang, B. (1988), *Heaven: A History*, Yale University Press.

McKnight, E. V. (1988), *Post-Modern Use of the Bible: The Emergence of Reader-Oriented Criticism*, Nashville, Tennessee: Abingdon.

Massey, D. (1994), *Space, Place and Gender*, Minneapolis, Minnesota: University of Minnesota Press.

Mayne, M. (1995), *This Sunrise of Wonder*, London: Harper Collins.

Merleau-Ponty, M. (1962), *The Phenomenology of Perception*, London: Routledge & Kegan Paul.

Merton, T. (1953), *The Sign of Jonas*, New York: Harcourt Brace.

——— (1977), *Confessions of a Guilty Bystander*, London: Sheldon Press.

Meyrowitz, J. (1985), *No Sense of Place: The Impact of Electronic Media on Social Behaviour*, Oxford: Oxford University Press.

Milbank, J. (1990), *Theology and Social Theory: Beyond Secular Reason*, Oxford, Blackwell.

——— (1997), *The Word Made Strange*, Oxford: Blackwell.

Milbank, J., Pickstock, C. and Ward, G. (1999), *Radical Orthodoxy*, London: Routledge.

Miller, J. H. (1995), *Topographies*, Stanford, California: Stanford University Press.

Mockler, A. (1976), *Francis of Assisi: The Wandering Years*, Oxford: Phaidon Press.

More, T. (1557), *The Works of Thomas More*, London.

Mortley, R. (1991), *French Philosophers in Conversation*, London: Routledge.

Mugerauer, R. (1994), *Interpretations on Behalf of Place: Environmental Displacements and Alternative Responses*, Albany, New York: State University of New York Press.

Muir, E. (1960), *Collected Poems*, London: Faber and Faber.

Murray, C. (1988), *In Pursuit of Happiness and Good Government*, New York: Simon & Schuster.

Nast, H. J. and Pile, S. (1998), *Places Through the Body*, London and New York: Routledge.

Niditch, S. (1985), *Chaos to Cosmos: Studies in Biblical Patterns of Creation*, Chico, California: Scholars Press.

Niebuhr, H. R. (1951), *Christ and Culture*, New York: Harper and Brothers.

Nisbet, R. (1953), *The Quest for Community*, Oxford: Oxford University Press.

Nolan, M.-L. and Nolan, S. (1989), *Christian Pilgrimage in Modern Western Europe*, Chapel Hill, North Carolina: University of North Carolina Press.

Norberg-Schultz, C. (1980), *Genius Loci: Towards a Phenomenology of Architecture*, New York: Rizzoli.

Novak, M. (1989), *Free Persons and the Common Good*, Lanham, Maryland: Madison Books.

O'Donovan, O. (1989), 'The Loss of a Sense of Place', *Irish Theological Quarterly*, **55**.

Oppenheimer, H. (1988), 'Making God Findable', in Ecclestone, G. (ed.), *The Parish Church*, London: Mowbray.

Origen, *Contra Celsum* (ET), introduction and notes by H. Chadwick, Cambridge: Cambridge University Press, 1951.

Origen, *De Principiis. On First Principles* (ET), introduction and notes by G. W. Butterworth, New York: Harper & Row, 1966.

Osborne, K. B. (1999), *Christian Sacraments in a Postmodern World: A Theology for the Third Millennium*, New York: Paulist Press.

Park, C. C. (1994), *Sacred Worlds: An introduction to geography and religion*, London: Routledge.

Parker Pearson, M. and Richards, C. (1994), *Architecture and Order: Approaches to Social Space*, London: Routledge.

Peacocke, A. (2000), 'Nature as Sacrament', *Third Millennium*, **2**.

Peters, M. (1996), *Poststructuralism, Politics and Education*, Westport, Connecticut: Bergin and Garvey.

Piaget, J. (1963), *The Psychology of Intelligence*, Totowa, New Jersey: Littlefield Adams.

Piaget, J. and Inhelder, B. (1960), *The Child's Conception of Geometry*, New York: Basic Books.

Pitter, R. (1968), *Collected Poems*, London: Macmillan.

Plato, *Timaeus*, trans J. Warrington, London: Dent, 1965.

Platten, S. (1996), *Pilgrims*, London: Harper Collins.

Platten, S. and Lewis, C. (eds) (1998), *Flagships of the Spirit: Cathedrals in Society*, London: Darton Longman and Todd.

Polanyi, M. (1967), *Knowing and Being*, London: Routledge & Kegan Paul.

Polkinghorne, J. (1989), *Science and Providence*, London: SPCK.

——— (1994), *Quarks, Chaos and Christianity: Questions to Science and Religion*, London: SPCK.

——— (1995), *Serious Talk, Science and Religion in Dialogue*, Valley Forge, Pennsylvania: Trinity Press International.

Power, D. N. (1999), *Sacrament: The Language of God's Giving*, New York: Crossroad.

Quick, O. C. (1916), *Essays in Orthodoxy*, London: Macmillan.

Rahner, K. (1963), *The Church and the Sacraments*, New York: Herder and Herder.

Raper, M. (1999), 'Refugees. Travel Under Duress', *The Way*, **39**.

Ravasi, G. (1999) 'My name will be there: Towards a theology and a Pastoral Care of Shrines', in *The Shrine a Privileged Place for a Meeting between God and His People, a Pilgrim in Time* (1999), Proceedings of the XIV Plenary Meeting of the Pontifical Council for the Care of Migrants and Itinerant People, The Vatican, 23–25 June.

Rees, E. (1992), *Christian Symbols, Ancient Roots*, London: J. Kingsley Publishers.

Relph, E. (1976), *Place and Placelessness*, London: Pion.

——— (1981), *Rational Landscapes and Humanistic Geography*, London: Croom Helm.

——— (1989), 'Geographical Experiences and being-in-the-world', in Seamon, D. and Mugerauer, R. (eds), *Dwelling, Place and Environment: Towards a Phenomenology of Person and World*, New York: Columbia University Press.

Richardson, M. (ed.) (1984), *Place: Experience and Symbol*, Baton Rouge: Department of Geography and Anthropology, Louisiana State University.

Ricoeur, P. (1984), *Time and Narrative, Volume I*, Chicago, Illinois: University of Chicago Press, Part II.

Robinson, E. (1977), *The Original Vision, Religious Experience Research Unit*, Oxford: Westminster College.

Robinson, E. and Jackson, J. (1987), *Religion and Values at 16+*, Oxford: Alister Hardy Research Centre and the Christian Education Movement.

Rodin, A. (1965), *Cathedrals of France*, Redding Redge, Connecticut: Black Swan Books.

Rodman, M. C. (1994), 'Empowering Place: Multilocality and Multivocality', in *American Anthropologist*, **94**.

Rogers, R. (1997), *Cities for a Small Planet*, London: Faber and Faber.

Rose, G. (1993), *Feminism and Geography*, Cambridge: Polity Press.

Ross, W. D. (1942), *The Student's Oxford Aristotle, Volume II*, Oxford: Oxford University Press.

Rouner, L. S. (ed.) (1996), *The Longing for Home*, Notre Dame, Indiana: University of Notre Dame Press.

Rumsey, A. (2001), 'The Misplaced Priest', in *Theology*, **CIV**.

Said, E. (1993), *Culture and Imperialism*, New York: Knopf.

Shafer, I. (ed.) (1988), *Essays in Theology, The Arts and Social Sciences in Honor of Andrew Greely: A Feschrift*, Bowling Green, Ohio: Bowling Green State University Popular Press.

Schaffer C. and Anundsen, K. (1993), *Creating Community Anywhere: Finding Support and Connection in a Fragmented World*, New York: G.P. Putnam's Sons.

Schama, S. (1995), *Landscape and Memory*, New York: A. A. Kopf.

Schillebeeckx, E. (1963), *Christ the Sacrament of the Encounter with God*, London and Melbourne: Sheed and Ward.

Schemmann, A. (1965), *The World as Sacrament*, London: Darton Longman and Todd.

——— (1973), *For the Life of the World: Sacraments and Orthodoxy*, Crestwood, New York: St Vladimir's Seminary Press.

Scott, J. and Simpson-Housley, P. (eds) (1991), *Sacred Places and Profane Spaces*, London and New York: Greenwood Press.

Seamon, D. (1984), in Richardson, M. (ed.), *Place: Experience and Symbol*, Baton Rouge: Department of Geography and Anthropology, Louisiana State University.

Seamon D. and Mugerauer R. (eds) (1989), *Dwelling, Place and Environment: Towards a Phenomenology of Person and World*, New York: Columbia University Press.

Selby, P. (1998), *Grace and Mortgage*, London: SPCK.

Sheldrake, P. (1995), *Living Between Worlds: Place and Journey in Celtic Spirituality*, London: Darton, Longman and Todd.

——— (1996), 'The Sacredness of Place', in *Spirituality Studies*, **6**.

——— (1998), *Spirituality and Theology: Christian Living and the Doctrine of God*, London: Darton Longman and Todd.

Sheldrake, P. (2001), *Spaces for the Sacred: Place, Memory and Identity*, London: SCM Press.

Shields, R. (1991), *Places on the Margin: Alternative Geographies of Modernity*, London: Routledge.

Smith, J. Z. (1978), *Map is not Territory*, Leiden: E. J. Brill.

——— (1982), 'The Bare Facts of Ritual', in *Imagining Religion: From Babylon to Jonestown*, Chicago, Illinois: University of Chicago Press.

Snyder, G. (1985), *Ante Pacem: Archaeological Evidence of Church Life Before Constantine*, Macon, Georgia: Mercer University Press.

Sobel, D. (1999), *Longitude*, London: Fourth Estate.

Soja, E. W. (1989), *Postmodern Geographies: The Reassertion of Space in Critical Social Theory*, London: Verso.

Sperber, D. (1975), *Rethinking Symbolism*, Cambridge: Cambridge University Press.

Staniforth, M. (ed.) (1968), *Early Christian Writings*, Harmondsworth: Penguin.

Steiner, G. (1989), *Real Presences*, London: Faber and Faber.

Stewart, A. (ed.) (1887), *Itinerary from Bordeaux to Jerusalem*, London: Palestine Pilgrims Text Society.

Stokes, M. (1994), *Ethnicity, Identity and Music: The Musical Construction of Place*, Oxford: Berg.

Stopford, J. (ed.) (1999), *Pilgrimage Explored*, Woodbridge, Suffolk: York Medieval Press.

Swan, J. A. (1991), *The Power of Place*, Wheaton, Illinois: Quest Books.

Sykes, S. (1996), Address given at a conference, *The Holy Place: Mission and Conservation*, Keele University, 25–26 June.

Taylor, J. E. (1993), *Christians and the Holy Places: The Myth of Jewish-Christian Origins*, Oxford, Clarendon Press.

Taylor, J. V. (1992), *The Christlike God*, London: SCM Press.

Teilhard de Chardin, P. (1970), *The Mass of the World*, London: Fontana.

Temple, W. (1935), *Nature, Man and God*, London: Macmillan.

—— (1949), *Readings in St John's Gospel*, London: Macmillan.

The Shrine, 'Memorial Presence and Prophecy of the Living God', distributed by the Pontifical Council for the Pastoral Care of Migrants and Itinerant People, The Vatican, 1999.

Tillich, P. (1951), *Systematic Theology*, Vol. 1. Chicago, Illinois: University of Chicago Press.

Tindall, G. (1991), *Countries of the Mind: The Meaning of Place to Writers*, London: Hogarth Press.

Torrance, T. F. (1969), *Space, Time and Incarnation*, Oxford: Oxford University Press.

—— (1974), 'The Relation of the Incarnation to Space in Nicene Theology', in A. Blane (ed.), *The Ecumenical World of Orthodox Civilisation*, The Hague: Mouton.

Traherne, T. (1966), *Centuries of Meditation*, II.20 in Ridler, A. (ed.), *Traherne, Poems, Centuries and Three Thanksgivings*, Oxford: Oxford University Press.

——, *The Kingdom of God*, unpublished manuscript, Lambeth Palace Library Manuscript 1360.

Traherne, T. (ed.) (1997), Julia Smith, *Select Meditations*, London: Fyfield.

Tournier, P. (1968), *A Place for You: Psychology and Religion*, London: SCM Press.

Tuan, Y.-F. (1971), 'Geography, Phenomenology and the Study of Human Nature', *Canadian Geographer*, **15**.

—— (1972), 'Topophilia: Personal Encounters with the Landscape', in English, P. W. and Mayfield, R. C. (eds), *Man, Space and the Environment*, Oxford University Press.

—— (1974), *Topophilia: a study of Environmental Perception, Attitudes and Values*, Eaglewood Cliffs, New Jersey: Prentice Hall.

—— (1977), *Space and Place: The Perspective of Experience*, Minneapolis, Minnesota: University of Minnesota Press.

—— (1984), 'In place, out of place', *Geoscience and Man*, **24**.

—— (1984) in Richardson, M. (ed.), *Place: Experience and Symbol*, Baton Rouge: Department of Geography and Anthropology, Louisiana State University.

Turner, D. (1999), 'The Darkness of God and the Light of Christ: Negative Theology and Eucharistic Presence', *Modern Theology*, **15**.

Turner, F. (1989), *The Spirit of Place: The Making of American Literary Landscape*, San Francisco, California: Sierra Club.

Turner, H.W. (1979), *From Temple to Meeting House. The Phenomenology and Theology of Christian Places of Worship*, The Hague: Mouton Publishers.

Turner, V. and Turner E., (1978), *Image and Pilgrimage in Christian Culture: Anthropological Perspectives*, New York: Columbia University Press.

Unger, R. (1984), *Knowledge and Politics*, New York: Free Press.

Van der Leeuw, G. (1967), *Religion in Essence and Manifestation*, Gloucester, Massachusetts: P. Smith.

Von Balthasar, H. U. (1958), *Science, Religion and Christianity*, London: Burns and Oates.

—— (1986), *The Glory of God, A Theological Aesthetics, Volume III: Studies in Theological Lay Styles*, Edinburgh: T. & T. Clark.

Vycinas, V. (1969), *Earth and Gods: An Introduction to the Philosophy of Martin Heidegger*, The Hague: Martinas Nijhoff.

Wainwright, G. (1981), *Eucharist and Eschatology*, Oxford: Oxford University Press.

Wainwright, G. (1997), *For Our Salvation: Two Approaches to the Work of Christ*, London: SPCK.

Walker, E. V. (1988), Placeways: *A Theory of the Human Environment*, Chapel Hill, North Carolina: University of North Carolina Press.

Walker, P. W. L. (1990), *Holy City, Holy Places? Attitudes to Jerusalem and the Holy Land in the Fourth Century*, Oxford: Clarendon Press.

—— (1996), 'Centre Stage: Jerusalem or Jesus?', in *Papers towards a Biblical Mind*, **5**.

Walker, P. W .L. (ed.) (1992), *Jerusalem Past and Present in the Purposes of God*, Carlisle: Paternoster Press.

Ware, K. (1979), *The Orthodox Way*, Oxford: Mowbray.

Waters, M. (1995), *Globalisation*, London: Routledge.

Webb, D. (1999), *Pilgrims and Pilgrimage in the Medieval West*, London: I. B. Tauris.

Weil, S. (1952), *The Need for Roots*, New York: G.P. Putnam's Sons.

Weiner, J. (1991), *The Empty Place: Poetry, Space and Being among the Foi of Papua New Guinea*, Bloomington, Indiana: University of Indiana Press.

Wells, S. (1998), *Transforming Fate into Destiny: The Theological Ethics of Stanley Hauerwas*, Carlisle: Paternoster Press.

Wesley, J. (1870), Janes, E. L. (ed.), *Wesley: His Own Historian: Illustrations of His Character, Labors and Achievements from His Own Diaries*, New York: Carlton and Lanahan.

Wiesel, E. (1996), 'Longing for Home', in Rouner, L. S. (ed.), *The Longing for Home*, Notre Dame, Indiana: University of Notre Dame Press.

Wilken, R. L. (1992), *Palestine in Christian History and Thought*, New Haven, Connecticut: Yale University Press.

Williams, R. (2000), *On Christian Theology*, Oxford: Blackwell.

Wilson, C. (1987), *The Essential Colin Wilson*, London: Collins.

Witherspoon, A. and Warnke, F. (eds) (1929), *Seventeenth-Century Prose and Poetry*, New York: Harcourt Brace Jovanovich.

Index